Journey Into the World of **SASE**

Rohan Naggi, VeloCloud BU,
Product Management

Ferdinand Sales, VeloCloud BU,
Product Management

Foreword by
Mark Vondemkamp,
Vice President Products VeloCloud BU, VMware

Spotlight Section for VMware SASE by
Craig Connors,
VP & CTO, VeloCloud R&D, VMware

Spotlight Section for Edge Networking Intelligence,
Abe Ankumah,
Senior Director, Product Marketing and Partnerships VeloCloud BU, VMware

First Edition

VMware Press

Program Manager
Rohan Naggi

Journey Into the World of SASE

First Edition
Printed in the United States of America
First Printing April 2021

Warning & Disclaimer

Every effort has been made to make this book as complete and as accurate as possible, but no warranty or guarantee is implied. The information provided is on an "as-is" basis. The authors, VMware, and the publisher shall have neither liability nor responsibility to any person or entity with respect to any loss or damages arising from the information contained in this book.

The opinions expressed in this book belong to the authors and are not necessarily those of VMware.

Table of Contents

Table of Contents - **Figures**

About the Authors

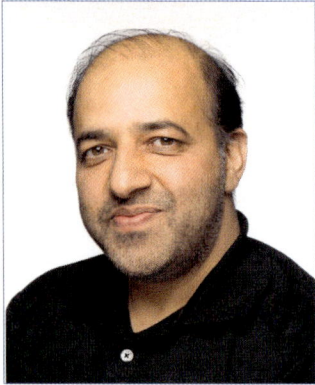

Rohan Naggi, Sr. Technical Product Manager at VMware, is an expert in networking, security arena, technical marketing, and enablement with a B.E. in Computer Technology paired with over 20 years of experience in this field. Rohan has expertise in content development, service provider/telco market enablement, and large enterprise deployment. He has been intimately involved with WAN technologies for over a decade in roles at VeloCloud and Cisco Systems. Rohan brings a passion for mapping technology to customer pain points, developing solutions incorporating routing, security, and SD-WAN. A sought-after public speaker, Rohan has presented at conferences, participated in panel discussions, and briefed analysts on many aspects of WAN technology. Follow Rohan on Twitter at @Lifeboy.

Ferdinand Sales, Product Management at VMware, has over 20 years' worth of experience in networking, security, Data Center, virtualization, application delivery, cloud computing, and Multi-Cloud infrastructures. He has played multiple roles as a Cloud Solution Architect, Product Manager, Business Development Manager, Technical Marketing Engineer, Systems Engineer, and Technical Assistance Center (TAC). Ferdinand has worked at Juniper Networks, Criterion Networks, Cisco Systems, and F5 Networks and maintains a wealth of connections within the networking, security, and multi-cloud infrastructure communities. Ferdinand has B.S. in Electronics and Communication Engineering and an M.S. in Engineering Management.

Technical Reviewers

Tim Van Herck, Director Technical Product Management at VMware, has over 15 years of experience in technical marketing, product management, and cloud service operations. He is currently the Director of Technical Product Management at VeloCloud, now part of VMware, where he leads the team responsible for writing product content and developing technical training. Tim previously worked for Aryaka, Cisco Systems, Allegro Systems, Assured Access Technology, and Alcatel. Tim holds an M.S. in Industrial Sciences from the University of Antwerp.

Acknowledgments

My gratitude goes out to firstly the Almighty God for everything I have accomplished in my life. I extend this gratitude then towards my family, that includes my parents, my wife, Nargis, and my kids, Ayaan and Rehan, for being by my side and for inspiring me to be driven. I am so thankful towards my colleagues, my friends, and largely to my co-writer, comrade, Ferdinand Sales, for his invaluable wisdom and efforts.

My appreciation for the readers is as important as well. Thank you for taking the time to read our book and dedicate yourselves to the pursuit of knowledge. I am humbled and encouraged by you all and seek to follow in your example to make the world a better place through continuous learning and growth and sharing knowledge.

Rohan Naggi
Sr. Technical Product Manager at VMware

This book was made possible through the assistance and dedication of so many colleagues and friends, whose invaluable feedback I gratefully acknowledge and humbly admire. I am deeply thankful for my co-author Rohan Naggi, whose vision, passion, persistence, and organization drove our efforts and our final SASE book. Rohan, I am indebted to you.

To my caring, loving, and supporting family: your untiring support and assistance have supported me all this way. You have my deepest gratitude.

Finally, to our readers: I extend to you my warmest thanks for taking the time to read our book and position yourselves at the forefront of this technological evolution. Our field would fall stagnant in your absence. We are indebted to you and would do well to follow your example and improve our world through continuous learning and growth.

Ferdinand Sales
Sr. Manager, Product Management at VMware

Our Gratitude

We would like to thank the VMware family for their guidance and support, with a special mention to the founders of VeloCloud—**Sanjay Uppal, Ajit Mayya,** and **Steven Woo** —for their vision and leadership.

A book is not complete without the support of reviewers. As authors, we partnered with this team at many levels, some reviewing the full book and some working on individual chapters. We would like to thank them all and are grateful for their contributions.

Our deepest gratitude to Amr Ayad, who has been involved in reviewing from the start. He has been instrumental in providing feedback for all the chapters in the book as well as offering guidance and structure for many diagrams.

Our heartfelt thanks to Tony Banuelos for reviewing chapter 7 and providing technical insights on the SASE traffic flow and global PoP. We are grateful to him for giving us confidence in writing the content for chapter 7 and his endless patience, positivity, and genuine help.

Our appreciation goes out to Sultan G Dawood for reviewing chapters 4 and 5, both challenging and helping us to develop new content for the SD-WAN and SASE. We deeply appreciate your guidance, constructive feedback, and wonderful humor.

A sincere thank you to Anand Srinivas, Jay Thontakudi, and **Murtaza Zafer** for writing, contributing, and reviewing all Edge Networking Intelligence-focused material. Chapter 8 on AIOps/ML would not have been possible without their dedicated, relentless efforts to help us complete this section, and on such short notice without hesitation.

Thanks again to **Chris Le** for reviewing and providing valuable feedback for VMware SASE chapter 6 and the conclusion in chapter 10.

Our gratitude to **Vivian Clark** and **Vernon Apperson** for proofreading the opening and closing chapters, ensuring that VMware messaging is not lost.

Thanks also go to **Hamza Ahmed** - genuine kindness for bringing his field experience into the deployment (chapter 9) and SD-WAN (chapter 4) topics.

Our deep gratitude to **Rajeev Singh** and **Rajendra Chayapathi,** who expertly guided us while reviewing chapters 2, 3, and 4.

We would also like to thank **Munir Dabaghi** and **Lin Huang** for reviewing SD-WAN chapter 4.

We are fully indebted to **Vinod Kumar Balasubramanyam** for his understanding, suggestions, patience, and focus while reviewing chapter 5 on SASE and chapter 3 on cloud security.

We would like to express our deep and sincere gratitude to **Ravi Sharma** and **Scott Calvet** for providing clarity and guidance during the entire writing process.

Our appreciation extends to **Aamir Akhter** for the VMware SASE chapter 6 review. We would like to thank **Bhanu Vemula, Nitin Kumar Ananda,** and **Jaspreet Bhatia** for reviewing cloud security chapter 3.

We owe our gratitude to **Abe Ankumah** and **Craig Connors** for their valuable and early insight on AIOps and SASE. This knowledge has been captured in the Spotlight sections.

Above all, we acknowledge **Tim Van Herck** with gratitude for his support in keeping us going. This work would not be possible without him.

Finally, Ferdinand and I would like to thank our readers. We hope you find this book a helpful resource in your own efforts to power business growth and success through technology. If you have any comments or suggestions about this book, we welcome your feedback.

Thank you all for your attention, your time, and your passion for SASE.

Let's start the Journey towards SASE, bringing together Cloud Networking and Security.

Foreword

This book is arguably overdue by a decade. This is not because of a delay of the authors but rather a lack of technical evolution and corporate vision. It was not held back out of a desire to protect existing markets; instead, it relied on the readiness of enterprises to warm to the capabilities of cloud-delivered networking and security solutions and workforce mobility.

VMware has spent more than two decades providing technology by inspiration and acquisition, through development and partnership. With a core focus on cloud computing, virtualization software, and services, VMware has fundamentally changed many technology landscapes – including compute, networking, security, storage, device management, application deployment, and cloud.

Advances in one area create challenges and opportunities in another. Cloud virtualization has placed extreme demands on networks, security, and storage solutions. They are facing management and capacity challenges far in excess of what their foundational designers intended. Long-standing organizational silos and processes are insufficient to address the speed and scale requirements users now expect.

These technical challenges do not exist in a vacuum; they intersect with business imperatives for networking and security, developer productivity, and workforce mobility. Technology must be advanced and compelling enough to empower the business without becoming so complex it restrains the business. Agile IT organizations need to focus their limited resources on delivering new solutions, not simply managing legacy infrastructure.

While not the genesis of the movement, the COVID-19 pandemic drove home the importance of working from home, the coffee shop, the local library, or most any location other than the office. Remote access has a long history of targeted solutions, but none have yet unified the simplicity, security, availability, and experience that can match the in-office experience. But as with many opportunities before, VMware is ready to challenge that reality.

This book is both a walk down memory lane for seasoned technologists and a look toward the road ahead in the IT journey for anyone interested in the Secure Access Services Edge (SASE) model. It will examine why established practices exist and how SASE brings its concepts into modern architectures. It highlights the importance of both connectivity and security in delivering on the user quality of experience promise. Readers should find both general references to build their understanding as well as specific use cases which may align with their own business challenges.

As the SASE model evolves and VMware enhances its SASE infrastructure and offerings, this book will remain a solid foundation for understanding the motivations, requirements, and technologies involved in modern access architecture. Its technologies and capabilities are the results of decades of collaboration between VMware developers, cloud architects, professional services, technology partners, product management, and customers. We look forward to showing you how SASE can simplify and secure your business' networking and security requirements.

Mark Vondemkamp
Vice President Products – VMware SDWAN / SASE

Chapter 1

Introduction: The Case for SASE Evolution

Introductions and Goals

This book is intended for any professional interested in gaining greater insight into the terms, concepts, and issues related to the ongoing evolution of security and networking. It has been developed for a range of readers: the executive seeking to understand how their business is changing, the IT leader responsible for driving the transition, and the technologist designing and implementing change. Upon conclusion of the book, the reader should have a better and deeper understanding of:

- The state of enterprise technology today – legacy systems and networks, cloud compute and service providers, hybrid operating models

- The ongoing evolution to hybrid models, bringing together disparate data center and cloud components under a single policy and security management umbrella.

- The individual components that make up networking and security ecosystems and how they come together to form an intrinsic security solution.

- The path to move enterprise networking and security blueprint towards SASE architecture.

- How the integration of SD-WAN and SASE will address latency, performance, and global policy

- The technical foundations, operational concerns, and business benefits of the SASE model and the VMware SASE Platform™.

SASE Vision

Traditional branch and data center networks evolve as enterprises embrace cloud-based/ hybrid solutions and employ an increasingly distributed workforce. Corporate IT must be ready to address the security mandates and evolving threat landscapes that come with these changes. Holistic visibility and control are essential to delivering a secure, optimized user experience.

Gartner's Secure Access Service Edge (SASE) model is a modern architecture that combines cloud networking and cloud security services to simplify connecting users to data reliably and securely. SASE brings policy and security to user sessions rather than routing them through multiple enforcement elements. It enables organizations to adopt cloud, embrace mobility, and deliver a superior user experience while protecting their users and data against emerging security threats.

VMware SASE Platform converges industry-leading cloud networking and cloud security providers to deliver agility, security, scale, and flexibility for cloud-first enterprises. Powered by core VMware technologies including VMware SD-WAN and VMware Workspace ONE®, VMware SASE Platform delivers on the vision of resilient connectivity combined with comprehensive intrinsic security in a single, integrated solution. By integrating advanced security capabilities such as Zero Trust Network Access (ZTNA), Secure Web Gateway (SWG), Cloud Access Security Broker (CASB), URL filtering, and Data Loss Prevention (DLP), it extends the security boundary beyond the data center and cloud to applications and users, minimizes the attack surface by trusting no one, and protects users, networks, applications, and data against both internal and external threats.

Enterprise Motivations

Regulations, costs, and skillsets once greatly restricted interest in cloud solutions. Market mindset is rapidly changing as businesses show an eagerness to benefit from promises of flexibility and scalability. Legacy systems and on-premises data centers will continue to exist; however, they will be a piece of a larger whole as they are joined by virtualized infrastructure, cloud platforms, and SaaS providers. Enterprise IT must be ready to meet users' ever-

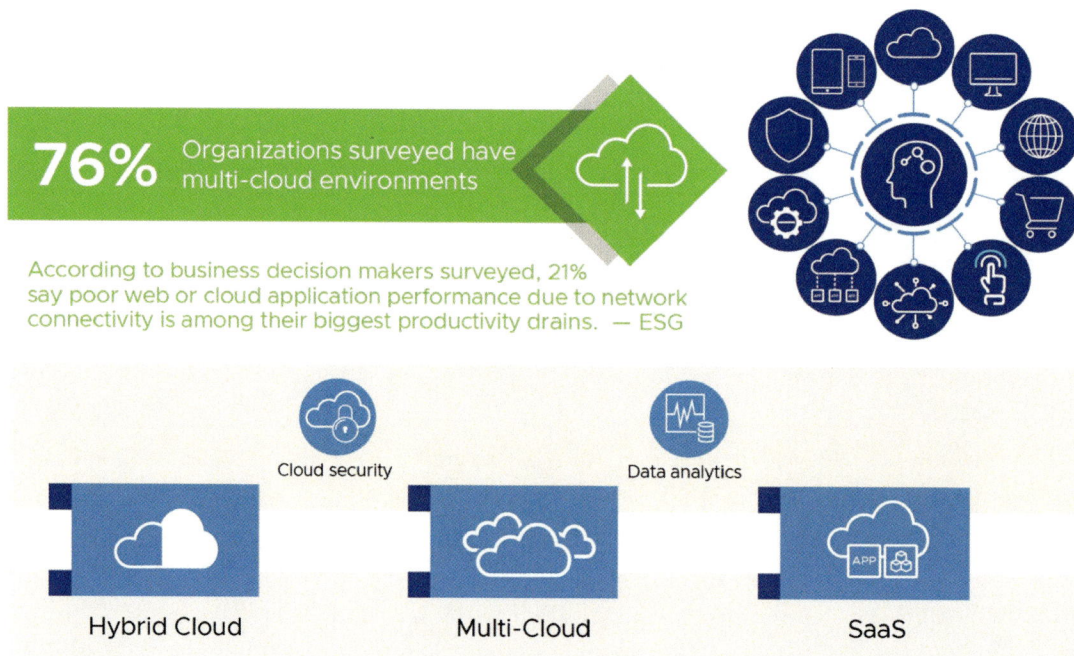

76% Organizations surveyed have multi-cloud environments

According to business decision makers surveyed, 21% say poor web or cloud application performance due to network connectivity is among their biggest productivity drains. — ESG

Cloud security   Data analytics

Hybrid Cloud   Multi-Cloud   SaaS

Figure 1.1: The Movement Towards Cloud

Source for ESG: http://wan.velocloud.com/rs/098-RBR-178/images/WP-ESG-Emergence-Network-Edge-Platforms-August-2019.pdf

increasing demands for security, resiliency, speed, and agility – delivered on any device, for any application, and in any cloud. Even highly regulated and data-sensitive verticals that were adamant they would never adopt cloud solutions are reconsidering their stances.

Individual motivations vary but the market will leave behind those unable to effectively transition to the new secure and flexible cloud paradigm. Continued adherence to a data center-centric connectivity model will slow the adoption of cloud and modern access solutions as more applications and data reside outside of the traditional enterprise boundary. Enhancing and assuring service quality will drive the need for consolidation of networking and security services to better support these workloads, wherever they may reside. The broader scope of hybrid IT operations raises the importance of global policy and management consistency. Central asks include enterprise-wide granular visibility, control, automation, and analytics. Understanding of terms, concepts, technology, challenges, and mandates of this evolving ecosystem are essential for transformation success.

Security Marketplace

The cybersecurity market is fragmented, bolted-on, siloed, and traditionally threat-centric. Enterprises need solutions that are built-in, unified, and focused on the context of protecting users, data, and applications; VMware's intrinsic security vision aligns with this requirement. The cybersecurity landscape also includes end-user devices which can access and store sensitive information outside of the traditional corporate perimeter.

Figure 1.2 demonstrates the scope of the problem: too many vendors are addressing too many unique problems with too many different products. The volume of moving parts and

Figure 1.2: Cybersecurity Vendor Landscape

different tools not only make an effective security solution complicated to design but also make creating, configuring, monitoring, and maintaining the corporate security ecosystem an unsolvable problem. The added complexity due to the number of components increases the attack surface, enhancing the challenge of delivering effective security solutions.

The current cybersecurity landscape includes exponential growth of remote end-users and devices which can access and store sensitive information outside of the traditional corporate perimeter. These end-user devices are not limited to corporate assets; employees, whether on site or remote, commonly use personal devices for work-related tasks. Global events and economic models have hastened the diaspora from the traditional office environment to permanent work-from-home expectations. In the home, there is an explosion of connected devices which collect data and communicate with services in the cloud.

Malicious actors need to find only a single vulnerability across the entire spectrum to put an entire corporation or country at risk. As recent intrusion events have demonstrated, even governmental security teams and the most talented corporate security vendors cannot guarantee they will stay ahead of the latest threats. Simplification of the landscape—from design to integration to operation—is imperative to a successful security strategy. An intrinsic security approach, as shown in **Figure 1.3**, leverages built-in capabilities combined with threat intelligence to shift from a reactive posture to a position of strength.

Security Evolution

Enterprise security strategy must evolve to treat the cloud as a central point of concern. An increasing volume of traffic will connect there rather than to legacy data centers while users will continue to demand responsive and resilient connectivity. The complexity of architectures needed to properly monitor, inspect, and secure this traffic will increase dramatically;

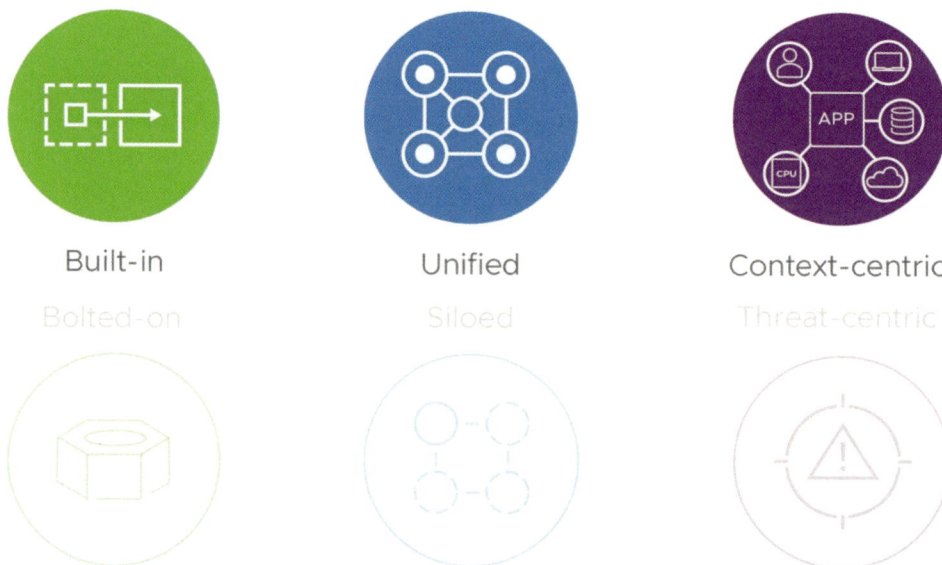

Built-in
Bolted-on

Unified
Siloed

Context-centric
Threat-centric

Figure 1.3: Intrinsic Security

corporate IT teams will be overburdened without a solution that unifies connectivity and security within a central management context. The SASE model brings this picture together; optimized cloud-native SD-WAN networking and cloud security, unified with intrinsic security, meeting user demands for modern cloud-based services while ensuring the security of corporate data and systems.

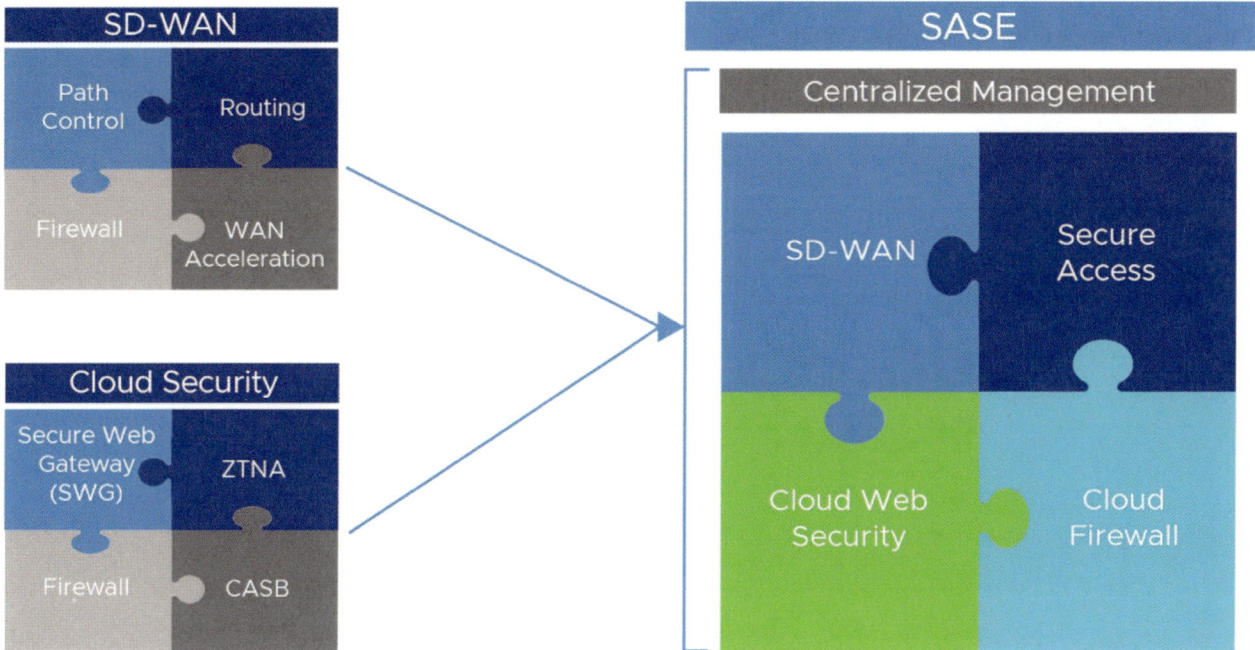

Figure 1.4: SASE- Integration of Cloud-Delivered SD-WAN and Cloud Security

Book Organization

Many of the foundational topics touched on are significant enough to have entire books written about them. This text can serve as a starting point for further exploration and research of both the fundamentals and emerging solutions of networking and security.

Chapters are organized around the following themes and seek to answer specific questions. While each can be read individually, they build on concepts over time to fully educate the reader on the motivations for the adoption of SASE design and architecture.

- **Chapter 1: Introduction - The Case for SASE Evolution.** An introduction to the current market landscape for on-premises, cloud, and hybrid IT.

- **Chapter 2: On-Premises Security Foundation:** An overview of on-premises security. What does traditional on-premises security look like? What are the capabilities and purpose of individual components? How do IT organizations manage and operate these systems?

- **Chapter 3: Cloud Security Foundation.** How do cloud security solutions differ from today's on-premises security infrastructure? What are various cloud security components? Why is cloud security about more than simply technology?

- **Chapter 4: SD-WAN Networking Foundation.** The evolution of traditional WAN into Software Defined Networking (SD-WAN). How VMware SD-WAN® simplifies WAN deployment with a cloud-delivered model? What are the different stages of WAN transformation that lead to SASE?

- **Chapter 5: Realizing Enterprise Digital Transformation through SASE.** What are the market trends forcing SASE evolution? How should adoption challenges be evaluated and addressed? Why should a business consider making this move, and why now?

- **Chapter 6: VMware SASE Platform.** What challenges does VMware SASE address in the market? How does the VMware SASE Platform differ from other implementations? What are the most significant benefits customers will realize? Which use cases are the most relevant and quickest to demonstrate value?

- **Chapter 7: Network Flow for VMware SASE PoP.** What does the SASE network flow look like? How should design principles and operational practices evolve? Why will this benefit both individual users and the enterprise as a whole?

- **Chapter 8: Edge Networking Intelligence and AIOps.** AIOps definitions and components. What is AIOps and what problems is it solving? What role does ENI play in the VMware SASE Platform?

- **Chapter 9: Rolling out SASE in the Enterprise.** What should IT security teams do to prepare for SASE? How will day-0 through day-N operations and management change? Migration Guidance to VMware SASE, Customer Case study for SASE Migration?

- **Chapter 10: Final Thoughts & Next Steps.** VMware SASE: Bringing it All Together VMware SASE Difference, What are the next steps, and key take-aways checklist.

Chapter 2

On-Premises Security Foundation

2.1 – Definition and Overview

Enterprise IT organizations have traditionally built out their technology infrastructures within boundaries of physical control while using a model of direct management. This chapter discusses the structures and components that secure these traditional enterprise branch/data center environments. The following explanation lay the foundation for the organization and expectations of this on-premises security model.

- **Premises:** The buildings and property directly under an enterprise's control. Premises could include corporate offices, manufacturing facilities, retail outlets, or sales offices. While the physical arrangements may vary, the enterprise is ultimately responsible for the control and oversight of all activities on its premises.

- **On-Premises Information Technology (IT):** Solutions residing on enterprise premises rather than sitting in a co-location facility or running on cloud provider systems. The enterprise is directly responsible for all design, operation, and maintenance of on-premises IT. A database installed on a server in the corporate data center is an example of on-premises IT software.

- **On-Premises Security:** The rules and tools in place to protect the security and accessibility of IT assets. This includes both hardware and software components. Examples include firewalls, Virtual Private Networks (VPNs), Intrusion Detection Systems/Intrusion Prevention Systems (IDS/IPS), and antivirus software.

2.2 – A Journey to Security

Access Lists

Firewall capabilities are often defined by generations. First-generation firewalls were simple packet filters using Access Lists (ACLs) to match packet headers at Open Systems Interconnection model (OSI) layers 2-4. Traffic traversing the first-generation firewall was inspected and processed according to a limited ruleset. The most common actions included

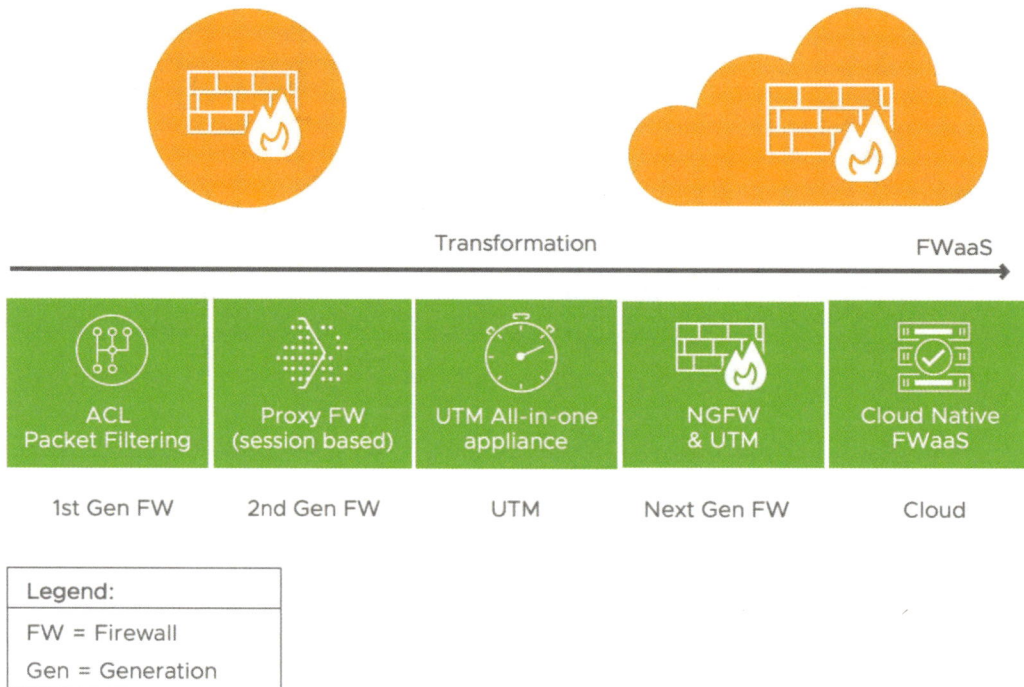

Figure 2.1: Firewall Evolution to Cloud-Native Firewall-as-a-Service (FWaaS)

allowing the traffic to pass (i.e., permit), rejecting the packet and notifying the sending protocol of the action, or silently discarding the traffic (i.e., drop). Additional functionality ranged from limited to nonexistent; many systems did not even identify established sessions since they could not match on TCP SYN flags. These evaluations were made simply based on the IP/network addresses or protocol ports of either the source or destination. Access control lists primarily operated on TCP, UDP, and associated control (e.g., ICMP) traffic.

This basic functionality was useful at the time but was inefficient as it required evaluation of each packet. Additionally, it did not maintain the concept of an ongoing communication session or monitor connection state. Operationally, design and maintenance of enterprise-grade access lists were difficult and cumbersome.

Stateful/Session-Based

Second-generation firewalls introduced the concept of stateful inspection. Stateful firewalls tracked connection details, allowing traffic to pass in both directions where a valid connection has been established. Maintaining this list of valid sessions helped improve network security. While this firewall track session flows, they did not validate traffic at the application level.

Denial-of-service attacks posed a direct risk to this generation of firewalls. An attacker could flood the firewall with connection attempts in order to fill the memory allocated for tracking the state of valid connections. Most second-generation firewalls in use today sit inside the corporate perimeter where these types of attacks are blocked or more easily mitigated.

Unified Threat Management

A Unified Threat Management (UTM) system is an all-in-one appliance or single device that provides multiple security features and services, simplifying the process of protecting users from security threats. UTM functionality includes common services such as antivirus, anti-spam, and web filtering. As opposed to a firewall that simply manages packet flow, a UTM appliance operates across a broader spectrum.

Processing power limits how much functionality can be included in a single appliance. Large enterprises often prefer specialized devices to perform each security function. Small businesses benefit significantly from the UTM model, where they have access to a broad suite of services managed through a unified, centralized interface at a much lower price point.

While UTMs brought together many different security capabilities, they remained distinct from services provided by newer generations of firewalls. IT organizations looked to next-generation firewall (NGFW) devices to further unify and simplify operations. Where UTM systems lacked performance, NGFWs used single-pass architectures to deliver high-performance throughput and low-latency network security.

Next-Generation Firewalls

As previously noted, stateful firewalls do not examine the application layer to determine the purpose of data and user activity. A new generation of firewalls evolved that offer layer 7 (i.e., the application layer of OSI model) inspection combined with other filtering capabilities (e.g., deep packet inspection or intrusion prevention).

Next-generation firewalls build on packet filtering and stateful connection tracking, bringing support for IPsec and SSL VPNs, IP-to-user identity mapping, network monitoring, and deep content inspection techniques that go beyond simple port and protocol inspection by inspecting the data/payload carried in network packets. These capabilities provide the ability to detect and block attacks from malware and outside threats with SSL inspection, application control, and intrusion prevention.

Operationally, many NGFWs can function in either in routed or transparent mode and are available integrated with SD-WAN edge devices.

Firewall-as-a-Service

The evolution of the cloud and the growing importance of workload mobility has changed the legacy networking and security mindset. The fluidity of infrastructure and movement of data places tremendous pressure on traditional physical security devices.

Physical devices cannot follow workloads. Physical devices cannot be moved around the network. Operational overhead is considerable where device maintenance is a race against time to maintain security. Evaluation, testing, staging, and deployment must all be performed across each device in the infrastructure before applying security patches. This is an ongoing process that must be addressed with each new vulnerability and security patch to prevent malicious actors from compromising the enterprise infrastructure.

Enterprises look for cloud-delivered security-as-a-service to provide a solution. Network security functions (e.g., FWaaS) are available from the cloud, offering IT teams centralized, managed offerings that address the enterprise's need for speed and scale.

2.3 - On-Premises Security Model

The traditional on-premises security model in **Figure 2.2** starts with authentication at an endpoint location (e.g., enterprise/branch user). Common On-Premises endpoint devices include desktops, laptops, and mobile devices – both corporate and personal. Other types of endpoints–cameras, card readers, environmental sensors–may not be associated with an individual user but must still be considered as part of the on-premises security strategy.

Traffic will flow from an endpoint through the enterprise network or enterprise security perimeter to access resources. These may be located in an on-premises data center, private cloud, or public cloud anywhere on the Internet. Throughout this journey, components at multiple layers inspect the traffic and act to enforce the security policy. This multi-layered

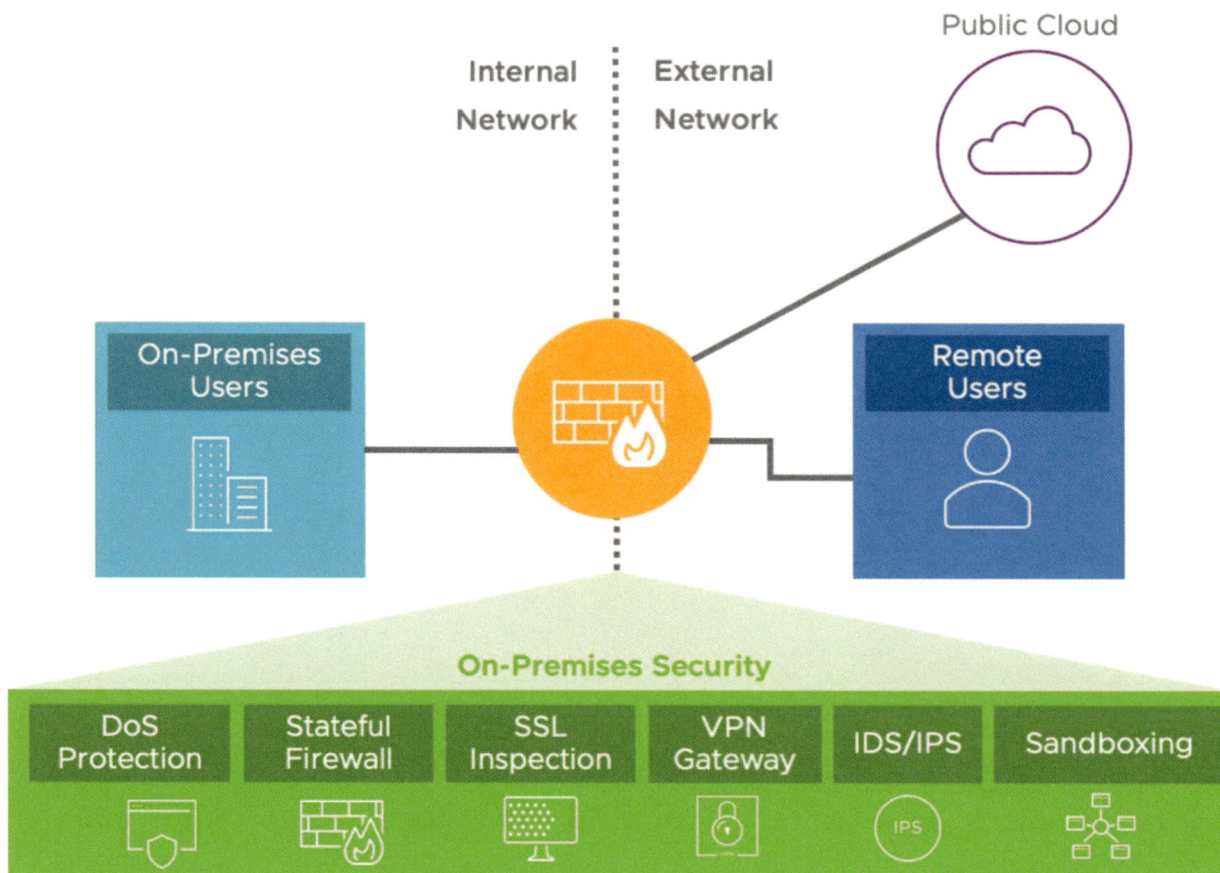

Figure 2.2: On-Premises Security Model

defense-in-depth approach is at the root of escalating security complexity – for policy consistency, architectural design, and ongoing management. The different layers and their individual components are shown in **Figure 2.3**.

Devices at each level frequently come from different manufacturers and operate independently. It is the responsibility of security professionals to ensure that the enterprise security architecture is well-designed, the policy is properly translated across a variety of platforms and protocols, and information is effectively passed between devices and across layers.

The following sections examine the layers of on-premises security, addressing aspects specific to the perimeter, networking, endpoints, applications, and data. Each section takes a closer look at the layer's purposes along with its components and capabilities, breaking these concepts down to address three questions:

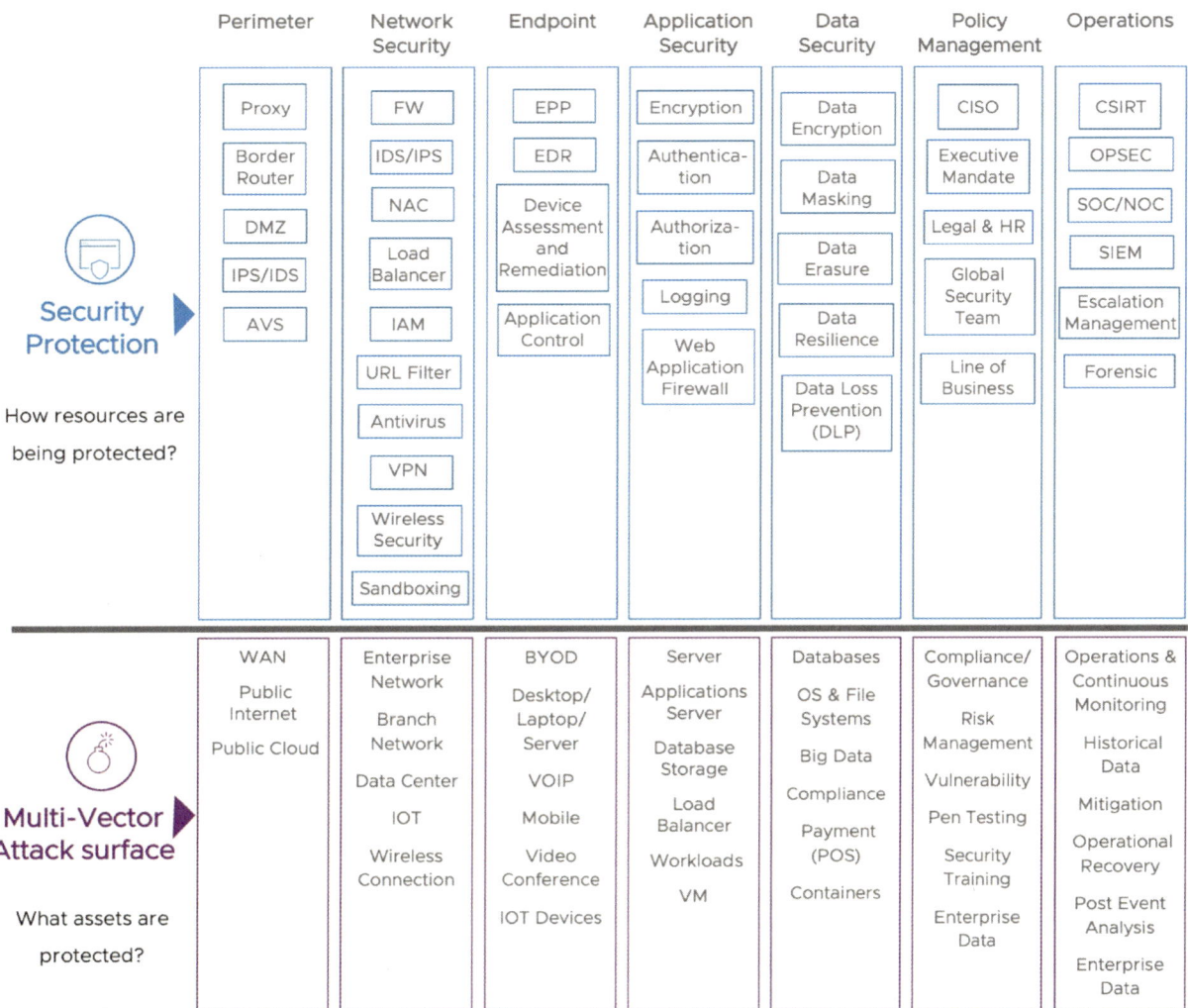

	Perimeter	Network Security	Endpoint	Application Security	Data Security	Policy Management	Operations
Security Protection — How resources are being protected?	Proxy	FW	EPP	Encryption	Data Encryption	CISO	CSIRT
	Border Router	IDS/IPS	EDR	Authentication	Data Masking	Executive Mandate	OPSEC
	DMZ	NAC	Device Assessment and Remediation	Authorization	Data Erasure	Legal & HR	SOC/NOC
	IPS/IDS	Load Balancer		Logging	Data Resilience	Global Security Team	SIEM
	AVS	IAM	Application Control	Web Application Firewall	Data Loss Prevention (DLP)	Line of Business	Escalation Management
		URL Filter					Forensic
		Antivirus					
		VPN					
		Wireless Security					
		Sandboxing					
Multi-Vector Attack surface — What assets are protected?	WAN	Enterprise Network	BYOD	Server	Databases	Compliance/ Governance	Operations & Continuous Monitoring
	Public Internet	Branch Network	Desktop/ Laptop/ Server	Applications Server	OS & File Systems	Risk Management	Historical Data
	Public Cloud	Data Center	VOIP	Database Storage	Big Data	Vulnerability	Mitigation
		IOT	Mobile	Load Balancer	Compliance	Pen Testing	Operational Recovery
		Wireless Connection	Video Conference	Workloads	Payment (POS)	Security Training	Post Event Analysis
			IOT Devices	VM	Containers	Enterprise Data	Enterprise Data

Figure 2.3: On-Premises Security Layers

- **What** does this layer involve?

- **How** does it accomplish its task?

- **Why** is this important to the business?

This policy management and operations sections are conceptual and are not focused on a specific product or technology. Each one is equally important to an effective security strategy.

2.3.1 – Perimeter Security (First Layer)

What is Perimeter Security?

Perimeter security is an essential component of any solution. It is the first layer of defense against external attacks and the last opportunity to prevent information from leaving corporate control. Where it was once well-established and fairly static, the corporate network perimeter is now undergoing significant expansion due to the variety and volume of devices demanding access.

How does Perimeter Security Work?

The perimeter security layer is traditionally implemented through multiple devices that comprise a perimeter firewall. A perimeter firewall sits between internal (e.g., enterprise) and external (e.g., Internet) networks, blocking undesired traffic flows. It is also the first contact for many external threats to the network. It serves as a gatekeeper to intrusion and is implemented through both hardware and software.

Why is Perimeter Security Important?

Employee-owned systems and IoT devices offer a broad landscape for the introduction of malware and active intrusion by cybercriminals and government actors. As the complex nature and volume of cyber threats continue to increase, advanced perimeter solutions offer capabilities that adapt to defend against new or previously undetected attacks.

An On-Premises perimeter layer may include:

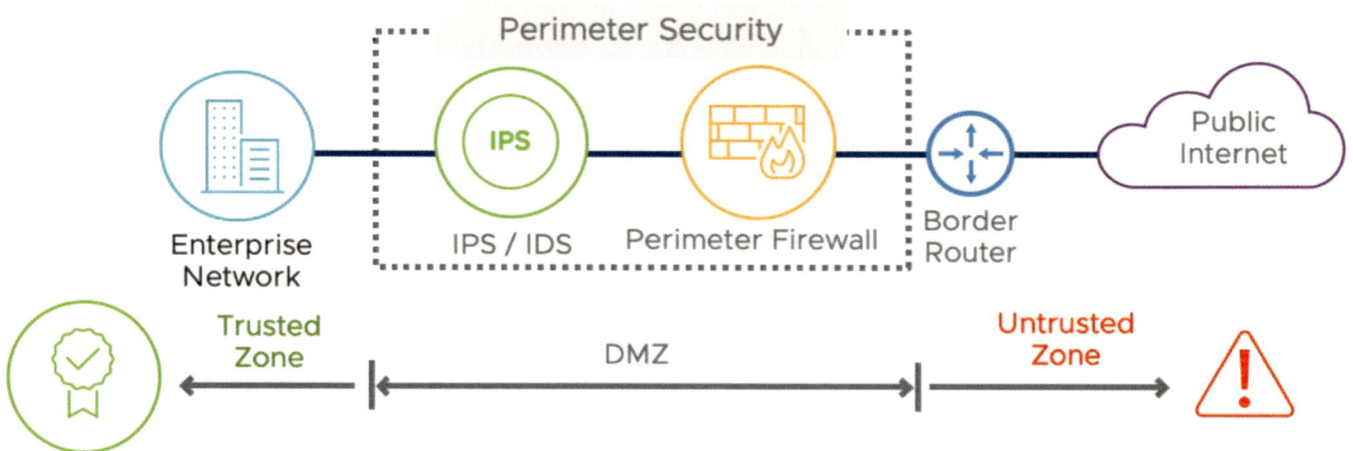

Figure 2.4: Perimeter Firewall

- **Border Router:** Border routers sit at the edge of the corporate network and are usually separate from the routers responsible for internal traffic. They move traffic into and out of the enterprise as well as manage peering relationships with service providers. Border routers can hide the internal network architecture, blackhole traffic to/from specific networks, and filter flows based on a variety of parameters.

- **Proxy Service:** Proxy servers are positioned between internal and external networks to act as intermediaries between the users and resources. When an inside end-user initiates a connection to an external resource, the proxy server will locally process (i.e., terminate) the connection, then establish its own connection directly to the external system. This prevents direct, unsupervised packet transfer between internal and external systems. There are many types of proxy servers, such as forward, reverse, and transparent proxies.

  Forward and reverse proxy servers are the most common. A forward proxy is used from inside the enterprise on traffic exiting the perimeter; it could block enterprise users from visiting certain websites or monitor user activity. A reverse proxy does the opposite, acting on traffic from external users destined for a server inside the enterprise. Some of the benefits of reverse proxy are load balancing, caching, SSL encryption/decryption, and content optimization. The forward proxy hides the identity of enterprise users/clients, while the reverse proxy hides the backend server's identity.

- **IDS/IPS/AV:** Active monitoring of traffic through intrusion detection (IDS), intrusion prevention (IPS), and antivirus (AV) systems provides real-time threat detection and remediation. These systems monitor flows crossing the perimeter and seeks to identify patterns and signatures that indicate malicious intent. They can respond with a notification to the Security Operations Center (SOC), actively block traffic deemed dangerous, or remove problematic data code from packet flows.

- **Demilitarized Zone:** A Demilitarized Zone (DMZ) provides a heightened layer of security by creating a network environment to perform additional traffic inspection and processing. DMZs offer a location for support services that directly interact with external users and require enhanced protection against attack; DNS, mail, and FTP servers are common examples. Logically they sit outside the enterprise perimeter and have additional security capabilities between them and external networks.

- **DLP:** Data Loss Prevention (DLP) tools guard against the accidental or intentional release of protected information by preventing sensitive communication and data from leaving the corporate environment. Similar to IDS/IPS systems, they inspect and analyze traffic flows to identify patterns (e.g., social security numbers, credit card details), keywords (e.g., project codenames, PII medical data), or other defined parameters of concern. DLP technologies provide content awareness through integration into existing infrastructure components such as mail and web gateways or packaging into independent, robust, fully-featured enterprise solutions.

2.3.2 – Network Security (Second Layer)

What is Network Security?

The next layer in the hierarchy is network security. This set of technologies and products prevents attack and intrusion of the network infrastructure–both physical and virtual components–as well as the applications that reside on it. Network security seeks to keep bad actors out of a network, prevent lateral movement when the network has been breached, and isolate any issue prior to its remediation.

How Does Network Security Work?

Best practices for network security employ multiple products coordinated through centralized management and automation to ensure consistent policy application and enforcement. Many of the same technologies and processes deployed in perimeter security are used in this layer but focus on different traffic flows and potential threats. In addition to looking for threats coming from outside the enterprise, these systems also protect against traffic flows between

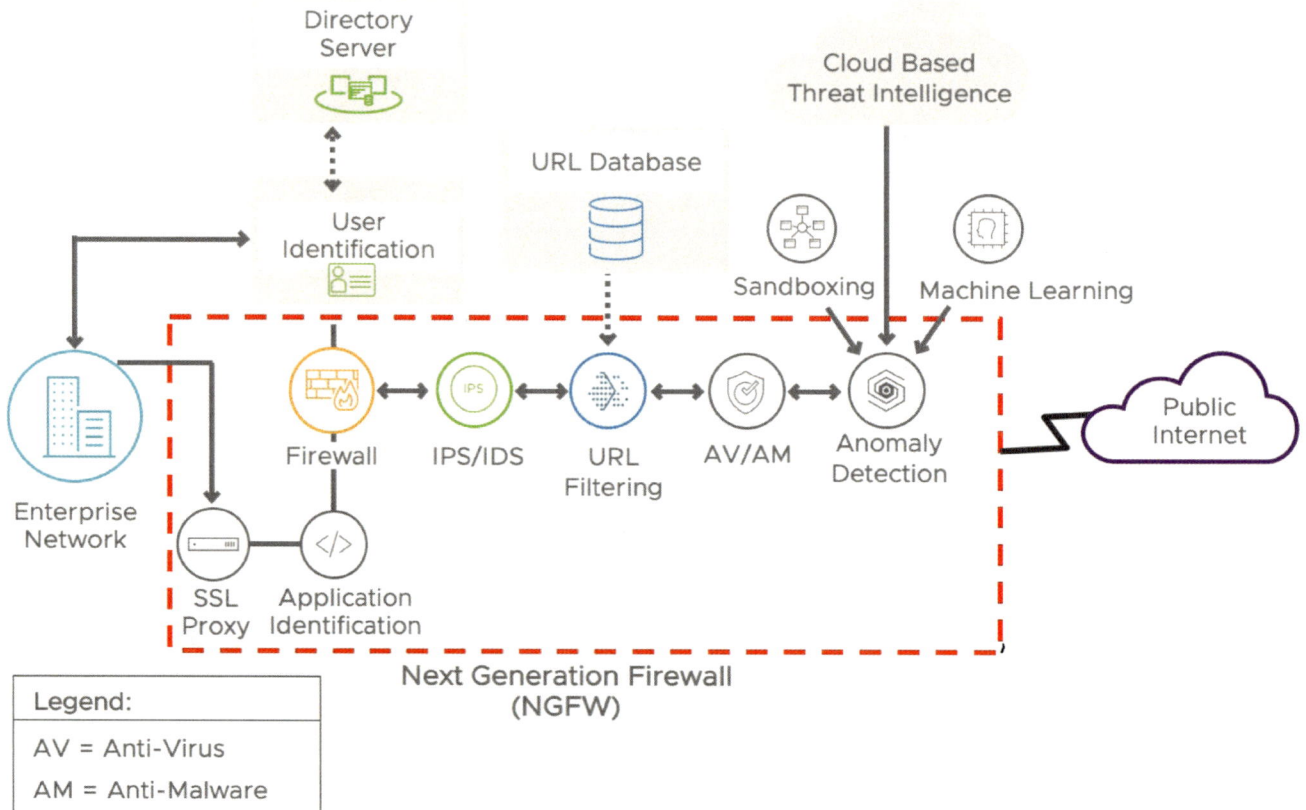

Figure 2.5: Next-Generation Firewall

the data center and other parts of the enterprise (i.e., north/south traffic) and between devices within an individual data center (i.e., east/west traffic).

Why is Network Security Important?

If intruders have compromised one part of the corporate environment, these efforts can prevent infiltration of additional, more sensitive resources. As on the perimeter, individual products and point solutions target different technologies and layers. Solutions such as next-generation firewalls combine many services across multiple layers – packet filtering, stateful inspection, Active Directory authentication, antivirus, URL filtering, threat detection and prevention, SSL encrypt/decrypt, etc.

Common network security components include:

- **Firewall:** Inside of the corporate perimeter, firewalls create zones of trust within the network. They are commonly placed at locations where traffic inspection and filtering are performed based on policy and organizational access rights. Examples include data center ingress/egress access rights, logical domain separation using segmentation such as site/campus branch, and lab environments. Individual firewall capabilities vary from coarse IP address/subnet filtering to fine-grained micro-segmentation.

- **Load Balancer:** Load balancers are proxies that distribute traffic to multiple systems based on policies and metrics. These systems provide resiliency against individual component failures as well as protection for the distinct systems behind the load balancer. Some load balancers have additional capabilities that can detect, mitigate, or fully prevent service-impacting attacks (e.g., DDoS) or block malicious connection attempts.

- **IDS/IPS:** IDS/IPS systems are deployed in conjunction with network firewalls to provide additional analysis of packet details and payload signatures. Protocol analysis validates the fidelity of addresses, ports, flags, and other processing control information. Signature matching examines the content of the payload data itself to identify known attacks (e.g., SQL injection) or infer malicious intent. Modern systems can also enhance deep packet inspection capabilities with the ability to evaluate the content or intent of encrypted traffic or zero-day attacks. The inspection of encrypted traffic requires a TLS proxy and for combating zero-day attacks, while an IDS/IPS needs a connection to a threat intelligence database and artificial intelligence/machine learning (AI/ML) resources.

- **NAC:** Network Access Control (NAC) ensures only authorized users and devices are allowed to connect to the corporate network. Controls can enforce a range of technical compliance policies, including connection location, resource access, device type, security profile, or time-of-day restrictions. These restrictions can be applied broadly or vary based on group membership or individual user specifics.

- **URL Content Filtering:** Content filtering secures web access by comparing web requests and results against block/allow lists and known malicious patterns. It can prevent active harm by blocking access to known malware/phishing URLs and permit access to only work-related websites. Today, URL filtering has expanded with threat intelligence and analytics.

- **Messaging Security/Antivirus:** Messaging Security provides content filtering and security for an enterprise messaging infrastructure (e.g., e-mail, chat). Similar to URL controls, these services eliminate spam and malicious content with a variety of block/allow list, network, reputation, and pattern-based techniques.

- **Wireless Security:** Wireless security is an implementation of network access control for devices not physically connected to the network. This traditionally involves IP-based devices and Wi-Fi protocols such as WPA2 and WPA3 (Wireless Protected Access), 802.1x, and Rogue Access Point (RAP) detection. However, its scope extends beyond this with the explosive growth of IoT devices and non-IP standards (e.g., Bluetooth, Zigbee).

- **Sandbox:** A sandbox environment disconnects a program from the rest of the infrastructure, providing another layer of protection against new security threats. It offloads the object into a controlled area (e.g., a virtual emulation of a target system) to evaluate its actions or traffic flow before allowing it to proceed within the network. Sandbox testing proactively detects malware by executing or detonating code in a safe and isolated environment to observe that code's behavior and output activity. Unlike an IDS/IPS, it is not signature-based, instead of relying on actual observation of behavior in a controlled environment.

- **VPN:** A virtual private network (VPN) is a networking construct that connects two disparate parts of a single network. VPNs usually consist of an encrypted session or tunnel that is intended to provide users privacy and anonymity. They are used to hide both connectivity information (e.g., source IP address) and user data. A VPN can help secure traffic when using an otherwise unsafe public connection such as a Wi-Fi hotspot or hide a user's true geographic location to circumvent content filtering. There are many protocols used to implement and secure VPN sessions; IPsec, SSL/TLS, PPP, and SSH are some of the most common.

- **SSL:** Secure Sockets Layer (SSL) and its successor, Transport Layer Security (TLS), are protocols for establishing authenticated and encrypted links between networked computers. SSL is used for servers and web browsers to make the communication private. SSL certificates are used to secure the connection by using an encrypted communication that connects the server and the browser.

2.3.3 - Identity Access Management (Third Layer)

What is Identity Access Management?

Identity Access Management (IAM) ensures that an individual user is appropriately identified and granted access to appropriate resources (e.g., applications, databases) within the correct context (e.g., who the user is and what access level). IAM controls this access to the corporate environment through authentication and authorization of individual user or device profiles. It is closely interconnected with network security while reaching out to directly interact with multiple other layers of security defense.

Figure 2.6 shows that the user is identified using privileged account management and continuous monitoring with User & Entity Behavior Analytics/Security Information and Event Management (UEBA/SIEM). Once the user is identified and authorized, they are allowed to access appropriate resources (e.g., applications, databases).

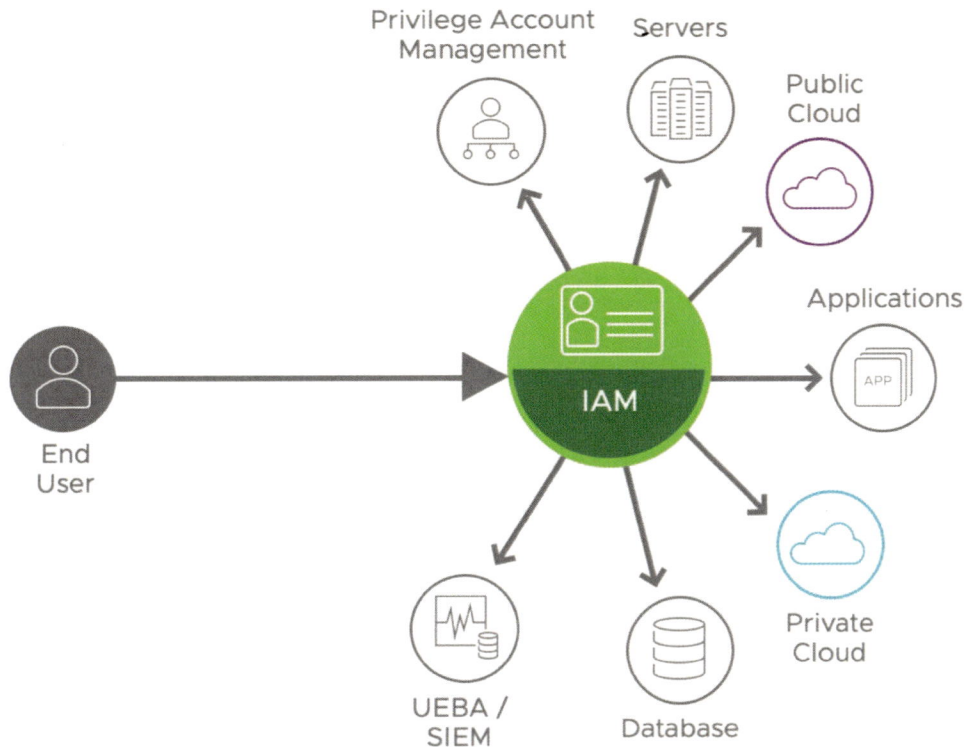

Figure 2.6 : Identity Access Management (IAM) Model

How does Identity Access Management Work?

An IAM solution is responsible for validating a user based on a set of credentials, matching this user to their set of approved resources, and enforcing access based on a set of policies. In addition to permitting or blocking access to resources, IAM also facilitates monitoring processes such as logging activity, metering consumption, and throttling traffic.

Why is Identity Access Management Important?

Businesses of all sizes must have effective IAM to allow for granular access to and control of sensitive resources. IAM can simplify user experience through Single Sign-On (SSO), where logging in from a central portal provides controlled access throughout all enterprise resources. The extension of SSO outside of the enterprise will be further explored in upcoming chapters.

2.3.4 – Endpoint Security (Fourth Layer)

What is Endpoint Security?

Endpoint security sits on individual devices such as laptops, desktops, phones, or even IoT modules. Common examples of endpoint security include OS firewalls, antivirus, anti-malware, and DLP. These solutions protect both system integrity and user data. Centrally managed and benefitting from vast databases of known threats, a complete endpoint security solution helps an endpoint protect itself while preventing it from spreading problems.

Why is Endpoint Security Important?

Endpoint Security is central to preventing previously compromised devices from launching attacks inside the corporate environment while also protecting clean devices from infection. With the prevalence of personally owned bring-your-own devices (BYOD) and multi-use devices on corporate networks, endpoint protection can partition distinct contexts for differing use cases. This approach blocks the flow of information from one context to another, preventing a compromised consumer context from accessing proprietary information or infecting the corporate context.

How does Endpoint Security Work?

Depending on the endpoint, controls can be embedded in hardware, integrated into the operating system, or deployed through the use of an agent. The policy is sent to this controller from a central manager that can report on compliance violations, apply required patches, block known-bad connections, and isolate compromised components. Advanced solutions provide capabilities to quarantine suspected zero-day attacks and other novel threats.

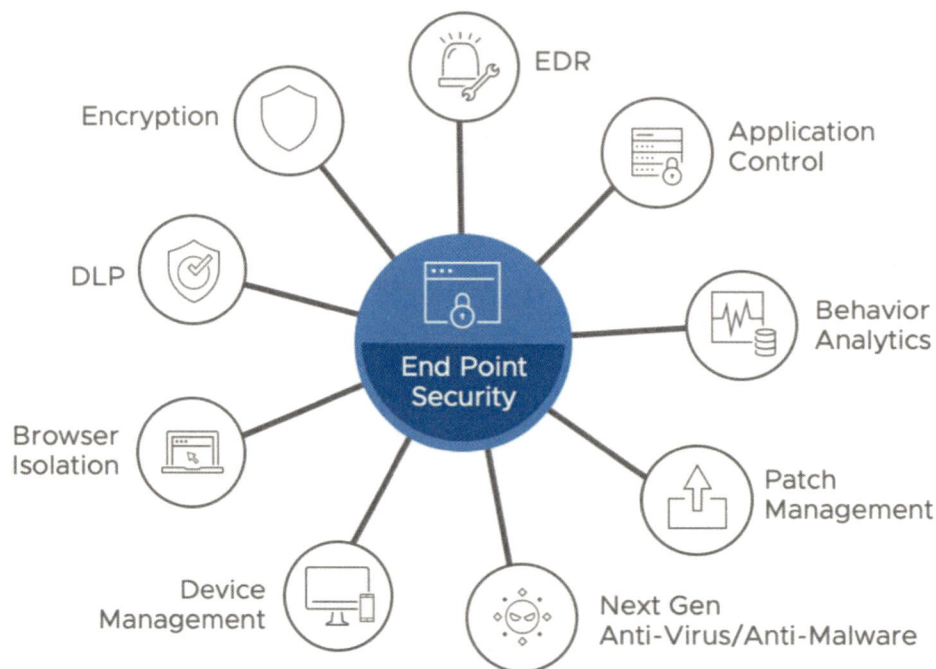

Figure 2.7: End Point Security

The following concepts are central to the construction of an effective endpoint security layer:

- **Endpoint Protection Platform:** An endpoint protection platform (EPP) is the central control point to deploy, manage, and operate endpoint security policy. An EPP can prevent security threats from both known and unknown forms of malware. It provides automation for operational tasks and raises the visibility of potential and ongoing threats. An EPP unifies operations of endpoint agents and distributed access controls. Modern EPPs are leveraging the power of the cloud to hold an ever-growing database of threat information. This frees endpoints of the bloat associated with local storage of all this information and the associated maintenance required to keep these databases up to date. Accessing this data in the cloud also allows for greater speed and scalability

- **Endpoint Detection and Remediation:** Endpoint detection and remediation (EDR) has evolved beyond traditional antivirus programs to incorporate defenses against malware, ransomware, destructive activities, and newly emerging threats. It offers capabilities that can detect and respond to threats that an EPP and other security tools did not identify. These solutions operate independently of the corporate environment and can protect a device regardless of the nature of the connection or the vector of the attack (e.g., USB media, laptop, IoT devices, Servers, Wireless devices, medical devices). Network Detection and Remediation (NDR) offers similar functionality for networking, while Extended Detection and Response (XDR) is a SaaS-based security model and operates from endpoint to the cloud.

- **Device Assessment and Remediation:** Real-time device assessment and remediation systems allow auditors to understand the current state of systems, investigate and analyze paths through which endpoints may have become compromised, and manage corrective efforts, including patching, encryption, and posture enhancement.

- **Application Control:** Endpoint application control allows system administrators to define and limit valid update sources (e.g., users, groups, applications) to ensure only trusted updates can be deployed. Application control solutions can lock servers and other critical systems to prevent unwanted changes and ensure continuous compliance with regulatory mandates. App control can protect both new and legacy systems and is applicable to embedded, virtual, and physical platforms as well as operating systems.

2.3.5 – Application Security (Fifth Layer)

What is Application Security?

Application security aims to prevent data or code within an application from being stolen or hijacked. Its specific requirements and implementation can vary widely based on the nature of the application itself. Security concerns exist not only on the front end of the application but the back end as well, where connections to databases, storage, network services (e.g., DNS, SQL DB, Active Directory) provide additional vectors for attack.

How does Application Security Work?

Proper deployment should encompass all stages of the application lifecycle, including design, development, deployment, operation, and maintenance. It may be implemented through both hardware and software as well as include processes that actively mitigate security vulnerabilities. Examples, respectively, include application address translation, application-level filtering, and regular penetration testing. Cloud environments share certain resources between tenants, so care must be taken to restrict the visibility of and control over data. Finally, applications should be designed with security considerations built-in. They may rely on platform-specific functionality unique to a specific environment, use existing industry standards (e.g., PCI, HIPAA), or take specific steps based on their individual nature and operational environment.

Why is Application Security Important?

Application protocols and data may cross networks with varying levels of protection and encryption, some of which exist outside of the corporation's physical zone of control. Internet applications add another layer of risk as IT departments cannot assume users employ secure connectivity methods (e.g., VPN) and do not have complete control over 3rd party applications. As legacy monolithic applications (e.g., IBM DB2, RDBMS) give way to container and microservice-based models such as cloud-native databases, management tools must scale at the same exponential rate to keep pace with the complexity.

Application security incorporates the following areas and technologies and is shown in **Figure 2.8**.

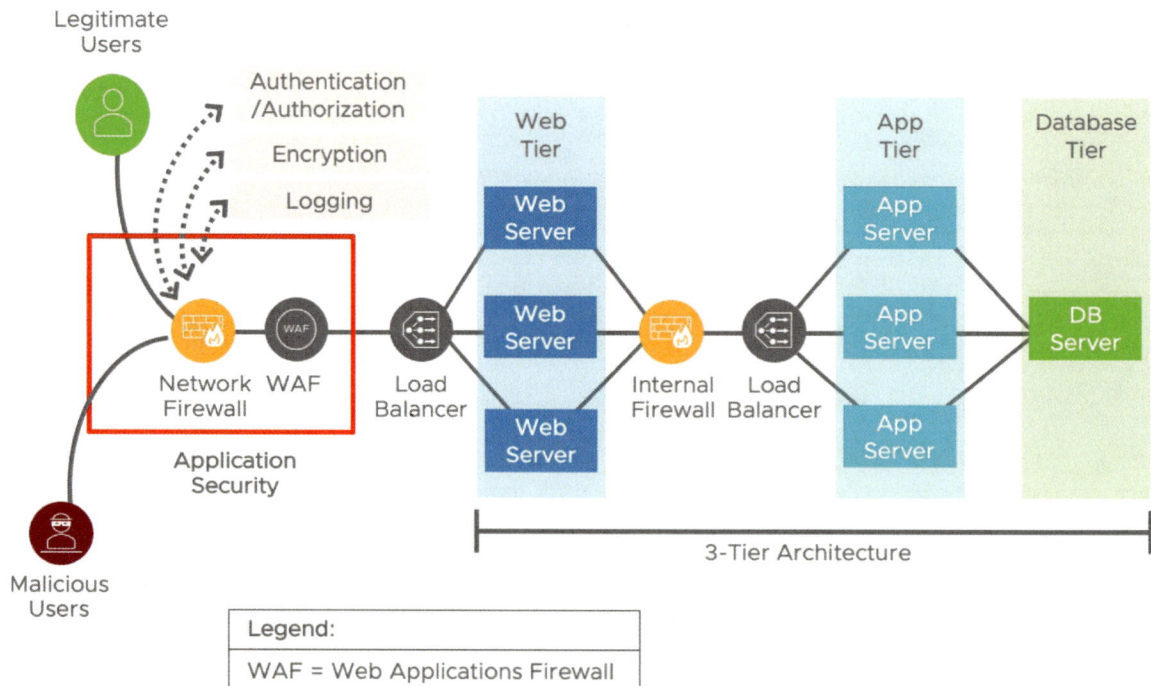

Figure 2.8: Application Security Protecting a 3-Tier Architecture

- **Authentication:** Authentication is the process of correctly identifying a user and determining whether they have access to a given application. The most familiar example of authentication is the request for a username and password. Multi-factor protocols require additional data for proper authentication, such as a security token. Biometric authentication uses factors that are nearly unique to any given individual (e.g., thumbprint). Location-based methods seek to understand where a person is known to be and restrict access from unlikely combinations. For example, if an end-user is already logged in from New York and shortly after attempts to log in from San Francisco.

- **Authorization:** After a user has been authenticated, the authorization process validates that they have permission to use a specific application and, if so, grants access. This check is performed against a list of authorized users and may be determined by additional attributes such as group membership, time/date details, or location. This step must necessarily follow authentication as it operates on a specific user attribute.

- **Encryption:** Applications can employ various layers and methods of encryption to shield sensitive data from both cursory inspection and cybercriminals. Corporations with sensitive or compliance-regulated data must take care where sessions may cross public carrier links or the Internet. Information can be encrypted before it is encapsulated, packet payload can be secured after creation, or standard encryption protocols such as TLS can be used to secure the entire end-to-end session. Encryption can also be performed at other layers of this security model, so application developers and network designers should work together to understand the implications of each approach.

- **Logging:** Logging is a fundamental component of all aspects of networking and security. Within an application, logging can identify who accessed processes and data, when individual components were used, what tasks were performed, and how the application responded. Security logs are used in active troubleshooting, problem remediation, and post-incident investigation.

- **WAF:** A Web Application Firewall (WAF) filters and monitors HTTP traffic between web application servers. They are usually placed at boundaries between zones of trust, especially where traffic will traverse the Internet. Web applications are popular targets due to their common use for e-commerce and other financial services. WAFs work by inspecting traffic and filtering data that is deemed dangerous. They operate at the application layer and protect against attacks, including cross-site forgery, cross-site scripting, malicious file transfers, and SQL injection.

2.3.6 – Data Security (Sixth Layer)

What is Data Security?

The final layer of this defense is data security – the process of protecting files, databases, and accounts throughout the enterprise. While this level focuses directly on base-level corporate information, it should not be viewed as more important than other layers; it is simply one part of a complete practice that comes with storing and processing any kind of data.

How does Data Security Work?

Data security uses a set of controls, applications, and techniques that identifies the relative importance of data sets, evaluates their sensitivities and compliance requirements, then applies the protection necessary to secure the information. Data security solutions centralize and simplify the process of creating and managing complex policies across the enterprise. They organize the complex tasks associated with protecting all data created, received, stored, and transmitted. Adherence to privacy, regulatory, and legal compliance is also a major consideration, especially in heavily regulated industries and specific geographies (e.g., HIPAA, Protected Health Information medical data, GDPR governmental compliance, and Payment Card Industry/Data Security Standard PCI/DSS).

Why is Data Security Important?

All digital businesses deal in data. Banks process massive volumes of personal and financial data. Sales teams rely on databases of customer contact and marketing information. Even one-person companies must store and secure information essential to their continued existence and may use a mobile device or cloud provider to accomplish this. News stories continuously demonstrate the risk and impact of security threats from both opportunistic cybercriminals and organized nation-states. Businesses can suffer not only data loss and financial repercussions; they also can lose the trust of customers and reputation in the marketplace. As businesses grow more connected and more dependent on data, bad actors will only increase their efforts. **Figure 2.9** represents Data Security key capabilities like Data Protection, Data Confidentiality and Data Compliance.

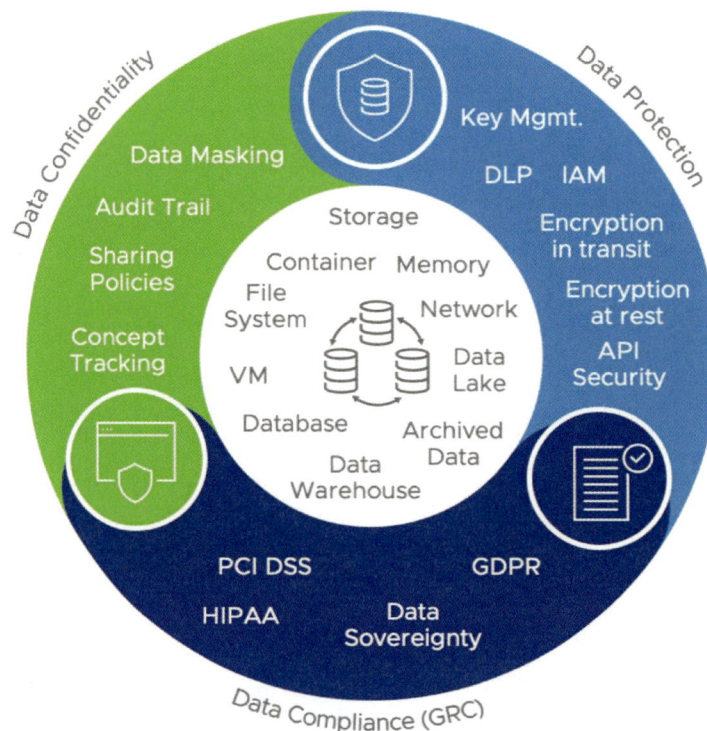

Figure 2.9: Data Security Representing Key Capabilities

Components of a proper data security solution include:

- **Data Encryption:** Encryption protects data by making it unreadable by those who do not have access to the decryption key. Different encryption models–symmetric vs. asymmetric–offer different processes for key generation, distribution, ownership, and management. Data can be encrypted at any point in its lifecycle – upon generation, while at rest, or when in motion. Security algorithms come in a wide range of strengths and implementations; it is important to understand the capabilities, limitations and select accordingly.

- **Data Masking:** A subset of data encryption, masking obfuscates sections of the original data to hide sensitive or restricted information while keeping uninteresting data readable. This process can allow the use of real data sets in less secure environments such as external reporting or IT operations. An example of data masking would be hiding the first 12 digits of a credit card or starring out a password while displaying the associated username.

- **Data Erasure:** Erasure ensures that data is properly destroyed after it is no longer required. Deletion of a file from a computer may not eliminate the data from the drive where it was stored or account for replications of the file on other systems. Proper erasure involves the tracking of a data element throughout its entire lifecycle.

- **Data Resilience:** In ways the opposite of erasure, resilience aims to ensure that data is always available and never at risk of loss – either through accidental or intentional means. At its most basic level, data resilience helps protect an individual system against compromise by a ransomware attack or an isolated hard drive failure. More complex solutions ensure availability in the event of failures of entire networks or data centers.

- **DLP:** Data loss prevention software detects potential data breaches. Touched on in other sections, DLP solutions inspect data wherever it exists – on a disk, in memory, or on the network. They apply policy to allow or block data movement onto, off of, or between systems. DLP solutions are most commonly deployed directly on an endpoint or at the corporate perimeter, but use cases exist at all security layers. For example, an IT administrator can create a policy for data files that contain intellectual property or copyrighted information that prevents them from being copied to removable media or transmitted outside the enterprise network.

- **Data Retention:** Data retention is the policies of persistent data and records management for meeting legal and business data archival requirements, also referred to as record retention. These capabilities may be required due to government mandates (e.g., European GDPR) or internal business continuity practices (e.g., recovery in case of fire or flood) for essential information.

2.3.7 – Policy Management (Seventh Layer)

Where the previous layers dealt with specific on-premises security practices, this final layer examines policy and day-to-day operational management.

What is Policy Management?

Security policy management is the process of identifying, implementing and managing the rules and procedures that control access to an organization's digital assets and resources. These policies are in place to harden the infrastructure against security threats, minimize the impact of intrusions, and speed recovery after an incident. They also provide guidance to employees on proper security practices, permissible activities, and consequences associated with deviation from standards.

How is Policy Management Implemented?

Chief Information Security Officers (CISO) are responsible for ensuring adherence to compliance and regulatory mandates (e.g., PCI, HIPAA, GDPR), managing risks and vulnerabilities, and working with lines of business to address their individual requirements and restrictions. They face a steady increase of responsibility and concern due to the rapid rise in scope and impact of business digitization.

Automation is increasingly important to helping security organizations scale their capabilities, maintaining quality without significantly increasing headcount. Businesses use automated policy management solutions for the evaluation, implementation, and ongoing operation of their security policies. Automation increases the accuracy of repetitive tasks while allowing staff to focus on higher-value efforts. Effective automation can provide continuous assurance of compliance, consistency for change management processes, and timely application of security patches and system upgrades.

Why is Policy Management Important?

Global security policy trends evolve rapidly. Regulation and protectionism will require greater control over and reporting on data. Supply chain vulnerabilities place business continuity at risk. Lack of standards and regulation for mobile and IoT systems can create a wild west of security solutions. Cybercriminals' increased access to nation-state-grade hacking tools will lead to more rapid patch cycles to address critical and zero-day vulnerabilities. For security teams that already struggle to meet security challenges on-premises, their threat landscape is about to be even more expansive as services move into the cloud.

2.4 – Operations

Organizational models for security teams vary widely. Security personnel can be integrated with IT technology silos, spread across lines of business, or organized into independent teams. Operations leadership must give careful consideration to charter and structure where they have a wide range of responsibilities, including threat awareness, policy management and maintenance, hands-on troubleshooting, and employee education. A proper examination of best practices for organizing and managing an operational security

Figure 2.10: Day-to-Day Security Operations

organization is beyond the scope of this book, but the following list details common terms and concepts that anyone working in the security space should be familiar with. Some of the day-2-day operations are shown in **Figure 2.10**.

- **OPSEC:** Operations Security (OPSEC) is a set of standards and practices through which a security organization can better identify, evaluate, and work to mitigate or eliminate vulnerabilities. Operations security is not a one-time checkbox or yearly audit requirement; it should be an ongoing practice that is constantly evaluating and responding to potential threats.

- **SOC:** The security operations center (SOC) is responsible for the ongoing operation of an enterprise security practice. It implements a strategy that aligns with line-of-business requirements and executive mandates, implementing the architecture and enforcing predefined policy. A SOC is not necessarily a physical war room with large monitors and global maps; it should be formed from security analysts and engineers with the charter to protect digital corporate resources against all threats.

- **CSIRT:** A computer or cybersecurity incident response team (CSIRT) is responsible for responding to an intrusion event. It commonly consists of members from cross-functional disciplines and is tasked with leading impact mitigation, operational recovery, and post-event analysis. While mainly focused on technical and business challenges, the team must collaborate with units across the company (e.g., HR, customer support, legal) to ensure clear communication and business continuity during an incident.

- **SIEM:** Security information and event management (SIEM) aggregate and analyzes information from systems and platform across the enterprise. A SIEM solution provides both real-time information to help identify threats and aggregated historical logs for audit or compliance requirements. It gives the SOC a unified, high-level view of the state of the security ecosystem and infrastructure.

2.5 – On-Premises Security - Putting it all Together

Even with its high-level perspective, **Figure 2.11** demonstrates the complexities and challenges faced by IT organizations. Added to this environment is the requirement to

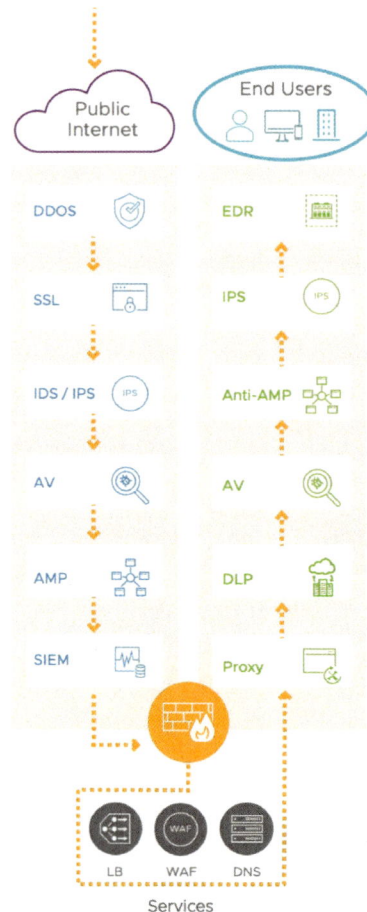

Figure 2.11: Logical Flow Diagram of On-premises Security

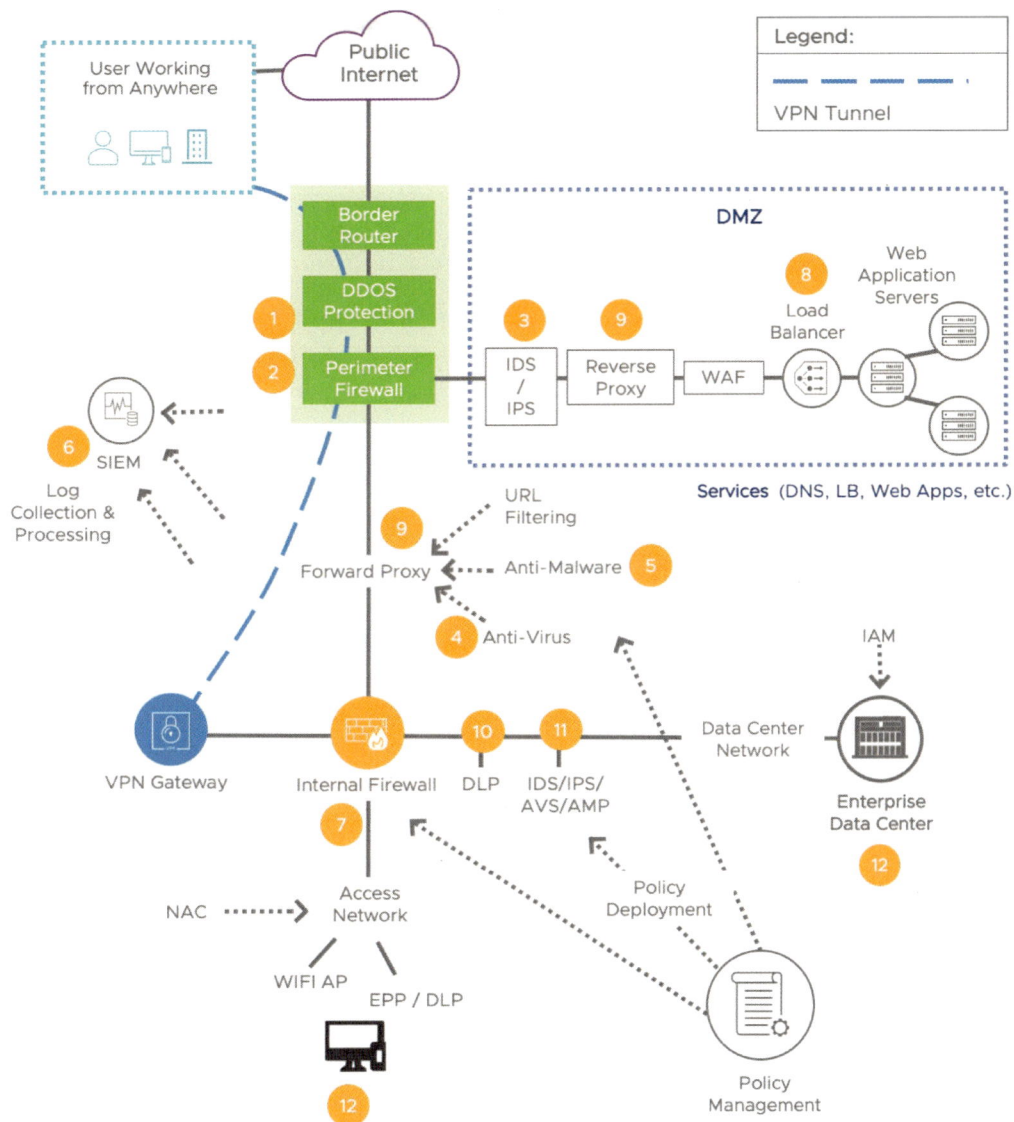

Figure 2.12: Physical Representation of Traditional On-Premises Security in Enterprise Network

define and implement security policy while working across the evolving requirements of the business landscape.

Figure 2.12 depicts a physical representation of the traditional on-premises security layer. It follows a sample traffic flow originating on the Internet (i.e., outside) through security controls on its way to an enterprise network resource (i.e., inside).

1. **DDOS:** Upon reaching the corporate perimeter, the flow is processed by the external firewall. DDoS protection will protect against any volume-based attacks, including UDP flooding, ICMP flooding, ping-of-death, and other spoofed packet floods.

2. **SSL:** SSL inspection is done by Perimeter firewall. Encrypted traffic (e.g., HTTPS) between the client and server is inspected to ensure it is legitimate. Border Router, DDOS Protection and Perimeter Firewall resides on the external network represented by the green shaded box.

3. **IDS/IPS:** An IDS analyzes the content to identify known cyber-attacks addressed by the IPS.

4. **AV:** Antivirus will prevent, detect, and remove viruses (e.g., worms, trojans) before passing through the perimeter.

5. **AMP:** Individual advanced malware processing (AMP) tools offer additional granular inspection. These systems can offload suspect traffic to a sandbox for further evaluation and will quarantine any malware detected.

6. **SIEM:** By analyzing data from multiple security products, the SIEM can provide real-time alerts about potential threats or security holes related to this traffic. The SOC can then follow up with a detailed investigation.

7. **Firewall:** Traffic next passes through the DMZ firewall. This system performs another layer of inspection at layers three and above while enforcing access lists that implement the enterprise's security policies.

8. **Services:** Service-specific (e.g., web application, DNS) inspection is performed. Load balancing also helps optimize the traffic flow and provides resiliency to the session.

At this point, the traffic has passed through the perimeter and is considered inside the enterprise boundary.

9. **Proxy:** The service proxy terminates the original session, then establishes a new one to the internal system. This helps control the traffic flow while protecting internal resources from external attacks.

10. **DLP:** DLP monitors the traffic flow in real-time to identify sensitive information, ensuring it only resides on or moves between authorized systems.

11. **IDS/IPS, AVS, AMP:** Similar to their external counterparts, these systems will examine traffic for specific threats and remediate/quarantine/block as appropriate.

12. **Destination:** The traffic finally reaches the end-user device, enterprise server, or network element, where it is processed or sent for further inspection by endpoint security solutions (e.g., EDR, NDR, XDR).

While this process is broken up into discrete steps, next-generation firewalls can combine many security functions into a single platform. Unified threat appliances provide not only traditional firewall capabilities but also aggregate many of these services into single hardware- or software-based solution with capabilities that include hardening, patching, or updating the operating system.

2.6 – Key Takeaways

Even as market analysts talk about corporations moving to the cloud, on-premises security is not going away. Individual areas and technologies may change in form or function as solutions move beyond the traditional perimeter boundary. The next chapter will examine security in the cloud, highlighting both common and unique challenges from the ones presented here.

Checklist: On-Premises Security Takeaways

✓ The marketplace for on-premises security solutions is diverse and fragmented. Point solutions target narrow problem spaces and rarely communicate well with each other.

✓ The layered model provides defense in depth to on-premises environments. Individual technologies and pinpoint products may exist at multiple layers (e.g., firewalls). No single layer is most important; they must all fit together like pieces of a larger, holistic strategy.

✓ On-premises security will remain critically important and will continue to evolve. As the enterprise landscape grows more complex with cloud platforms and SaaS providers, developing and maintaining consistent policy becomes a more significant challenge.

✓ Automation is critical to environmental stability. It helps eliminate human error, aids inconsistency across diverse infrastructure, scales as device count and network complexity proliferates and maximizes staffing efficiency.

✓ Do not neglect security policy or organization structure while pursuing technology and strategy.

✓ An effective intrinsic security solution must be built-in rather than bolted-on.

Chapter 3

Cloud Security Foundation

3.1 – Overview, Definitions, & Motivations

Cloud security implements traditional and advanced security services for branches, clients, and cloud workloads. It does this while maintaining most of the processing in the cloud and as a service. Security in the cloud as a service provides the advantage of scale and allows for intelligence sourcing across multiple customers. Cloud security is the practice of securing and protecting cloud environments through the deployment and management of technologies and operational standards. It considers the requirements of networking, applications, storage, and data when defining and implementing the processes that ensure security across an online infrastructure.

Ownership of individual components of a cloud security solution varies, which can complicate the holistic visibility and ongoing policy management.

Distinct audiences bring differing opinions and perspectives on what defines the cloud and how models are organized. The following definitions from the US Department of Commerce National Institute of Standards and Technology (NIST) describe fundamental terms that will be used in this chapter.

- **Cloud:** NIST defines cloud computing as "a model for enabling ubiquitous, convenient, on-demand network access to a shared pool of configurable computing services (example includes networks, servers, storage, applications, and services) that can be rapidly deployed with minimal IT operations". Essential characteristics include on-demand self-service, broad network access, resource pooling, rapid elasticity, and measured service.

- **Public Cloud:** A deployment model where third-party providers offer the infrastructure as a service over the public web (internet), making them available to anyone who wants to use or purchase them. They may be free or sold on-demand, allowing customers to pay only per usage for the CPU cycles, memory, storage, or bandwidth they consume. Hardware and software resources reside on the provider's premises and are accessed over the public Internet. Public Cloud is a multi-tenant environment where each cloud tenant's allocated resources are logically isolated from the other tenants. Popular public cloud providers include AWS, Azure, Google Cloud, and Alibaba Cloud.

- **Private Cloud:** A private cloud infrastructure is designated for use by a single enterprise or entity but is not necessarily owned or managed by that group. It may be located either on or off-premises. Private clouds can also be accessed over the public Internet using VPN technology to segregate traffic and prevent tampering. Enterprise IT is responsible for all the management, operations, maintenance, and updates in the private cloud infrastructure.

- **Hybrid Cloud:** The hybrid cloud model uses a mix of on-premises, public cloud, and private environments for a single enterprise, unifying them under a standard set of practices such as management, workload mobility, or security policy. A hybrid cloud approach could involve a public cloud environment and a private cloud environment.

- **Multi-Cloud:** A multi-cloud model uses clouds from more than one cloud provider. A multi-cloud approach could involve two or more public cloud environments or two or more private cloud environments. The main benefit of multi-cloud is its high availability; if one cloud goes down, an enterprise can still be up and running with connectivity to the other cloud infrastructure.

- **Cloud Security:** Security must be a core concern of modern, cloud-focused businesses. Traditional security practices are no longer sufficient as IT resources shift to the cloud. Business-critical data lives outside of the corporate perimeter, beyond the bounds of guaranteed physical and technical control. Cloud-centric models increase the distance between individual components and the velocity with which the environment scales. The complex web of connectivity between users, applications, and data offers a rich landscape for intrusion and exploitation. Understanding and monitoring corporate and governmental compliance mandates are no longer possible with internal skillsets. Ensuring business continuity remains a primary IT responsibility regardless of the location of systems and control of services.

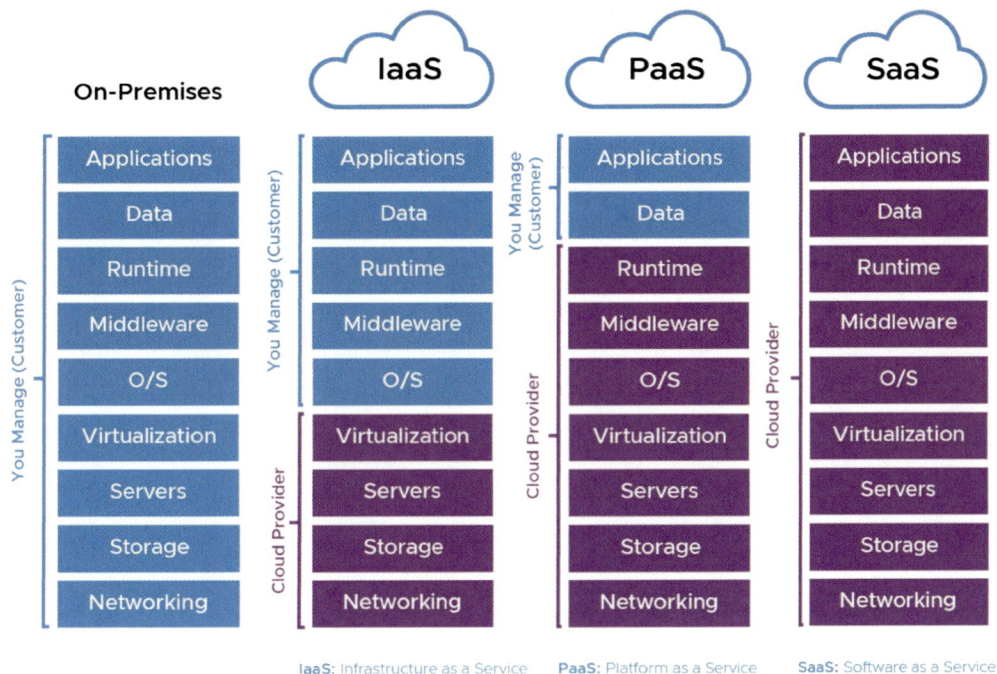

On-Premises   **IaaS**   **PaaS**   **SaaS**

On-Premises (You Manage – Customer): Applications, Data, Runtime, Middleware, O/S, Virtualization, Servers, Storage, Networking

IaaS — You Manage (Customer): Applications, Data, Runtime, Middleware, O/S; Cloud Provider: Virtualization, Servers, Storage, Networking

PaaS — You Manage (Customer): Applications, Data; Cloud Provider: Runtime, Middleware, O/S, Virtualization, Servers, Storage, Networking

SaaS — Cloud Provider: Applications, Data, Runtime, Middleware, O/S, Virtualization, Servers, Storage, Networking

IaaS: Infrastructure as a Service   **PaaS:** Platform as a Service   **SaaS:** Software as a Service

Figure 3.1: Cloud Service Types

3.2 – Cloud Services and Environments

Cloud providers tailor their services and offer models to meet businesses' demands from all verticals. Solutions range from basic bare metal hosting that simply provides foundational hardware up through integrated turnkey offerings which eliminate most traditional IT tasks. Each draws distinct ownership lines and responsibility for networking, compute, virtualization, security, storage, and data. Some of the most common service-based models are described in the following list. **Figure 3.1** shows IaaS, PaaS , SaaS.

- **Infrastructure-as-a-Service:** An IaaS provider offers access to fundamental infrastructure–hardware, connectivity, and core cloud services–creating a foundational platform on which to build. It eliminates the burden of managing physical hardware and maintaining a data center facility. While the service provider retains direct control of the underlying cloud infrastructure, the consumer can be granted access to specific components through APIs or other processes. Customers must implement and manage their own operating systems, networking, services, storage, user administration, and applications. IaaS offerings include Amazon Web Services and Microsoft Azure.

- **Software-as-a-Service:** SaaS hosts a specific software application within the service provider's environment. Instead of purchasing and installing an off-the-shelf product or developing a solution in-house, the customer subscribes to the service, and the provider takes responsibility for everything from the hardware through the Application. This places the burden on tasks such as OS patching, software upgrades, and data backup on the SaaS provider. SaaS applications may have their own user administration tools or connect to a corporation's centralized directory system. Common examples of SaaS are Salesforce and Office365.

- **Platform-as-a-Service:** PaaS provides an environment for customers to develop and/or host applications of their choice. These resources such as applications are built on top of the operating system and development environment from the provider, with the client managing end-user connectivity (e.g., networking, user access) and workflow components (e.g., applications, data). The lines between PaaS and other as-a-service models are not hard and fast; solutions in this space often bridge the gaps and cross into adjacent areas such as offerings from ServiceNow and Google Cloud Platform.

- **Other Models:** Additional as-a-service models are tuned to address market-specific segments of control, functionality, and operation – including bare-metal-as-a-service, function-as-a-service, data-as-a-service, and disaster-recovery-as-a-service.

3.2.1 - Shared Responsibility Model

Unlike traditional corporate data center management, cloud environments offer an opportunity for IT to offload a significant amount of technical and operational functions to the provider. Where before it may have only been possible to outsource physical security or hardware replacement, as-a-service models allow the responsibility for almost any element to be delegated to a service provider.

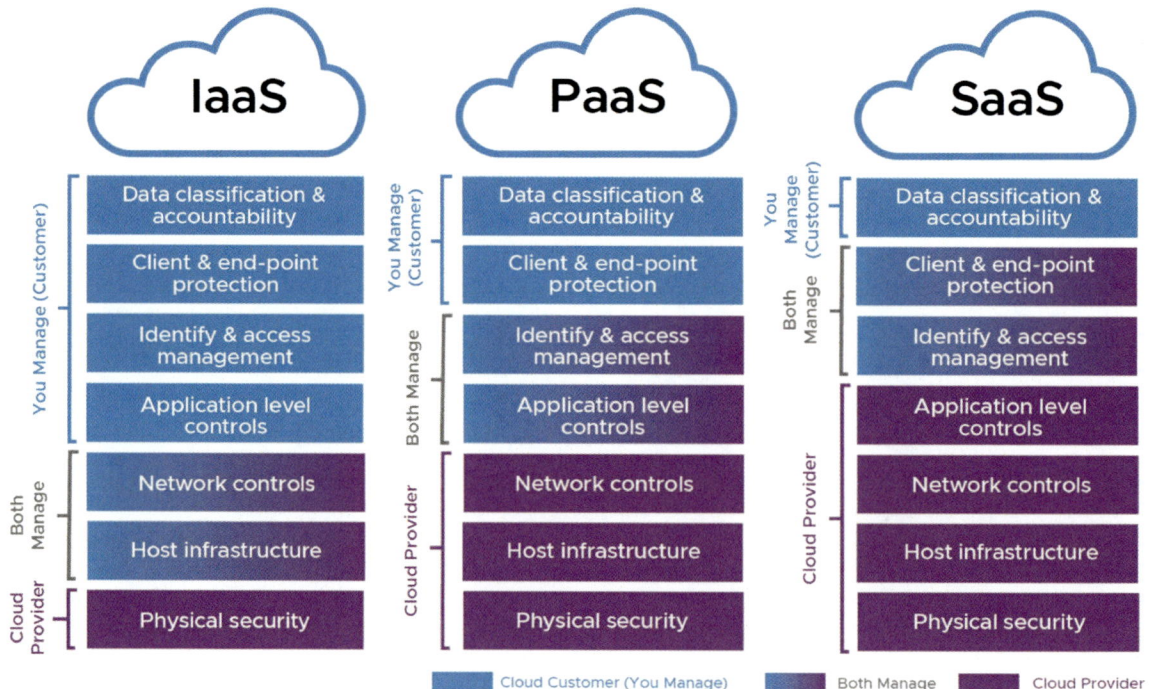

Figure 3.2: Shared Responsibility Model

Central to the success of this model is a clear definition of the ownership, processes, and communication associated with the service. In this shared responsibility model, each party has specific obligations they must fulfill. Roles and responsibilities vary based on customer, provider, and model – the only constant is clear communication and consistent oversight of the service lifecycle.

3.3 – Cloud Security Implementation

Similar to on-premises security, cloud security forms from a layered technology, process, and policy approach. Unlike that model, the notion of a progression inward from the perimeter must be adjusted as there is no single boundary from which to begin. Instead, the cloud security layers overlap, forming a self-reinforcing circle around the infrastructure rather than a protective outside-in shell. For an enterprise business goal, the security principles apply anywhere and should be consistent regardless of what is being protected – users, devices, data, or applications.

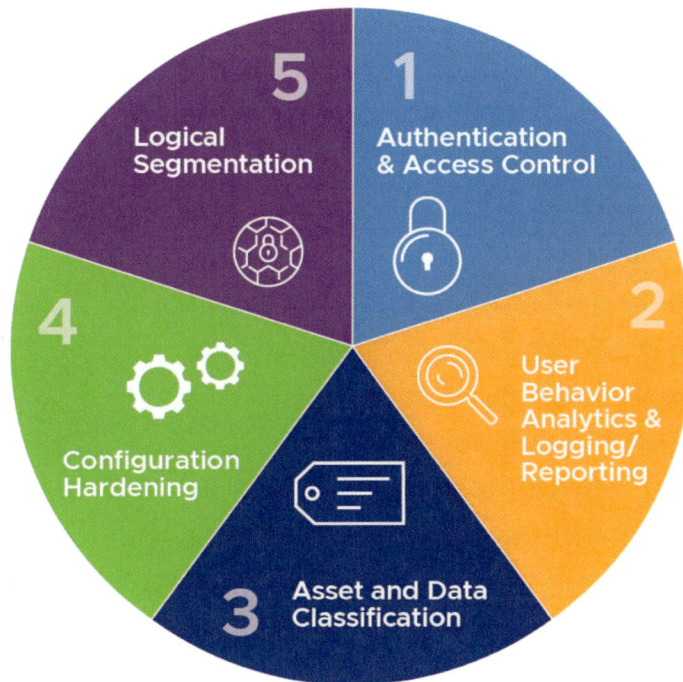

Figure 3.3: Circular Security Layered Approach

3.3.1 - Authentication & Access Control (First Layer)

What is Access Control

Identity, authentication, and access management systems are responsible for properly identifying users, matching them to a proper set of resources, and controlling access based on corporate policy. These solutions bring together a variety of individual components to allow proper users access while either restricting access to those who fall outside of specific permissions or preventing it entirely for unauthorized attempts.

How is Access Control Implemented?

Authentication is the first step of this process and takes the same approach as for on-premises solutions. User credentials are submitted and verified with varying sets of requirements and validations. A username/password combination is the most common authentication process but remains significantly insecure. The importance of multi-factor solutions is increased for cloud services due to increased exposure to threats outside of the corporate environment. Smart tokens, user certificates, and one-time validation codes are common examples used to enhance security when connecting across the Internet. Single sign-on solutions also enhance security by allowing the user to strongly authenticate to a single, central source responsible for confirming user details to individual federated services.

After confirming a user's identity, access control matches their profile against a set of resources to permit or deny access. The system's granularity depends on the Application; it could take a hard deny/permit approach—such as permitting full access to a financial application—or apply more granular controls by allowing viewing but not editing of router configurations.

Authentication

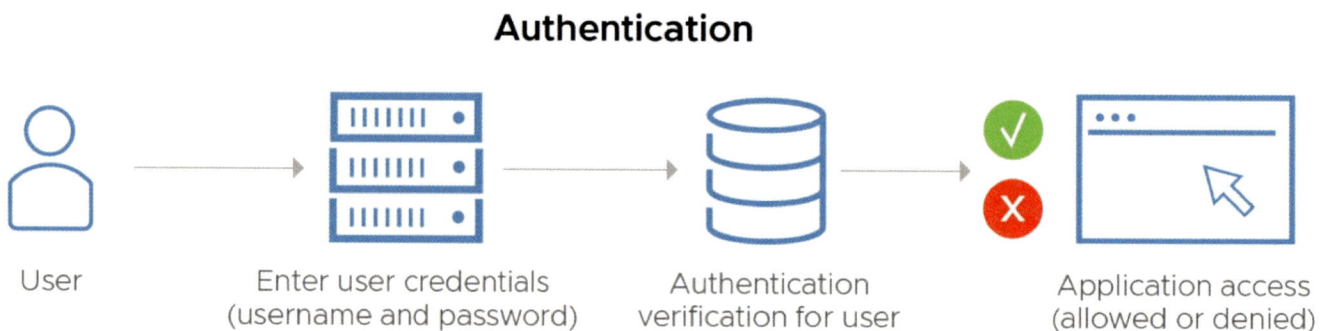

| User | Enter user credentials (username and password) | Authentication verification for user | Application access (allowed or denied) |

Figure 3.4: IAM: Identity and Access Management

Why is Access Control Required?

Authentication and access controls allow the enforcement of IT policy and can help establish a Zero Trust model that aligns with effective cloud security principles. Modern applications are built with the expectations of user and group roles and responsibilities; AAA/IAM systems are the engine that powers that control.

3.3.2 – User Behavior Analytics & Logging/Reporting (Second Layer)

What is User and Entity Behavior Analytics?

User Entity Behavior Analytics (UEBA) practices create a baseline of expected behaviors and practices of individual users or other entities (e.g., machines), then use analytical systems to identify deviations and anomalies from these standards. The goal is to discover potential threats and ongoing security incursions. Rather than identifying known issues or matching existing patterns, UEBA highlights the unexpected to allow for closer review.

> **User Behavior Analytics (UBA) is all about monitoring patterns of user behavior and applying algorithms to detect anomalies that could indicate potential threats.**
>
> **User and Entity Behavior Analytics (UEBA) Entity here means BYOD, end-user devices, applications, servers, or any entity associated with IP address.**

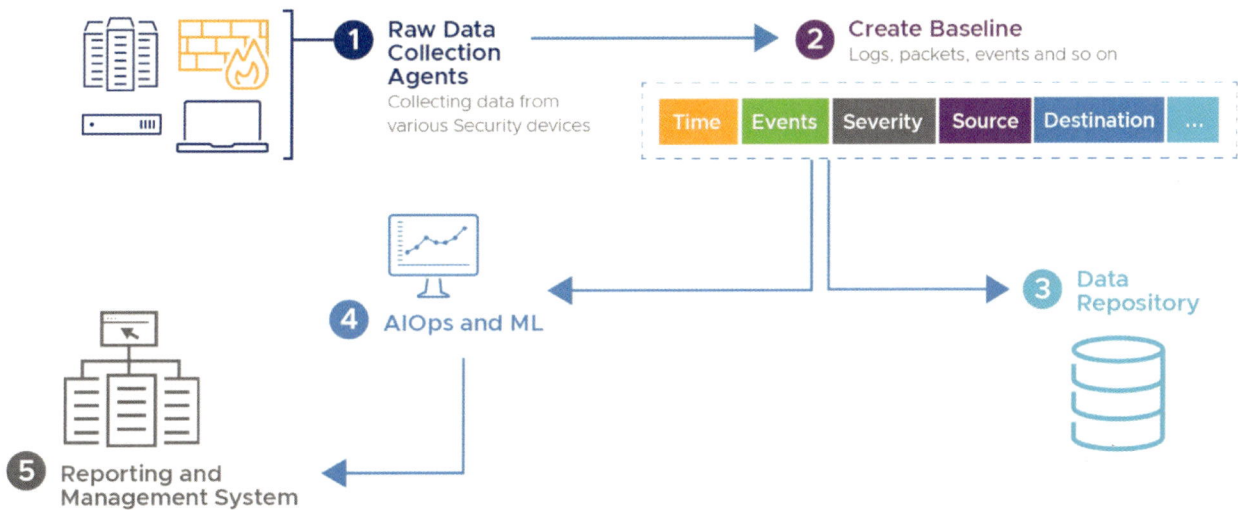

Figure 3.5: Threat landscape UEBA addresses

How is UEBA Performed?

A UEBA system will build its baseline from data collected throughout the corporate environment. Training data is not collected and processed in real-time from live networks; it is imported from infrastructure components, SIEM systems, log servers, and other data repositories. This full set of data is then integrated into a singular view of standard environmental behavior. As new information is processed by UEBA, AI analytics and statistical models evaluate its conformance to expected patterns. Based on standard thresholds and IT-defined criteria of interest, traffic is flagged, and alerts are created for manual evaluation. Depending on system capabilities and preferred best practices, traffic may be immediately blocked, quarantined, or permitted to flow pending review.

Why is UEBA Important?

The threat landscape continuously evolves and expands. No single threat matrix or set of policies will protect against emerging threats. UEBA reduces the time required to identify and respond to novel attacks, complementing layers that rely on more deterministic techniques.

3.3.3 – Logging and Reporting

What does Logging and Reporting Entail?

Logging is a fundamental operational component of networking and computing. Logging information is generated and sent to central servers for storage, analysis, and audit. Working from this pool of operational data, SIEM solutions mine volumes of information to create trending data and actionable insights.

How do SIEM Systems Work?

SIEM systems are a significant source of centralized information. They can directly collect information from sources throughout the infrastructure or review and aggregate data from log collectors. SIEM systems apply security policies, rules, and analytics to identify potential or confirmed threats. Important areas of detection include brute force hacking, impossible user travel events, excessive information copying, DDoS attacks, and file integrity changes. Connectivity to the broader management and alerting ecosystem allows the SIEM to automatically generate alerts/tickets and initiate security review protocols.

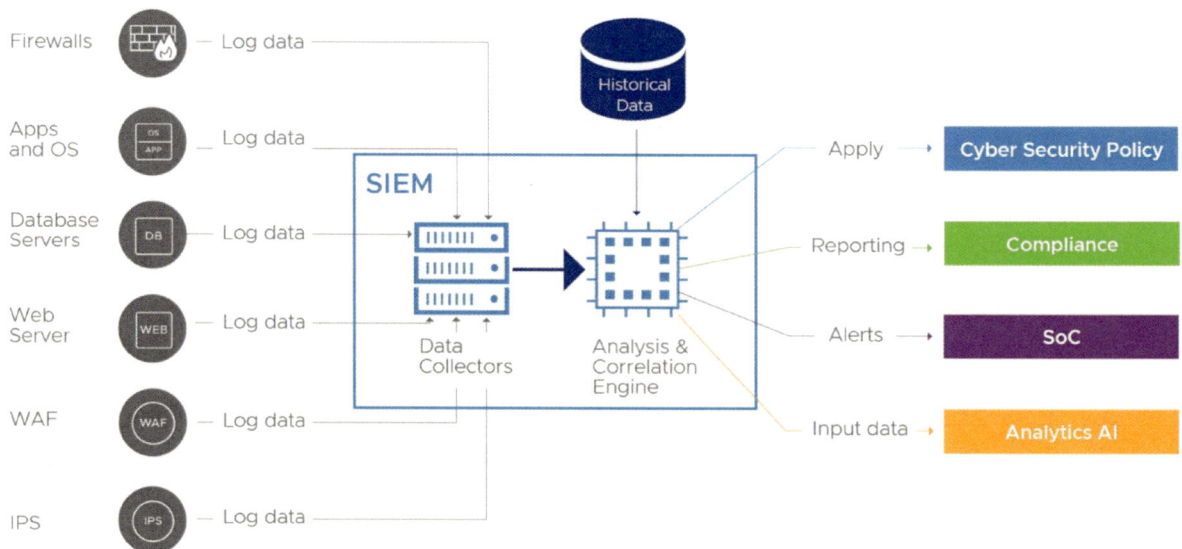

Figure 3.6: Security Information and Event Management (SIEM)

Why is SIEM Important?

An ongoing, comprehensive review of environmental events provides a baseline of confidence in the overall quality of the corporate security posture and awareness of threats to the enterprise. A longer-term historical archive of data aids in post-event analysis and informs audit/compliance processes. Centralization of archival controls with the full set of data allows for tuning of retention policies to align with corporate standards and government regulations.

3.3.4 – Asset and Data Classification (Third Layer)

What is Classification?

Before actively securing and protecting assets, IT must identify what assets the business has, where they are located, why they are important, and how they should be classified. A framework is necessary to evaluate the relative rank of each piece and provide ongoing guidance for future assessments.

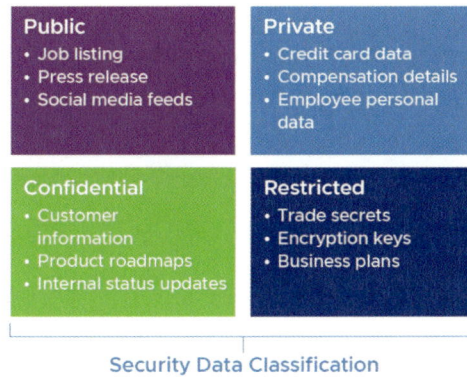

Public
- Job listing
- Press release
- Social media feeds

Private
- Credit card data
- Compensation details
- Employee personal data

Confidential
- Customer information
- Product roadmaps
- Internal status updates

Restricted
- Trade secrets
- Encryption keys
- Business plans

Security Data Classification

Figure 3.7: Types of Data Classification

How does classification work?

The creation of a consistent, meaningful system of labels/tags is the first step. Assets can be grouped under a variety of layers, each of which may require specific protections. Physical asset attributes may be related to location, service, or criticality. Data labels can indicate the value and sensitivity of general categories or specific records. The scope of this system should not limit itself to only current assets or business practices but should allow for growth as the business evolves.

In parallel with the establishment of the system, assets should be identified and grouped based on similar characteristics. With assets identified and labels applied, appropriate policies can be determined and protection solutions designed.

Note that the classification process is not a one-time effort; it is ongoing by nature. Changes to the environment require constant oversight, while validation of the entire system against evolving corporate and legal standards should be performed on a regular basis.

Why is Classification Necessary?

Companies acquire, change, and dispose of large volumes of assets. Establishing an automated, formal process for tracking and securing these resources is central to complying with corporate directives and government mandates. Proper classification ensures that each asset is protected not only appropriately but also cost-effective.

3.3.5 – Encryption

What is Encryption?

While encryption is a familiar concept, understanding the specifics of cloud encryption requires additional context. Effective cloud encryption ensures that data can only be consumed by authorized parties at each step of its journey. Data may take many forms – a file, video stream, or database. Whether the data resides on a single system or moves through an extensive service environment, it must always be protected from theft or manipulation.

How is Encryption Implemented?

Cloud encryption must address the needs of data at rest, data in motion, and data in use. Data at rest can be secured with an encryption key, then decrypted by an authorized party with an associated key. Policies associated with key ownership and management are an important consideration regardless of the cloud deployment model used; utilizing a CASB can assist with this process. Proper protection of data in motion requires encryption along its entire path. While each link may be expected to be encrypted, traffic routing changes or configuration errors on a single link put the entire session at risk. End-to-end encryption can be performed at different layers (e.g., application, network) using different protocols, but it is the ultimate responsibility of IT to ensure that the policy is properly understood and enforced. Data in use is a challenging area due to the interdependent reliance on Application, operating system, and physical system constructs and security. Remain aware of the risk for viewing, modification, and deletion of data while it is being processed in memory.

Why is Encryption Necessary?

A significant portion of cloud data's lifecycle exists outside of the traditional corporate perimeter. It may be created by a cloud application, moved across a cloud network, or stored in a cloud repository. It may pass back and forth between a cloud provider and the client or between multiple cloud providers. Whether at rest or in motion, cloud data is never far away from compromise.

3.3.6 – Configuration Hardening (Fourth Layer)

What is Hardening?

Configuration, system, or application hardening is the process of understanding the state of, then securing, the environment. Its purpose is to reduce or eliminate known vulnerabilities and minimize the general attack surface. The process will prevent unnecessary communication while ensuring best practices are applied on an ongoing basis.

How is Hardening Performed?

Common tasks involved with hardening include applying security patches, removing unnecessary programs and services, reviewing authentication protocols and user rights, and restricting traffic to known-required ports/addresses. Operating systems have standardized best practices for hardened deployment; these should be implemented and updated to remain current with the latest security risks. Cloud providers are responsible for many of the technology components which required hardening; actively monitor and regularly review compliance against published standards. Ethical hacking and penetration testing should be part of a hardening validation regimen.

Why is Hardening Important?

Common operating system and application vulnerabilities are low-hanging fruit for cybercriminals. Unhardened systems present easy targets both for data exfiltration as well as lateral movement within the cloud environment. Increasing the time and effort required for malicious actors to access corporate resources will encourage them to move to easier targets or risk more aggressive strategies which are less likely to evade detection.

3.3.7 – Logical Segmentation (Fifth Layer)

What is Logical Segmentation

Logical segmentation involves partitioning the cloud environment into distinct zones of trust to limit the impact of an intrusion. Distinct from the hardware underlay, logical segmentation allows complete control of traffic flows without modifying the physical infrastructure. Cloud firewalls and micro-segmentation are common tools used to secure and protect cloud-based assets.

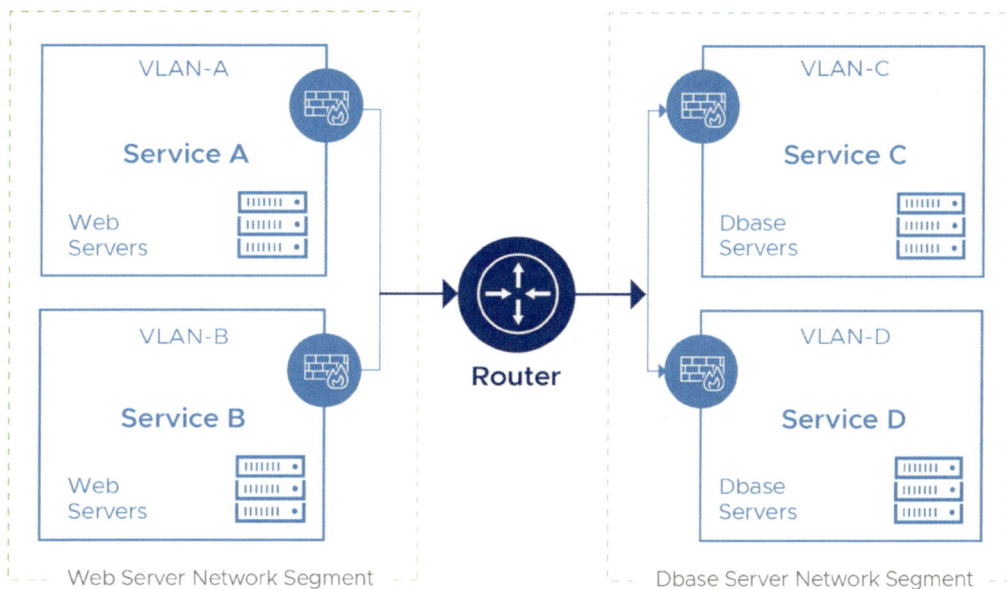

Figure 3.8: Logical Segmentation

How is Logical Segmentation Managed?

Firewalls remain a straightforward, effective solution to preventing traffic between zones of trust. Cloud-based firewalls protect cloud platforms in the same manner as traditional firewalls on-premises. They also can defend individual workloads with next-generation functionality tailored to the requirements of the cloud. A firewall-as-a-service may include many services familiar from the on-premises environment: packet filtering, IPS/IDS, payload inspection, proxy functionality, and layer-7 analytics.

Micro-segmentation takes a more fine-grained approach at traffic filtering than a classic firewall. As the name implies, the zones of trust created are small in scale. They are defined by rules that permit and/or deny communication between specific services, ports, and addresses. Best practices promote an organizational structure that allows the movement of micro-segmentation rules with workloads. This lets security policy follow a workload as it moves within, and potentially, out of an individual cloud provider.

Why should Logical Segmentation be Implemented?

Risk mitigation and compliance requirements are the primary drivers of segmentation. In environments where a set of applications or data must have enhanced security (e.g., HIPAA, PCI), segmentation can limit the work and expense required to adhere to regulatory mandates. Segmentation is central to the Zero Trust model's implementation, allowing for tight control over which users have access to which resources. It can also provide strict ownership and responsibility boundaries, helping organize management and operational tasks around corporate structures.

3.4 – Cloud Security Challenges

The volume of challenges that security organizations face only increases as their business' cloud footprint grows. Many of these areas are not unique to cloud environments, but their scope and impact are greatly enhanced.

- **Visibility:** With a significant amount of the technology infrastructure out of sight, IT cannot let what happens there be out of mind. Cloud provider monitoring solutions rarely provide the deep insights and complex customizability that on-premises operators expect. Lack of direct visibility should not directly correlate to a lack of confidence, so it is essential to understand what is happening behind the scenes. Fundamental requisite knowledge includes who has access to services, what actions they can perform, what actions have been taken, and what the results were. IT needs to understand how data is accessed, where it is moved, and how it is secured. The same concepts that apply on premises must be observed in the cloud while considering the distributed, highly mobile nature of the environment.

- **Compliance:** One of the most common blockers raised to cloud adoption is compliance. Whether only a perceived concern, strict corporate mandate, or governmental regulation, adherence to compliance requirements can be a complex task, data security is at the heart of compliance directives – ensuring sensitive information is only accessible and accessed by appropriate parties. Cloud providers have developed services that are certified to align with these standards, lowering barriers to adoption (e.g., GDPR-certified cloud compliance). While these services offer new options, ensuring compliance remains the ultimate responsibility of IT security.

- **Insider Threats:** The definition of an insider expands as service providers and business partners contribute and operate inside of the trust zone. According to NIST, almost 70% of modern attacks can be classified as insider threats. Threats are not only overt attacks that security solutions work to prevent; they can also be unintentional breaches or accidental configuration errors. Properly securing data through encryption reduces the risk if a business partner's database is breached. Tightly limited user access controls limit the damage a compromised user account can achieve. The business relationship with a service provider is all about trust and accountability; they ultimately have direct control over all processes and data. Understand the rules they have in place and design security policies accordingly.

- **Liability:** Legal, contractual relationships must be in place with any cloud partnership. These define the expectations for performance standards and penalties when they are not met. They should also address what will happen in the event of data loss or theft. While service level contracts may define compensation to a business, they cannot fully account for the liability to those whose data was affected or the impact on a company's reputation. Understand the potential risk to the overall business beyond simply the relationship to the provider. Recent cyberattacks have demonstrated that the most lasting impact of such incidents falls on the victim of the breach, not the service provider; plan accordingly from the perspectives of business continuity, insurance, and marketing.

3.5 – The Multi-Cloud Journey

What is Multi-Cloud?

As enterprises adopt and expand cloud strategies, the risk of reliance on a single vendor or concentration of resources with a single point of failure becomes significant. Adopting a multi-cloud strategy involves spreading cloud resources and operations across services from multiple public cloud vendors (e.g., AWS, Azure, GCP).

> **Despite the many benefits of taking a multi-cloud approach, challenges do remain. Complexity was cited as the biggest challenge by even more survey respondents (74%) this year than last year. Security followed at 60%, then managing costs and migrating apps tied at 40%. Last year, migrating apps and security were a challenge for 48% of respondents, while managing costs was an issue for 43%.**
>
> **Source:** https://www.zdnet.com/article/research-multicloud-deployment-increases-among-enterprises/

How should an Enterprise Adopt Multi-Cloud?

While offering significant benefits, a multi-cloud strategy comes with additional risks if not properly designed and implemented. Operational complexity is significantly increased as the organization's attack surface broadens. Expertise is required across multiple providers to ensure a common security policy is implemented consistently and adequately. Many providers have distinct authentication methods and mechanisms for securing their own systems, solutions which rarely integrate cleanly. Differing providers' means of securing their environments can be mutually incompatible or even incompatible with the software that an organization uses internally to manage this issue.

Why is Multi-Cloud Important?

Operating a multi-cloud environment offers flexibility in workload placement and service functionality. Workloads can be deployed in the most optimal location based on cost, latency, performance, or other factors. When business criteria or technical details change, they can be reprovisioned to take advantage of the new numbers. Workloads designed for portability are less likely to be based on proprietary protocols and capabilities, reducing the need to rewrite/refactor as offerings change. Multi-cloud models also reduce the overall corporate failure domain by spreading resources across multiple providers and geographies. Proper design of availability and redundancy policies can ensure business continuity even in the event of severe provider issues.

3.6 – Cloud Security Governance

What is Cloud Security Governance?

Certification and Governance of cloud security involve alignment of security practices with business mandates. It brings together executive direction, financial standards, operational policies, and corporate culture to deliver on the enterprise goals. Effective Governance should establish the scope and degree of risk, quantify the impact of potential incursions, validate the performance of security efforts, and reinforce the importance of security policy throughout the business.

How is Governance Crafted?

Governance is adherence to a set of policies rather than the implementation of a specific set of technologies. It is built from clearly defined corporate directives that incorporate the operational culture, business requirements, and customer expectations. Governance must consider external legal mandates and applicable security standards. Participation is required from across the entire business to properly understand the impact and ensure proper implementation.

Why do Businesses need Governance?

Organizations may lack direction or structure to move into cloud environments properly. Without clear corporate direction, efforts will be fragmented, met with resistance, or fail to account for the best interests of the business. Cloud adoption need not be performed on a grand scale or mandated for every Application, but it should be approached with a commonly understood set of requirements, restrictions, and policies.

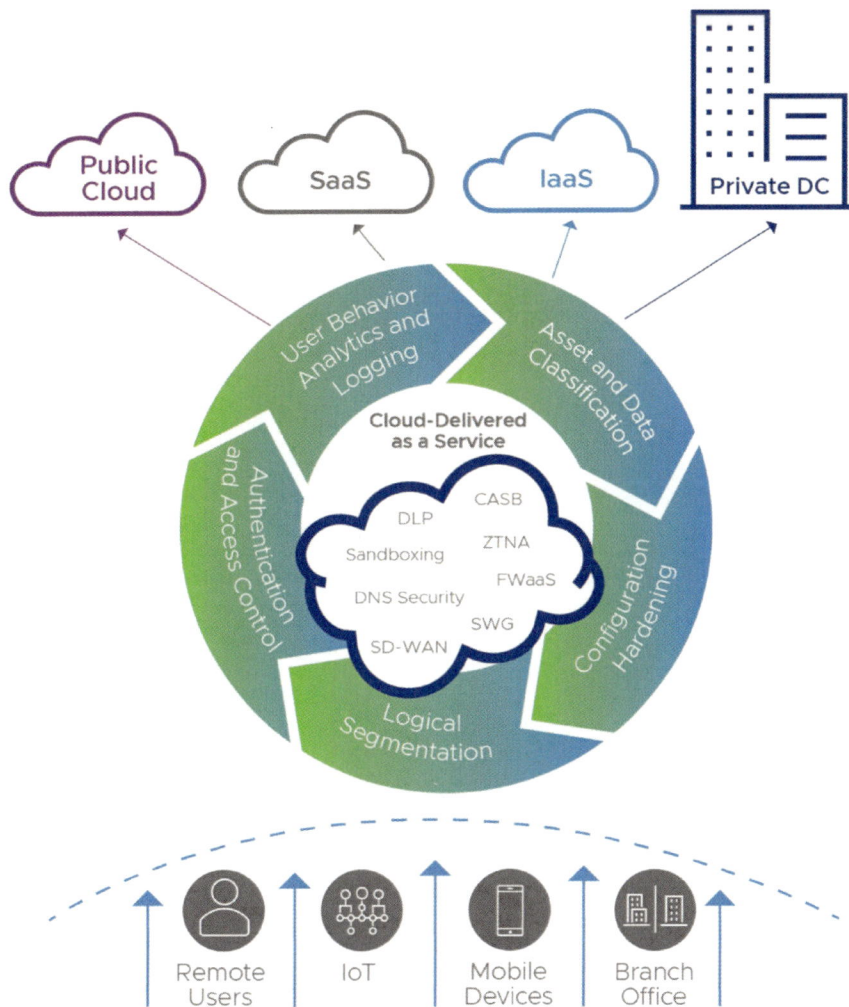

Figure 3.9: Cloud-Delivered as a Service

3.7 – Cloud-Delivered Security Services

In addition to cloud-based services that protect cloud systems, providers also offer cloud-based security solutions for on-premises infrastructure. This model is commonly referred to as cloud-delivered security or security-as-a-service. Cloud security services case provide protection for both on-premises and cloud infrastructure, applications, data, and users throughout an enterprise. Many of the same technologies available on-premises can be consumed from the cloud as-a-service, including SWG, CASB, DLP, and sandboxing. These cloud-based delivery services will be discussed in greater detail later in the book.

3.8 – Cloud Security Summary

This chapter shared a framework for cloud security, examining common elements and differing requirements from on-premises models. With the increasing acceptance of public, multi, and hybrid cloud solutions in the marketplace, an awareness of cloud trends and challenges is essential to establishing and growing an effective cloud security practice. In addition to areas already touched on—such as CASB, encryption, and penetration testing— solutions that unify many components to offer a more refined, fully functional service offering are growing in prominence. These include richer IAM solutions that provide greater organizational visibility and, as the later parts of this book will explore, SASE offerings that unify security, connectivity, and performance.

Figure 3.10 depicts several components that come together to deliver effective cloud security. In this example, an end-user accessing a SaaS application is authenticated and authorized with the least privileges access control using technologies like SSO or ZTNA. Once the user is authenticated and authorized, all the activities are continuously monitored in real-time through the threat detection and prevention layer using elements including UEBA and SIEM for security alerts. At the same time, data and application protection is provided by encryption, data classification, and cloud-delivered services like CASB.

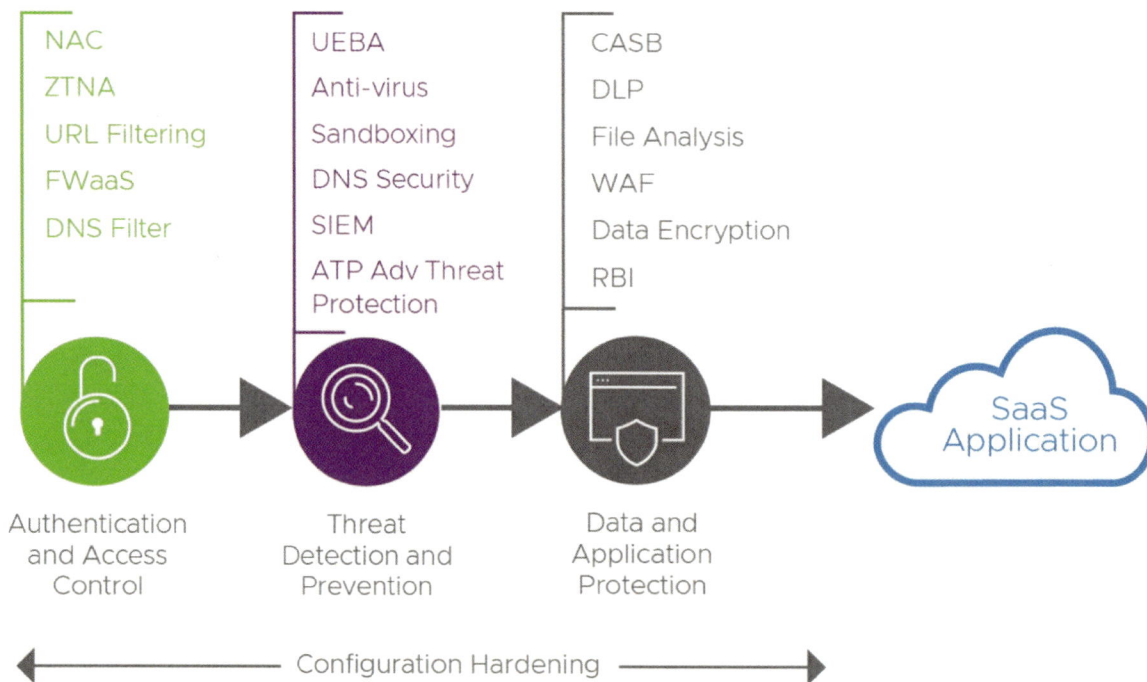

Figure 3.10: Cloud Security: Putting it all Together

3.9 – Key Takeaways

Enterprises see a significant shift from on-premises security towards cloud security when access SaaS applications. On-premises security will never go away, but with fewer guarantees for direct inspection (e.g., IoT devices), it is important for the complete environment to be secured through comprehensive, real-time inspection.

Checklist: Cloud Security Takeaways

✓ Align the security model with corporate compliance mandates and business goals. A combination of policy, process, technology, and culture are required for success.

✓ Inventory, understand and categorize corporate assets. If a business does not know its assets, it cannot understand its value or put controls to protect them.

✓ Cloud data requires enhanced use of encryption solutions – at rest, in motion, and in use. Understand each's implications and how they work together to deliver end-to-end privacy.

✓ Monitoring and logging solutions provide visibility into the security ecosystem, feeding tools and processes that watch for abnormal behavior, detect ongoing incursions, and document events for after-action analysis and audit mandates.

✓ Cloud-delivered security services include SWG, CASB, DLP, Sandboxing, and more.

✓ Effective cloud security is a partnership between a client and their providers. Understand roles and responsibilities. Keep in regular contact. Constantly check and validate commitments. Follow emerging security trends and remain vigilant.

Chapter 4

SD-WAN Networking Foundation

4.1 – Introduction

Today's applications and network architectures require a novel approach. The emergence of cloud, virtualization, and as-a-service models have upended traditional enterprise networking. In this multi-cloud world, organizations have been forced to reconsider how they design their wide area networks to connect and unify their dispersed sites.

Management trends and practices are changing. Networking teams are under increased pressure to simplify the network, make it more flexible, and centralize controls while simultaneously optimizing application performance. Companies want to reduce costs through network simplification, cloud adoption, improving IT support and troubleshooting, and increasing software licensing efficiency. Improving security remains an overarching goal to ensure critical data is protected. Changing government and industry regulations mandate a continued focus on compliance.

The modern WAN must support connectivity for traditional applications and latency-sensitive real-time services such as voice-over-IP (VoIP) and videoconferencing. Bandwidth-intensive applications are not limited to the office/campus environment; connectivity is needed not just for communication and collaboration but also for digital signage, physical security, and surveillance.

The importance of agility has increased with the pace of business. The IT infrastructure is a crucial enabler of innovation and business growth. Stakeholders expect rapid access to technology resources and the ability to quickly scale up or down as business requirements change. In this fast-paced world of digital transformation, it is unacceptable for the network to be a bottleneck in delivering on-demand infrastructure. The network is expected to always be available and ready to deliver on any requirement; even a brief outage can cause significant disruption to the business.

This chapter explores challenges and opportunities in wide-area networking – where it started, how it has evolved, and why SD-WAN presents an opportunity for the future.

4.2 – The Networking Journey

Wide Area Networks are composed of both networking and security stacks, with each moving through several phases of significant evolution. Historically, networking and security trends have often been thought of in terms of silos.

Networking began with the router, introduced new technologies such as WAN optimization, and then saw the evolution of the Edge and introduction of SD-WAN. In the security space, firewall offerings have evolved, and increasing consumption of cloud offerings has made new security-as-a-service models more relevant. Today's digital transformation journey brings together networking and security in the cloud, aligning them to address the needs of modern applications and users.

Router

Traditionally routers have been used at the enterprise edge to provide WAN connectivity. These routers lack policy-based control and automation as well as the intelligence for cloud connectivity. Routers generally do not consider the details of underlying transport infrastructures; this lack of abstraction capability limits their flexibility when connecting to the cloud.

To support a redundant WAN design, complex BGP tuning is required to support load balancing. In this model, path attributes may not allow for the selection of the best-performing path, and path length is not necessarily correlated to performance. Additionally, WAN routers do not have insight into enterprise application SLAs and policies, leading to unpredictable performance.

Private Link, MPLS and VPN

MPLS and private line services are dedicated connections delivered by service providers. These services offer predictable performance and come with SLAs providing guaranteed traffic performance and delivery. Unfortunately, they tend to be significantly more expensive than broadband Internet services, which offer the benefit of being easier to procure and deploy than MPLS and private line services. While MPLS delivers key benefits, including scalability, performance, improved bandwidth utilization, and reduced network congestion, it is not designed for the cloud and SaaS. This is primarily because all traffic must be backhauled, adding latency that ultimately impacts user experience.

VPN links offer a cost-effective and secure remote connectivity alternative. These connections establish an encrypted tunnel across the public Internet for security, connecting remote users to the corporate network through a VPN client. While VPNs continue to be widely used, this technology still has the bandwidth, scaling, and security challenges. New approaches are being put in place to provide alternatives to VPN.

WAN optimization

MPLS costs and application-specific requirements (e.g., latency sensitivity) were early factors driving WAN optimization over international links. With the rise of real-time voice and video traffic, services highly sensitive to latency and jitter, this capability was a welcome feature.

WAN optimization includes basic inline compression and a range of TCP optimizations, data deduplication, application proxies, and protocol-specific optimizations. These capabilities proved effective at managing latency-sensitive applications and transfers of large amounts of data across the WAN, especially for global transmissions.

Deploying WAN optimization solutions is complex and requires physical appliances at each end of the connection. These systems are limited to application proxy support and encryption applications such as TLS and SSL-based solutions. WAN optimization devices do not improve users' experience outside of the traditional office environment.

SD-WAN

Over time, applications became smarter and less chatty on WAN links. Services began moving to the cloud (e.g., SaaS) while the public Internet became more economical and available. Additionally, SD-WAN made broadband Internet connections more reliable, higher-performing, and secure for business communications and services; they were no longer viewed as only best-effort connections. Being transport-independent, SD-WAN could focus on application performance. It used application recognition, bandwidth aggregation, dynamic path selection while providing security and minimizing routing complexity. SD-WAN allowed enterprises to adopt software-defined networking (SDN) practices that separated.the data, control, and management planes.

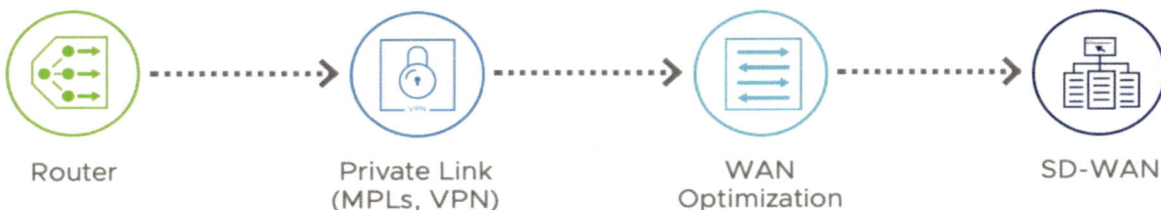

Router   Private Link   WAN   SD-WAN
(MPLs, VPN)   Optimization

Figure 4.1: Transformation for WAN Router to SD-WAN Edge device

4.2.1 – Traditional WAN Challenges

Corporate WAN infrastructures have built up over time. They were designed to support applications and models that have since evolved. Problems with legacy applications are often evident, while issues with the underlying infrastructure—such as the WAN—are rarely obvious or prominent.

The traditional WAN faces challenges in many areas: complexity, scalability, quality of experience, architecture, and security. This section examines these issues in detail before exploring how SD-WAN capabilities address problems facing the modern wide-area network.

Complexity: Traditional management tools lack the visibility and control to unify the operational experience. Configuration is performed device by device, often through a CLI, requiring customization for each site while being prone to human-induced errors. Important

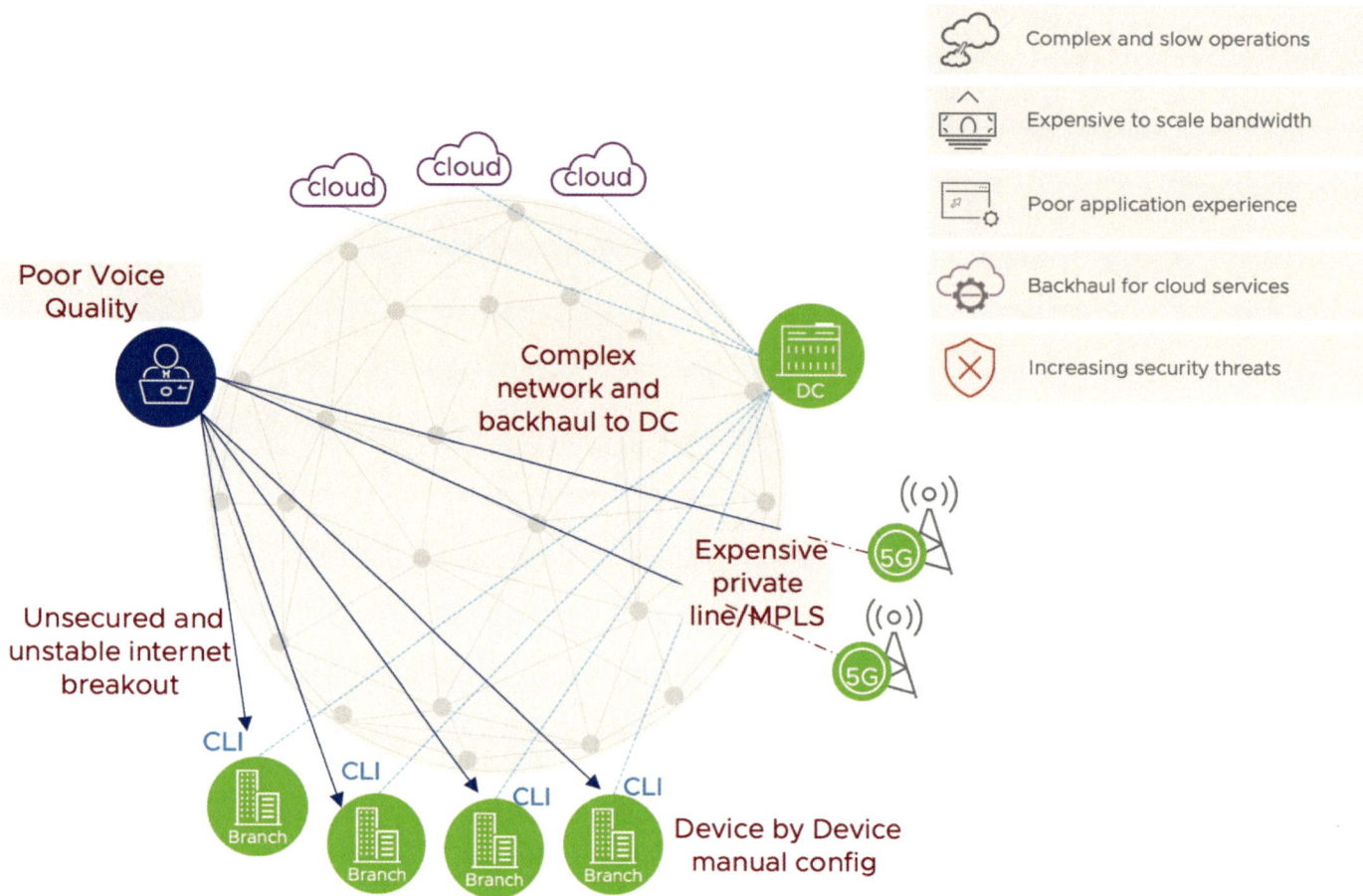

Figure 4.2: WAN Challenges: Expensive, Complex, and Inefficient

QoS policies are inconsistently defined and challenging to implement appropriately. Troubleshooting is a manual, time-consuming process that impacts availability and reliability. Network teams must deliver solutions that drive faster time-to-market, aid in quick adoption of new technologies, and move beyond manual operational processes to provide a more automated and agile infrastructure. A single solution is needed that configures, manages, monitors, and analyzes across the entire infrastructure.

Increasing Cost: Businesses are forcing IT to reduce expenses. As budget reductions impact both CAPEX and OPEX, there are insufficient funds to put toward additional traditional MPLS and private line circuits. Broadband connections do not provide the reliability and security that enterprises have come to rely on; SLAs are insufficient to address latency, packet loss, and jitter concerns that degrade modern application performance. Traditional WAN offerings do not provide high-quality, cost-effective solutions reaching from the branch edge through to the data center.

Quality of Experience: Traditional networks are not designed to address the needs of applications at the Edge or in the cloud. As more users connect to the cloud to access their applications from anywhere, they must have an infrastructure that can deliver delay-sensitive traffic and reliable connectivity that provides the best user experience. Today's existing WAN infrastructure cannot support this type of user experience. Simply upgrading the existing infrastructure with additional bandwidth is merely a bandage solution that is disruptive, costly, and ultimately delays application modernization in other areas.

Architecture: Cloud solutions are everywhere – deployed as IaaS in cloud providers (e.g., AWS, Microsoft Azure, Google Cloud), at peering points (e.g., Equinix, Rackspace), with application providers (e.g., Office365, Salesforce), and as storage solutions (e.g., Box, Dropbox). The wide-area network must bring together the corporate data center, campus, branch sites, cloud connectivity, and remote workers efficiently, cost-effectively, and securely. Legacy architectures and complexities hold organizations back. Backhauling of traffic from the branch to the data center and then to the cloud impacts performance by adding latency. Visibility is limited outside the corporate perimeter, where traffic routing is left to the Internet's whims. A solution is needed that can help with the challenges of managing WAN circuits, addressing last-mile quality issues, and steering traffic based on application policy and performance.

Security: The cloud's global reach opens a new wave of security threats and breaches. The traditional corporate security perimeter is no longer sufficient. Enterprises need to be bold and think about an integrated approach beyond just on-premises security. Security organizations must look for solutions that encompass the corporate environment, including mobile access and the cloud.

4.2.2 – SD-WAN Advantages

As networks have become more complex, organizations have turned to software-defined networking to improve infrastructure efficiency, manageability, and scalability. SDN abstracts the network to a set of functional capabilities independent of the physical implementation. Interaction with the network does not need to address specific networking equipment or other physical aspects that may regularly change.

One of the first practical SDN applications, SD-WAN applies these software-defined principles to the wide-area network to deliver similar advantages. SD-WAN segregates control and data planes to independently use the scaling and redundancy mechanisms best suited for each. Virtualized resources provide accelerated service delivery, better performance, and improved availability by automating network deployment and management while reducing the total cost of ownership.

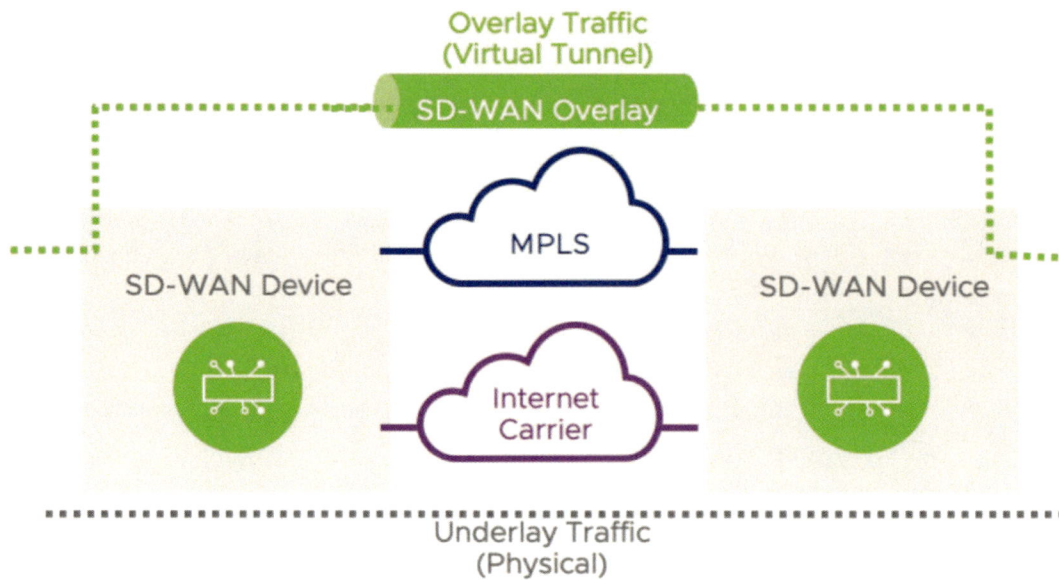

Figure 4.3: SD-WAN Overlay Tunnel on Multiple Links

SD-WAN provides a software abstraction layer to create a network overlay layer and decouple network software services from underlying hardware WAN circuits, as shown in **Figure 4.3**. This new abstraction layer lets network administrators control and manage networks more efficiently than possible using traditional approaches to address the underlying WAN hardware.

SD-WAN empowers organizations to address business-critical priorities at the Edge by enabling rich deployment, management, and scaling capabilities. It allows network teams to cost-effectively provide the connectivity and performance that dispersed organizations need while maintaining deep controls and visibility across the infrastructure.

These capabilities unleash several benefits:

Optimized Cloud Architecture: SD-WAN addresses the performance problems associated with the need to backhaul network traffic required with MPLS and other traditional models. It lets organizations utilize broadband Internet links to provide secure, high-performance connections from the branch to the cloud. This architecture also supports local Internet connectivity breakout with firewalling.

Business Agility & Flexibility: SD-WAN makes it fast, easy, and cost-effective for organizations to deploy the WAN services needed to support branch offices. It minimizes the need for onsite IT services, eliminates unnecessary truck rolls, and offers the ability to leverage broadband Internet services, which are cheaper and easier to procure and deploy.

Broadband Internet Economics: SD-WAN delivers the power of choice, freeing organizations to select from a variety of Internet connectivity options. These options are quick and easy to set up, allowing an organization to augment network connectivity with secure, dependable WAN services at a much lower price point than equivalent MPLS links.

Rapid Adoption, Simplified Manageability: Speed and business agility are essential. SD-WAN solutions are easy to deploy, powered by automation and centralized provisioning that accelerate deployment and minimize requirements for dedicated personnel at remote sites.

Hybrid WAN: Most distributed organizations already have MPLS connecting their branch offices. SD-WAN complements existing technologies, allowing the deployment of additional broadband links without modifying the existing WAN infrastructure. As business requirements change, an organization can migrate traffic toward cost-effective Internet bandwidth, freeing up MPLS links for applications that have distinct performance or compliance requirements.

Automation & Traffic Steering: SD-WAN supports traffic prioritization, providing tuning tools and the ability to dynamically modify flows to align with changing network conditions. The automation capabilities also enable faster provisioning and onboarding of new sites and users, eliminating redundant, time-consuming, error-prone manual processes. With SD-WAN, enterprises have complete visibility of their network, including detailed real-time analytics that provides actionable insights.

4.2.3 – WAN Evolution

Wide-area network architecture and design have undergone a continuous transformation over the past few decades. In recent iterations, optimized access to cloud resources and application-tailored performance has become critical to enterprise productivity. Internet WAN evolution can be grouped into three distinct generations: private connectivity, cloud-ready, and modern multi-cloud architectures. The following sections examine the transition from foundational WAN models to current solutions and best practices.

First Generation WAN Transformation: Private Networks

The first generation wide-area networks were private links and MPLS services connecting branch offices to central campus and data center sites. Most, if not all, applications were located on-premises with predictable traffic patterns. Architectures commonly followed a hub/spoke model with branch-to-data center traffic flows. The enterprise managed several remote networking and security devices, including routers, switches, firewalls, load balancers, and IDS/IPS appliances. Distinct tools were required for remote management, further adding to operational expenses.

Private line and MPLS circuits were the primary forms of connectivity for the branch to data center connectivity; public Internet connections were only considered as emergency backup links. Despite their inherent reliability and security, MPLS links proved to be costly as traffic demands grew. Traffic could not be effectively load-shared across public Internet links due to their lack of enterprise-grade performance; these links were an ongoing expense for rarely used backup capacity.

Traditional WAN design was static by nature; traffic flowed from branch offices to the data center and was secured by on-premises solutions. With the rise and rapid transition to cloud provider solutions, this architecture was not ready to address new challenges posed by the public Internet. Routing complexity further complicated the situation. Specialized technical skill sets were required to manage, configure, and support WAN devices properly. Lack of visibility created troubleshooting challenges. While larger corporations may have managed connections to multiple service providers, Internet connectivity was often a single pipe in and out of the network. There was rarely planning for proximity or performance related to providing services.

In summary, characteristics of first-generation enterprise WAN included:

- Expensive, point-to-point links connecting sites;

- Inactive broadband Internet solely as a backup.

- Static network topology, not focus on Internet and cloud-ready connectivity.

- All traffic backhauled to the corporate data center for security/processing, creating delay and bandwidth contention.

- Discrete systems with multiple points of management. Multiple User Interface (UI) for management.

- Traditional routing (e.g., OSPF, BGP) was key to traffic management.

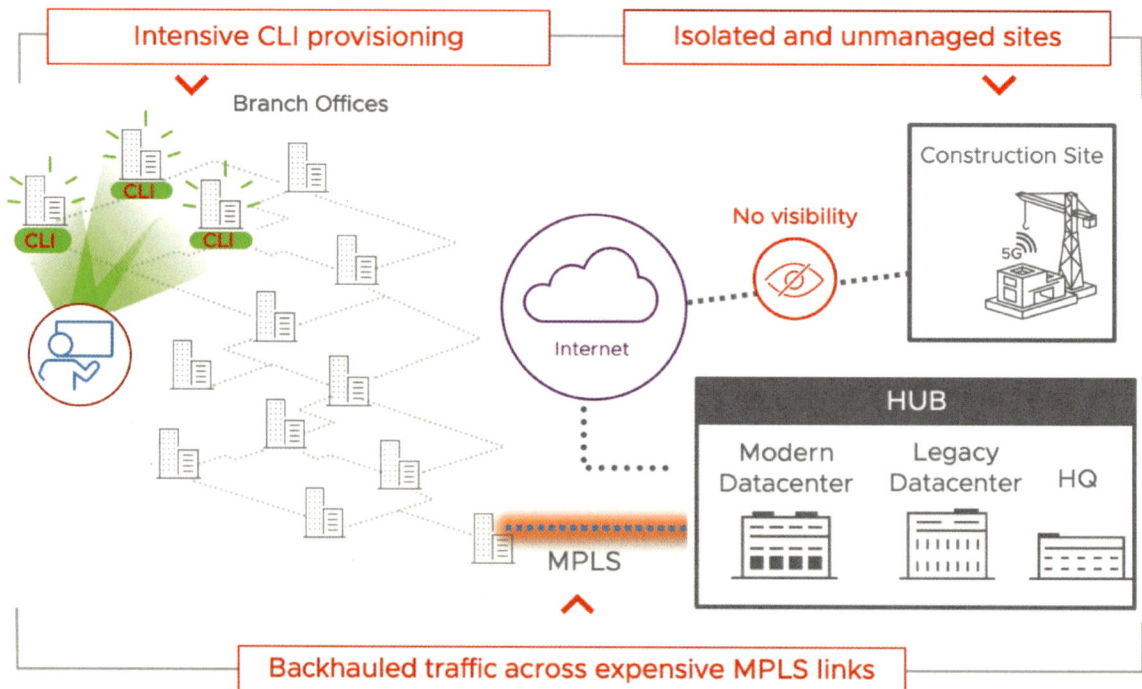

Figure 4.4: First Generation WAN Transformation: Private Networks

Second Generation WAN Transformation: SD-WAN & Cloud-Ready

SD-WAN entered enterprise networks and marked the second generation of transformation. It was based on SDN principles that segregated the control, management, and data planes. SD-WAN provides a richer application experience combined with centralized management. Key to adoption was the deterministic application performance, end-to-end visibility, and integrated security. Individual solutions offered automated templates to speed cloud onboarding and delivering on promises of rapid time to deployment (e.g., zero-touch provisioning).

SD-WAN provided predictable and reliable performance across public broadband connections at a much lower price point. This allowed the Internet to become the de facto transport standard across which SD-WAN controls provide application awareness and routing, quality of experience (QoE), intelligent link remediation, and consistent security. At the same time, SD-WAN helped enterprises augment both public (e.g., broadband) and private (e.g., MPLS circuits) links for SaaS applications and cloud-based services.

As applications and platforms move to the cloud, SD-WAN removes requirements to backhaul traffic to the corporate data center. It enables direct branch-to-cloud connectivity with policy-based controls to ensure a fast and responsive SaaS experience.

Highlights of second-generation WAN capabilities include:

- Simplified operations through centralized management and zero-touch deployment, applicable to both green and brownfield environments.

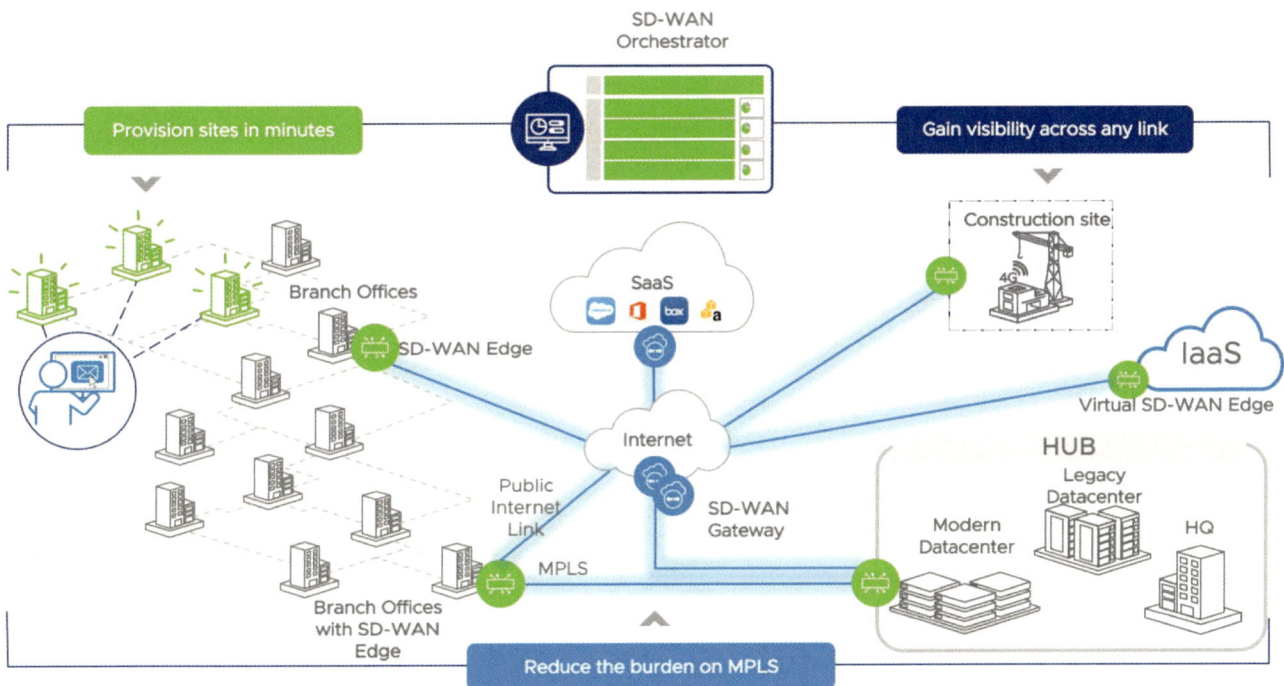

Figure 4.5: Second Generation WAN Transformation towards SD-WAN

- Fully functional APIs enable integration of 3rd party components (e.g., security services) and streamline connectivity to enterprise management tools.

- It assures Application performance over any WAN link by providing link monitoring, dynamic traffic steering, policy-based prioritization, and real-time remediation.

- Direct access to SaaS, hybrid, and multi-cloud solutions reduces latency and improves user experience.

- Provides customization for implementing security, supporting security service insertion for third-party firewall services as virtual network functions (VNF), redirecting branch site traffic to cloud security services, and enabling end-to-end Segmentation.

- Support for universal customer premises equipment (UCPE) for various network and security functions.

- Cost-effective connectivity with enterprise-grade performance.

Third Generation WAN Transformation: Modern Multi-Cloud

As enterprises move into the third generation, embracing and leveraging multiple cloud providers, they must invest in a network that provides seamless cloud infrastructure connectivity. Business drivers, including a dramatic increase in remote workforce demands, have accelerated the urgency and adoption of new technologies. The corporate perimeter continues to dissolve as applications are moving to the cloud and can be accessed from anywhere. As the complexities of connectivity and security continue to grow, it is essential to bring technologies and solutions together to deliver seamless access to the end-user.

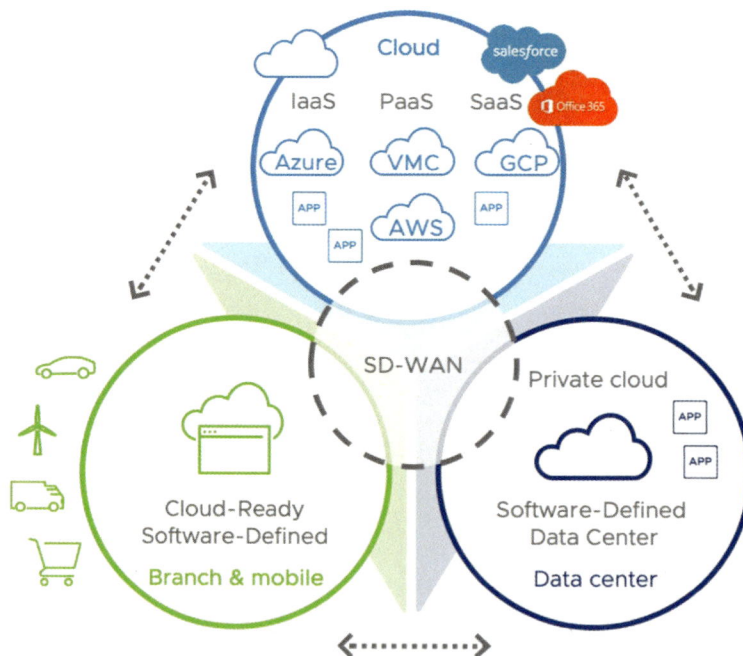

Figure 4.6: Third Generation WAN Transformation towards Multi-Cloud

SD-WAN solutions are expanding to address multi-cloud connectivity demands. 5G is proving viable for WAN connectivity. Automation and AI are delivering self-healing networks. Vendors are unifying and simplifying end-to-end management with intrinsic security and Zero Trust network architectures.

With applications operating in a multi-cloud world, businesses must establish tight integration with the public cloud infrastructure. APIs are the preferred model to deliver an enhanced cloud experience and ensure cross-cloud compatibility. Cloud offerings such as infrastructure-as-a-service and software-as-a-service can be effectively implemented through specific API integrations with cloud provider platforms (e.g., AWS, Microsoft Azure, Google Cloud Platform).

Infrastructure-as-a-Service: Through API integration, enterprises establish automated connectivity to the cloud to reach workloads directly from the data center or branch locations (e.g., AWS Transit Gateway, Microsoft Azure Virtual WAN). WAN edge instances are automatically deployed in the public cloud and become part of the SD-WAN overlay, establishing data plane connectivity to the existing data center and branch infrastructure. This, in turn, pushes full SD-WAN capabilities into the cloud and establishes a common policy framework across the enterprise environment. This architecture eliminates the need for traffic from SD-WAN sites to traverse the data center, improving the performance of the public cloud applications. It uses path redundancy across commodity connectivity to deliver high availability in a cost-effective model.

Software-as-a-Service (SaaS): Branches have traditionally accessed SaaS applications through centralized data centers. This led to increased application latency and unpredictable user experience. As SD-WAN has evolved, enterprises have established direct branch-to-cloud connectivity and access through regional gateways or colocation sites. This approach creates a lack of visibility and performance of SaaS applications from remote sites. In turn, it is challenging to identify the best path for SaaS applications and deliver an optimal end-user experience.

Additionally, when network changes or link impairments occur, there is no easy way to move affected applications to an alternate path. An integrated API infrastructure allows enterprise customers to quickly and easily configure access to SaaS applications. This can be done directly from the branch or through gateway locations. By continuously measuring and monitoring each path's performance to SaaS application and choosing the best-performing path based on loss and delay, traffic can be dynamically and intelligently moved to an alternate, higher-quality path.

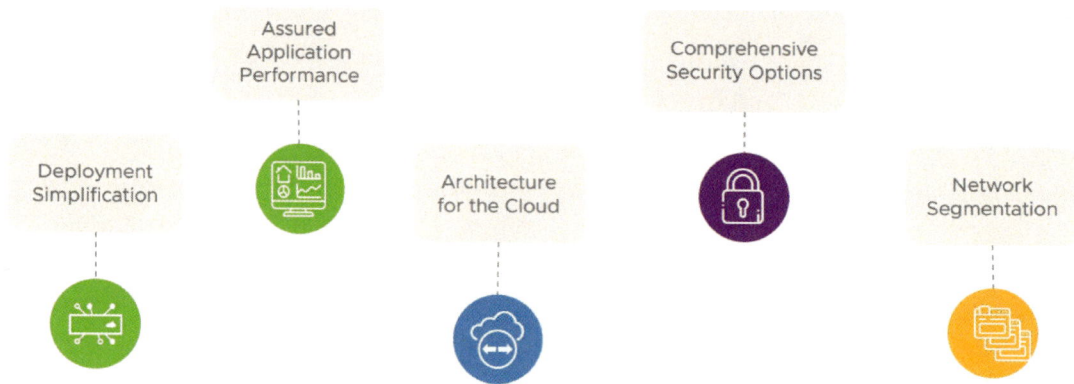

Figure 4.7: Five Ways Your Networks Needs to Evolve using VMware SD-WAN

4.3 – SD-WAN Transformation

SD-WAN was developed to simplify and transform networks by making them more responsive, scalable, and cost-effective.

VMware SD-WAN Cloud-delivered Model

VMware SD-WAN® simplifies WAN deployment with a cloud-delivered model. The solution is built on three components:

- The VMware SD-WAN Edge is deployed in the branch locations. It provides WAN connectivity and replaces the branch office router. SD-WAN Edges are also installed at data center sites and configured as hubs. An SD-WAN Edge can be deployed as physical hardware, a virtual appliance, or instantiated from a cloud provider marketplace. The Edge provides SD-WAN data plane functionality.

- VMware SD-WAN Gateways are hosted in points of presence (PoPs) around the globe. Traffic is sent to the Gateways and then routed to the destination, which may be a corporate data center hub, cloud provider, or a SaaS application. The SD-WAN Gateway offers control plane functionality and plays a role in the data plane.

- The VMware SD-WAN Orchestrator is a cloud-hosted centralized management system. The Orchestrator is not customer-installed; it is a VMware-managed system that is available for direct customer connection. The Orchestrator operates across the SD-WAN management plane.

The components are delivered as a subscription service with the management and cloud interconnect gateways hosted in the cloud. The service is also available with all three components on customer premises.

The VMware SD-WAN solution is strategically designed as a transport-independent overlay that can work across any circuits to connect branch locations to applications. It enables connectivity to enterprise data centers, SaaS applications, and IaaS in the cloud, dynamically optimizing traffic over multiple links.

4.3.1 – Deployment simplification

A VMware SD-WAN deployment starts with the deployment of a VMware SD-WAN Edge device at a location (e.g., branch office) and a larger Edge device, called the hub, in the data center. The SD-WAN Edge simplifies site deployment, enabling quick and efficient network expansion to new sites.

Edge devices are available as a hardware appliance, as a virtual appliance that can run on common hardware, or as a virtual instance on a uCPE (i.e., 3rd party off-the-shelf hardware) from various vendors. They are also available for cloud deployments and can be procured from providers for deployment in their respective clouds.

The Edge device connects a site to the service provider's WAN, routing through to the Internet to connects to an application's location – enterprise data center, service provider, or cloud. A smaller device at the remote location communicates with the larger hub device in the data center. The hub devices aggregate connections from all the Edge devices.

Figure 4.8: VMware SD-WAN Edge Simplifies Site Deployment

Edge devices communicate with each other to optimize the traffic flow. These devices are automatically configured via profiles from the VMware Orchestrator, so they are quick and easy to install. Their deployment cost is much lower than typical routers that must be configured manually, device-by-device.

Figure 4.8 depicts high-level deployment for VMware SD-WAN Edge devices in branches, data centers, and multiple verticals like a construction site, kiosks, and retail stores. Deployment across this wide variety of environments remains rapid and efficient due to the zero-touch provisioning capabilities of the SD-WAN Edge.

Multiple Deployment Options

Edge devices offer flexible deployment options. There are three deployment choices for an Edge in branch offices:

- Coexist with the existing deployed switch or router to support existing network connections.

- Become the default device and provide failover capabilities to the branch using Virtual Router Redundancy Protocol (VRRP). The Edge can coexist at Layer 3 and use routing protocols such as BGP or OSPF to support failover.

- Replace the existing router and firewall. Elimination of devices can lead to greater cost savings. VMware SD-WAN Edges are provided on a subscription basis rather than requiring the purchase of new hardware.

Enterprises can deploy SD-WAN on their choice of vendor appliances. Alternately they can choose to deploy the VMware SD-WAN Edge as a VNF and choose from a list of tested and approved vendor appliances. APIs and SDKs support integration with a list of partner virtual CPE management systems.

4.3.2 – Assured Application Performance

VMware SD-WAN increases the performance of applications over the WAN with real-time remediation and traffic steering. The VMware SD-WAN Edge bonds multiple links and virtualizes them to act as one. If an existing link does not have enough throughput, a second link can be added to increase bandwidth without changing anything in the network.

VMware SD-WAN supports combining links of different types (e.g., broadband Internet with MPLS), enhancing options for connecting a branch site to the corporate data center. If there

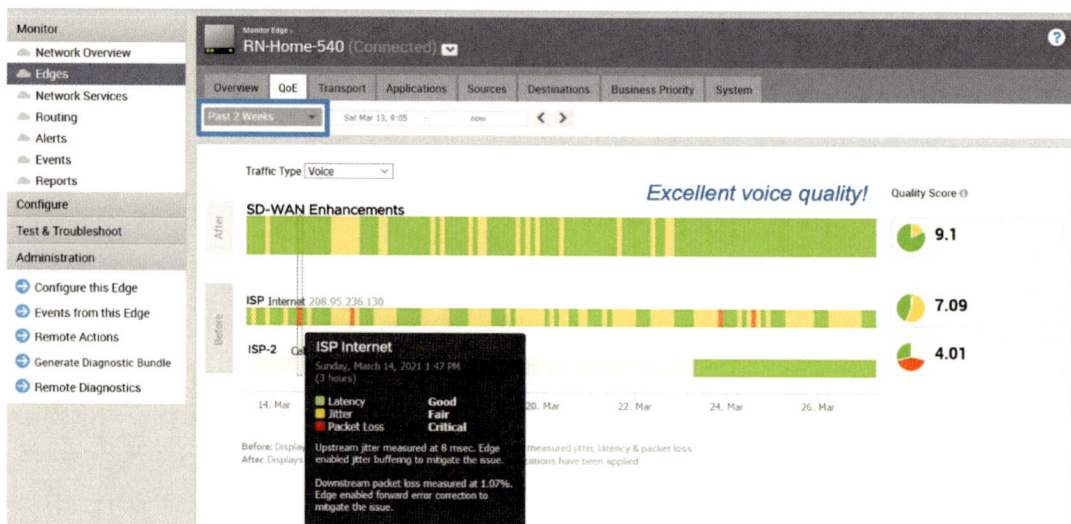

Figure 4.9: VMware SD-WAN Quality of Experience (QoE) Score

is a quality issue on one of the links, the Edge device immediately steers traffic to the other link. This ensures that the performance is never compromised, even if the links are of varying quality. With this arrangement, enterprises can increase throughput while reducing the cost per unit of throughput and still maintain the reliability of connections.

Dynamic Multi-Path Optimization

Dynamic Multi-Path Optimization (DMPO) provides continuous real-time link monitoring on a per-packet basis. If a link experiences packet loss, latency, or jitter, DMPO moves traffic to the best available link. **Figure 4.10** refers to VMware SD-WAN DMPO capabilities.

Deep Application Recognition	Secure Overlay	Link Qualification	Application Steering	On-Demand Remediation & Aggregation
What is on the network?	What paths are available?	How are the paths performing?	What is the best path for the application?	Reacting to deteriorating link conditions

Figure 4.10: VMware SD-WAN Dynamic Multi-Path Optimization (DMPO)

DMPO enables sub-second failover response to any brownout (e.g., packet loss, jitter, latency) or blackout (e.g., link failure) condition. In the event customers have a single link or all the links experience brownout conditions, DMPO initiates Forward Error Correction (FEC) and remediates the brownout condition.

Network Visibility and Agile Troubleshooting

The VMware SD-WAN Orchestrator makes it easy to monitor Edge devices and the performance of applications on the network, providing visibility across the entire WAN. The Orchestrator can save hours of time normally spent on device management because it can configure all devices from the central console using defined policies.

VMware SD-WAN comes with smart default for business application traffic. The VMware SD-WAN Orchestrator is used to set policies for the prioritization of applications on the network to make sure that the most important applications get the top priority. The Orchestrator provides a dashboard to monitor the performance of network connections and applications, gaining firsthand benefits of VMware SD-WAN.

The application monitoring features in the VMware SD-WAN Orchestrator allow IT organizations to quickly troubleshoot and resolve issues and, in turn, prevent poor application performance and downtime.

4.3.3 – Architecture for the Cloud

A significant benefit of the VMware SD-WAN solution is high-performance access to applications in the cloud and IaaS services. This is accomplished by connecting branch locations directly to the cloud through a VMware SD-WAN Gateway. These Gateways are hosted by VMware in PoP close to where the target application/IaaS. The VMware SD-WAN Gateway optimizes connectivity to the Edge device in the branch office location; no matter where the application resides, it provides a high-quality network connection with consistent policy across the enterprise.

Customers do not need to own or manage these Gateways. They are hosted by VMware and provided as a service as part of a subscription. There are two options available for connecting into the SD-WAN environment:

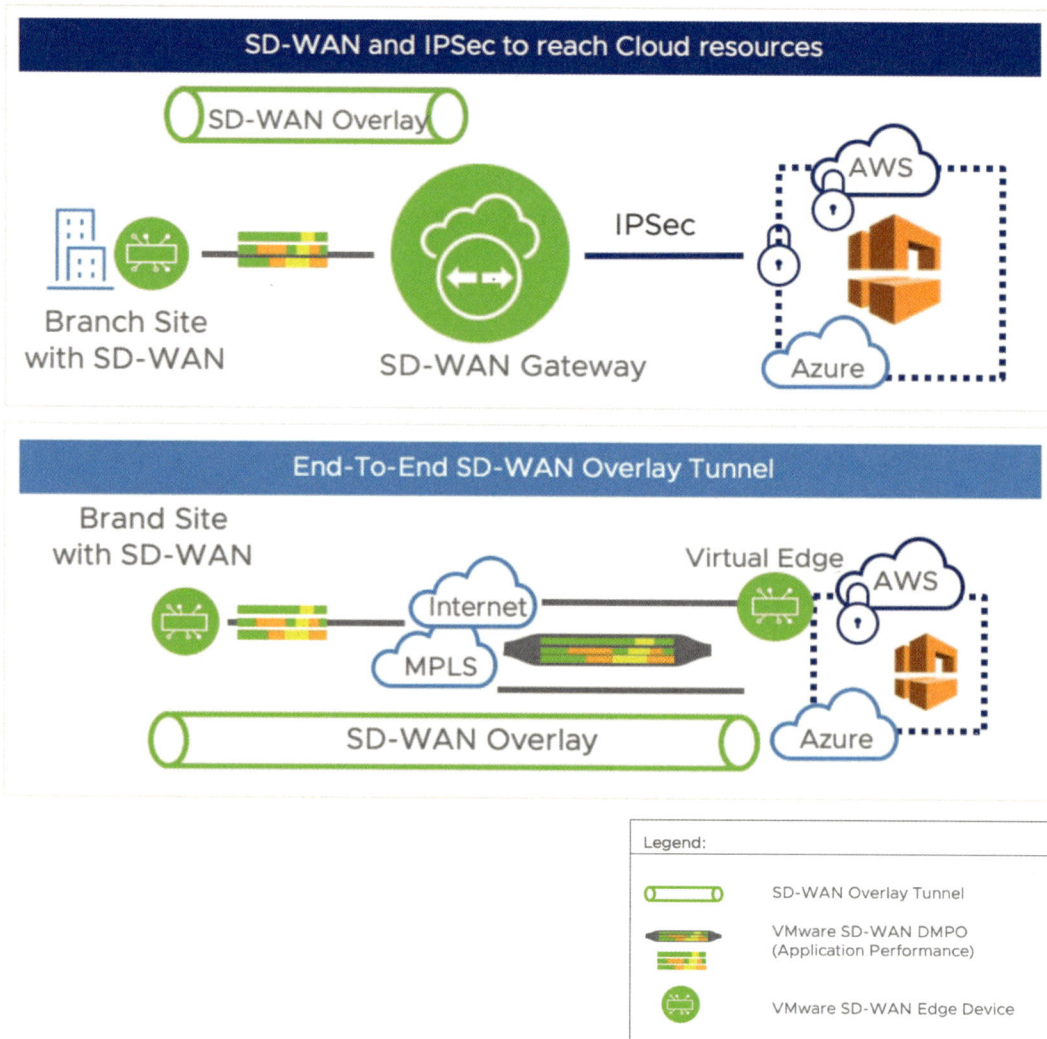

Figure 4.11: VMware SD-WAN connectivity to Cloud

- Connect over the Internet using IPsec tunnels for a secure connection without any SD-WAN. The connection between the branch Edge device and the VMware SD-WAN Gateway is always optimized.

- Connect using SD-WAN and connect with a virtual Edge instance in the cloud. The virtual Edge is available from cloud marketplaces such as AWS and Azure.

4.3.4 – Network Security

Security is a critical component of enterprise networks. The SD-WAN Edge has several built-in security functions, including a firewall, network segmentation, and the ability to run 3rd party security functions as VNFs. This functionality provides options to reduce the attack surface and minimize breaches. It also reduces costs and allows the flexibility to choose solutions from alternate security vendors. Customers can combine all these functions with existing on-premises security devices (e.g., firewall, IPS/IDS, SWG) and cloud web security solutions to build a comprehensive, network-wide—and cloud-inclusive—security solution.

Distributed Services Insertion via Service Chaining

Security services can also be built by automating and service chaining capabilities. Service chaining can be implemented to direct traffic to cloud-hosted security services. Service chaining can provide any type of protection, including website URL filtering or firewalling. It automates tunneling, eliminating the need for site-by-site configurations. It also offers single-click, application-aware policies for service insertion. Using this method helps secure traffic going over the Internet.

4.3.5 – Network Segmentation

Network security is not complete unless without the ability to isolate critical data traffic. Segmentation is the process of dividing the network into logical sub-networks using isolation techniques on a forwarding device such as a switch, router, or firewall. Network segmentation is essential when traffic from different organizations and/or data types must be isolated.

Segment-aware policies allow for rules to be set so specific traffic can be isolated, such as isolating guest Wi-Fi traffic or point-of-sale system data for better data integrity. Enterprises can configure a single physical network with multiple segments to address the need where a specific department in a company requires secure application access. Segmentation can be used to aid onboarding during mergers where IT wants to avoid overlapping IP addresses. Network services such as QoS and firewall policies can also be set per segment.

There are many use cases for Segmentation:

- Line of business separation by departments for security/audit

- User data separation: guest, PCI data, employee traffic

- Enterprise uses overlapping IP addresses for different groups

- Carrying Segmentation to VPNs for connecting off-network sites

Network segmentation is essential when traffic from different customers and/or business entities must be isolated from each other. Full support for Segmentation includes the isolation of management, control, and data plane traffic. For instance, VMware SD-WAN provides a simple configuration for Segmentation across the WAN. Segmentation can be enforced by an organization by data type and location. Organizations can isolate guest and employee-facing applications. Payment card data can be isolated for PCI audit compliance. Overlapping IP addresses can be provisioned to support acquired organizations.

4.4 – Key Takeaways

As applications move to the cloud, enterprises need a network that can keep up. To address the application performance issues of traditional wide area networks, SD-WAN provides simplified and flexible deployment options, improved application performance, security, and complete visibility at the network edge.

SD-WAN solutions streamline management and deliver cost savings to the enterprise. They provide the foundation for cloud connectivity and modern operational models, allowing IT to deliver a new level of enterprise-wide service and user experience.

Checklist: SD-WAN Takeaways

✓ The software-defined networking model unifies management of hardware, routing, and security components to reduce WAN complexity while improving user experience.

✓ Broadband connectivity can coexist with or replace expensive MPLS and leased line circuits, dramatically lowering bandwidth costs and hardware expenses.

✓ Integrated architecture provides granular, end-to-end visibility and control for both underlay and overlay networks.

✓ The cloud-ready architecture eliminates backhaul traffic and supports local Internet traffic breakout.

✓ Centralized management enables network segmentation, streamlines operations, reduces errors, and drives consistent security policy.

✓ Automation and AI intelligently steer traffic to deliver predictable application performance.

✓ Full support for Segmentation includes the isolation of management, control, and data plane traffic.

Chapter 5

Realizing Enterprise Digital Transformation through SASE

Objective

This chapter will frame the current challenges and trends impacting cloud networking and security. It will define the problems that the Secure Access Service Edge (SASE) is designed to address while looking at its benefits, architecture, components, and technical implementation.

5.1 – Current Trends

Digital transformation is rapidly changing corporate culture, business processes, and technology. The introduction of and increasing demand for cloud services combined with employees working from anywhere—office, home, or coffee shop—places new demands on networking and security architectures. Users are becoming more mobile and accessing business systems off-premises. The digitalization of business processes has also driven the use of thousands of outsourced business applications, most of which reside outside the corporate data center. SaaS business applications have drastically changed the volume and nature of network traffic. This explosion in the amount of data and the number of locations has significantly increased the attack surface. Networking traffic flows are shifting from data center backhaul to cloud direct. Traffic inspection is moving from on-premises security appliances to cloud-delivered security services. As such, enterprises are rethinking their existing network and security architectures as they look toward a comprehensive overhaul and digital transformation.

5.2 – Challenges with Today's Networking and Security Infrastructure

Fundamental churn and changes of infrastructure are underway due to cloud and virtualization. The demand for cloud and remote work trends is driving the need for WAN transformation. The existing WAN architecture is inefficient, expensive to maintain, and does not provide the expected application user experience. The static nature of the existing WAN architecture wastes bandwidth, limits business continuity, and lacks end-to-end visibility, analytics, and automation, all of which are ultimately detrimental to achieving enterprise digital transformation. The enterprise security landscape is also changing and evolving in concert with network transformation. While data is exponentially growing, it must be classified and protected. The number of threats and attacks is increasing, becoming highly sophisticated and targeted.

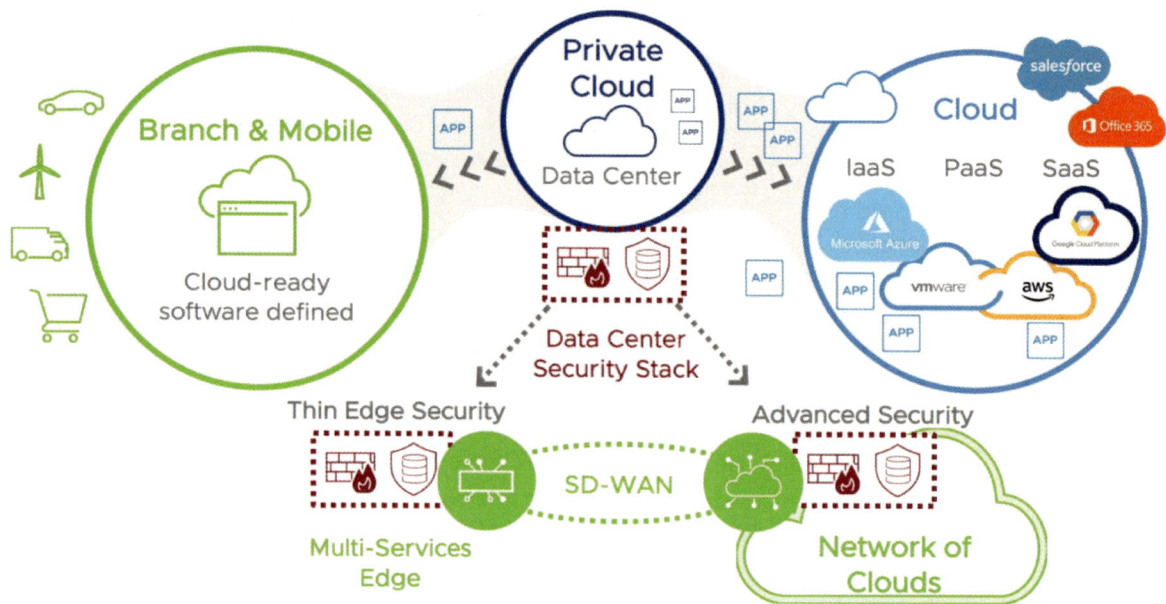

Figure 5.1: Transformation for the On-Premises Datacenter Application and Security to Cloud

Endpoint practices are evolving. Enterprise-managed devices and controlled assets have been joined by the bring-your-own-device (BYOD) model. In all cases, IT must be able to onboard remote users quickly while providing seamless access to enterprise resources.

IT departments are overwhelmed with network and security challenges. Some of these include but are not limited to:

- **Supporting Remote Access Security:** An increasingly heavy burden on enterprises with the growing number of users working remotely. While VPNs have been the common remote access technology, cost and bandwidth limitations combined with security limitations have created new challenges. IT must protect remote users, the devices they use to connect, and the apps they are accessing in the cloud.

- **Operations (CAPEX):** High network operational cost supporting the VPN infrastructure and associated security is increasingly complicated and rigid.

- **Policy:** Distinct policies that align with the business and users are trends for enterprises. IT must define policy to ensure users' data, applications, and cloud connections are simple, consistent, automated, and secure.

- **User Experience:** Service level agreement (SLA) enforcement remains a challenge to guarantee application predictability and availability regardless of where it is located or accessed from.

- **Cost:** Increases in operational costs due to the number of IT specialists required to understand, design, implement and support networking and security solutions.

The transition to remote work was well underway before the seismic changes of 2020. SaaS is expected to be the preferred model for application delivery within a few years. Users, data, and compute are increasingly located outside of the corporate perimeter. New capabilities are needed to secure any user, device, app, and cloud.

Traditional WAN models that backhaul traffic over MPLS links are financially expensive and architecturally inefficient in this modern environment. Decentralized models address these issues but place new burdens on security and performance. Traditional concepts of control and visibility no longer exist; with traffic crossing multiple provider networks, consistent implementation of policy and validation of compliance is a huge concern. The volume of security threats and the associated tools that protect against them is too large for effective oversight by enterprise security. Many areas may go completely unexamined, while those that are tracked may be lost in the noise of copious log data and false positives.

While corporate boards are more willing than ever to commit to security spending, they rarely focus on increased staffing. Technology and services must be able to take the place of larger teams, simplifying operations and management while improving the overall security profile.

SASE can help the enterprise address central challenges arising from both the shift to cloud and the exodus of users from the traditional office, including themes of management complexity, solution pricing, and user experience.

5.3 – Introducing SASE: Combining SD-WAN and Cloud Security

Gartner's original definition for SASE identified the central components that brought together networking and security as a unified service, including SD-WAN, SWG, CASB, ZTNA, and FWaaS.

> **Gartner has branded the Secure Access Service Edge (SASE), Convergence of Networking and Security.**
>
> **Source:** https://blogs.gartner.com/andrew-lerner/2019/12/23/say-hello-sase-secure-access-service-edge/

Today more users, data, and applications reside outside of the traditional enterprise perimeter—including the data center—due to cloud adoption. Enterprises need SASE, the emerging integrated network and security framework.

The SASE architecture integrates security functionality into software-defined wide-area networking to provide a cloud-delivered service that simplifies deployment, unifies management, and controls user/application experience.

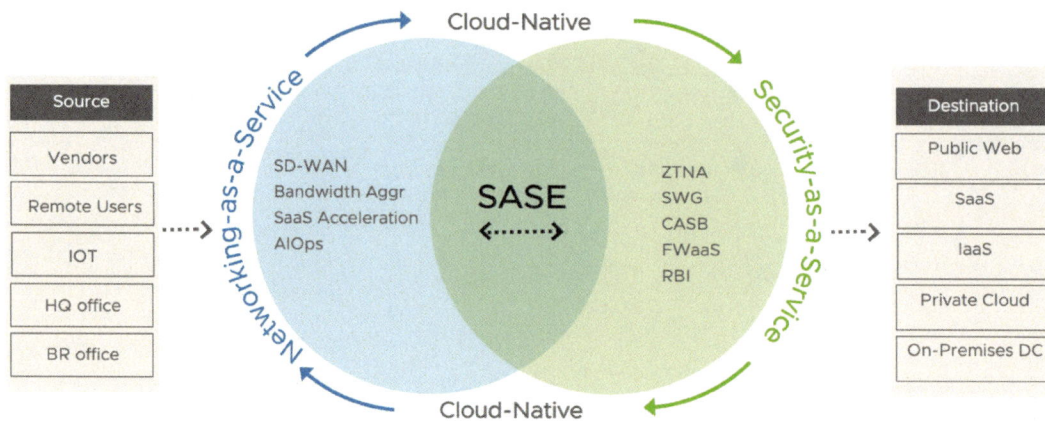

Figure 5.2: Cloud-Native SASE= Networking as a Service + Cloud Security as a Service

SASE brings together networking and security into a unified offering, as shown in **Figure 5.2**, connecting previously siloed functionality. It offers both technical capabilities and operational simplification at a price significantly reduced from high-cost point solutions and expensive private WAN links.

SASE is an architectural concept, and not all SASE offerings are created the same. Vendors may lack expertise in either security or WAN implementation. The design may be focused on traditional (i.e., on-premises) infrastructure rather than modern cloud requirements. A solution may be cobbled together from individual components and offered without a unified management system or operational experience. PoP locations may be limited, impacting application performance or regional access restrictions (e.g., data locality mandates).

The SASE model offers necessary security services like secure web gateways (SWG), cloud access security brokers (CASB), data loss prevention (DLP), advanced threat protection (ATP), which are converged in the cloud-native model and utilize a global, high-capacity, low-latency SD-WAN edge network for optimal performance.

Effective adoption of SASE concepts and practices goes beyond just installing technology; it will require a mindset shift and practical training throughout an organization to break down operational silos and established practices. The strategy must start from the top of the organization to encourage networking, security, and cloud teams to put aside turf wars and work together.

5.4 – Benefits of SASE

Implementation of a SASE model for the enterprise brings significant benefits to simplified management, security, network performance, user experience, and budgets.

Simplified Management: A single user interface providing simplified configuration, provisioning, real-time monitoring, fault management, and granular visibility for networking and security components.

Driven by fully functional APIs, SASE components are built from the ground up to align with corporate management and automation tools. Tasks that were previously labor-intensive (e.g., branch site deployment, workflow template, automated network optimization, event correlation, and active remediation) can now be addressed without any need for manual intervention. End-to-end connectivity simplifies the process of delivering complete visibility and ensuring policy consistency throughout the enterprise.

Security: Implementation and enforcement of policy are unified while being brought closer to users and applications. Regardless of location, the same tools and practices are used. End-to-end encryption allows for a heightened compliance level, while cloud-scale security capabilities enhance detection and remediation of even advanced threats. Security policy can follow users as they move between locations and devices to assure consistent implementation and enforcement while corporate resources are protected through ZTNA.

Network Performance: SD-WAN technology is used to deliver latency-optimized connectivity both through efficient path selection and optimized traffic processing. Elimination of hair pinning and streamlining of data inspection tasks further reduces the network's impact on application performance.

User Experience: The channeled nature of SASE connectivity reduces the number of endpoint agents needed. Equivalent security controls can be applied without regard for user location or device access, creating a more transparent, less intrusive experience.

Budget: SD-WAN already offered the opportunity for dramatic cost reductions over traditional circuits (e.g., MPLS expenses). Integration into the SASE framework further enhances this potential through consolidation into common management tools and automation frameworks. Cloud-based security services offer cost-efficient approaches for scaling and bursting based on usage while providing flexibility to shift based on technical requirements.

5.5 – Early Drivers for SASE Adoption

How should a business proceed when considering SASE adoption? To realize the benefits of SASE, enterprises must be prepared to act upon challenges and commit to overcoming them. Functionality and performance vary widely between offerings, while implementation can be challenging even for experienced networking and security teams.

Significant barriers to adoption include:

- **Market expertise:** SASE solutions remain on the leading edge. New vendors without market expertise are rushing into space. Existing point-solution vendors may offer partial solutions that maximize their market position rather than address fundamental customer challenges. Industry leaders may be slow to bring compelling offerings to market, wary of the impact on their legacy hardware, or struggling to adapt to the new cloud-native reality.

- **Technical expertise:** Required to drive the proper processes and identify the appropriate solutions, including the necessary evaluations without bias.

- **Solution capabilities:** Cloud-native networking and security services are undergoing constant evolution. SASE offerings will continue to evolve with them. A business must adopt an operational strategy that accepts ongoing change and implement an architecture that can upgrade and grow with the broader SASE ecosystem. PoP prevalence and peering relationships are other components that loom large for both application performance and user experience.

- **Corporate readiness:** Technology is rarely the most significant barrier to corporate change, and this reality will apply to the adoption of SASE principles and practices. Organizational silos must be broken down for networking and security. Processes will need to be rewritten. Corporate practices and assumptions must be re-examined and modernized. Leadership and vision at the highest business levels are essential for successful adoption.

- **Baked-in solution flexibility:** Allow for a foundation built upon for future expansion and growth. Security is an ongoing journey, not a one-time solution.

5.6 – SASE Architecture and Components

The modern workforce is much more dynamic and distributed than a decade ago. Companies are using more cloud-based applications, and user mobility has become the norm rather than the exception. In this new normal, traditional wide-area network models where everything revolves around a central data center no longer make sense.

SASE combines networking-as-a-service with security-as-a-service. This streamlines IT management and operations while providing quality service for applications and consistent quality of experience for users. As stated earlier, SASE is a framework that brings together networking and security services to provide an integrated policy-based solution that is

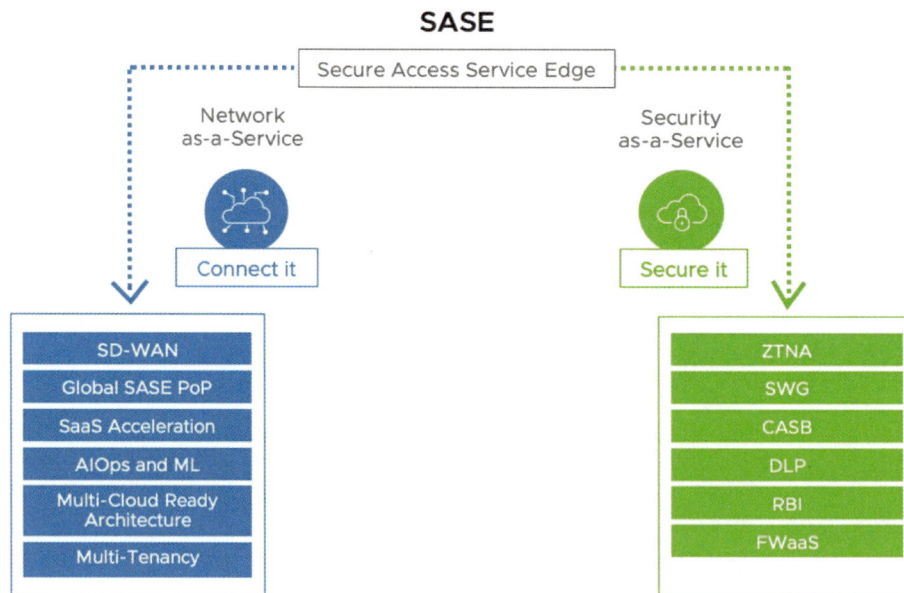

SASE

| Secure Access Service Edge |

Network as-a-Service — Connect it

SD-WAN
Global SASE PoP
SaaS Acceleration
AIOps and ML
Multi-Cloud Ready Architecture
Multi-Tenancy

Security as-a-Service — Secure it

ZTNA
SWG
CASB
DLP
RBI
FWaaS

Figure 5.3: SASE Framework

SASE is a general-purpose architecture that supports customization of functionality and components to support individual business requirements. The following sections discuss its networking and security components, grouping them into the core, recommended, and optional categories. Where individual technologies have been discussed earlier in this book, these sections will example, their importance to the greater SASE and cloud environment.

5.6.1 – SASE Core Components

Figure 5.4 highlights the core components in each vertical. The following sections take an architectural and technical look at each area.

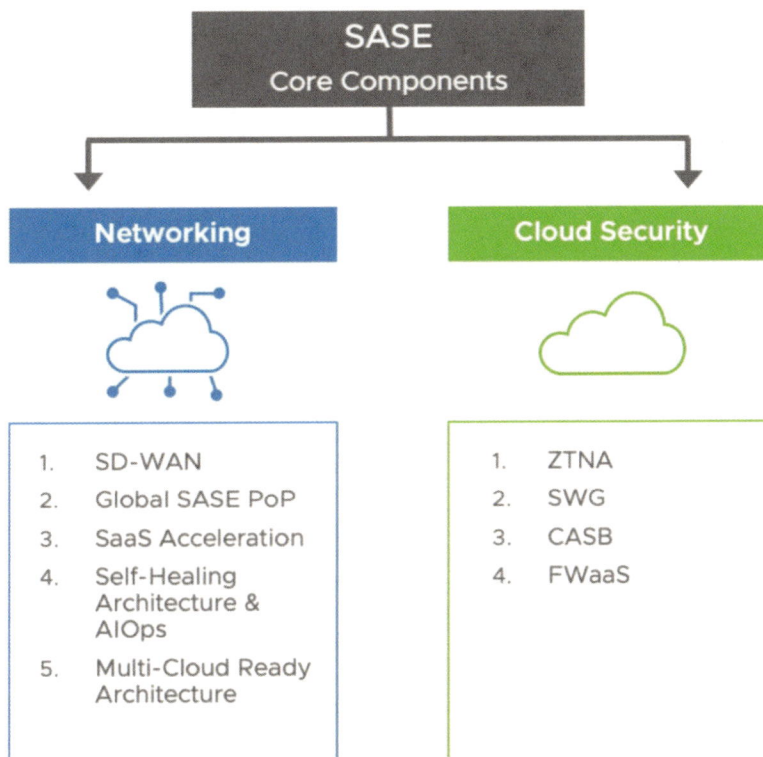

Figure 5.4: SASE Core Components for Networking and Security

Core Networking Components

SD-WAN

SD-WAN is the key building block for SASE. It is responsible for providing reliable transport by controlling the connectivity, management, and services that connect its users and branch locations to cloud services. SD-WAN transforms connectivity, simplifying remote user and branch office networking while assuring optimal application performance and cost-effectiveness. SD-WAN is delivered as a cloud service with a separate management plane, control plane, and data plane. This separation improves service network agility by moving the intelligence from the data plane into a programmable control plane. The management plane simplifies day-to-day operations and creates a flexible architecture that addresses the demands of modern SASE implementations.

Some of the capabilities for SD-WAN include transport independence, secure overlay, application performance, proactive network remediation, and simplified operations.

- **Transport Independence:** Operates independently of any underlying transport technology (MPLS, Broadband, 3G/4G/LTE/5G). SD-WAN provides the structure for SASE transport. Its overlay operates independently of any connection technologies. An enterprise can use its existing WAN infrastructure, public Internet connections, commodity broadband links, or a combination of these and other technologies (e.g., LTE, 5G, Wi-Fi). The SD-WAN service will identify the proper network paths for each application to ensure optimal performance and secure connectivity. This offers a business greater control over properly mixing link cost and performance parameters.

- **Secure Overlay:** Connections between SD-WAN endpoints are protected with secure encrypted tunnels that carry traffic across the multiple transport underlays. These are virtual overlays based on tunnels that carry traffic across the multiple underlay networks – typically a mixture of private carrier services and public Internet connections. SD-WAN provides an additional layer of security over the public Internet, protecting traffic on its journey to SASE cloud security and then to its final destination. Furthermore, network segmentation and unified threat management capabilities ensure secure branch-to-cloud communications.

- **Application Performance:** SD-WAN technology ensures the performance and availability of applications regardless of user location or network changes. It utilizes dynamic, intelligent link steering to direct traffic based on application requirements and business policy. It can operate simultaneously across multiple WAN transport technologies and incorporates information about link capacity, latency, quality. Sessions can be redirected in real-time, preventing loss of information for even sensitive voice and video applications. High bandwidth sessions can take advantage of link aggregation to speed data transfer.

- **Proactive Network Remediation:** Intelligence at the network edge provides deep visibility into the client's wireless or wired state and proactively manages end-user and IoT device issues across the entire network stack. It offers complete fault detection, isolation, and remediation using ML algorithms to tackle application problems caused by network services, security services, and applications. It proactively remediates faults isolated with each application performance measured at vantage points between distributed workforce and distributed cloud applications.

- **Simplified Operations:** SD-WAN leverages a policy-based solution to ensure the network complies with the enterprise business needs. It allows specification of application definition parameters and resource usage. The service supports zero-touch provisioning for automatic authentication and configuration for secure branch connectivity and faster onboarding of new locations.

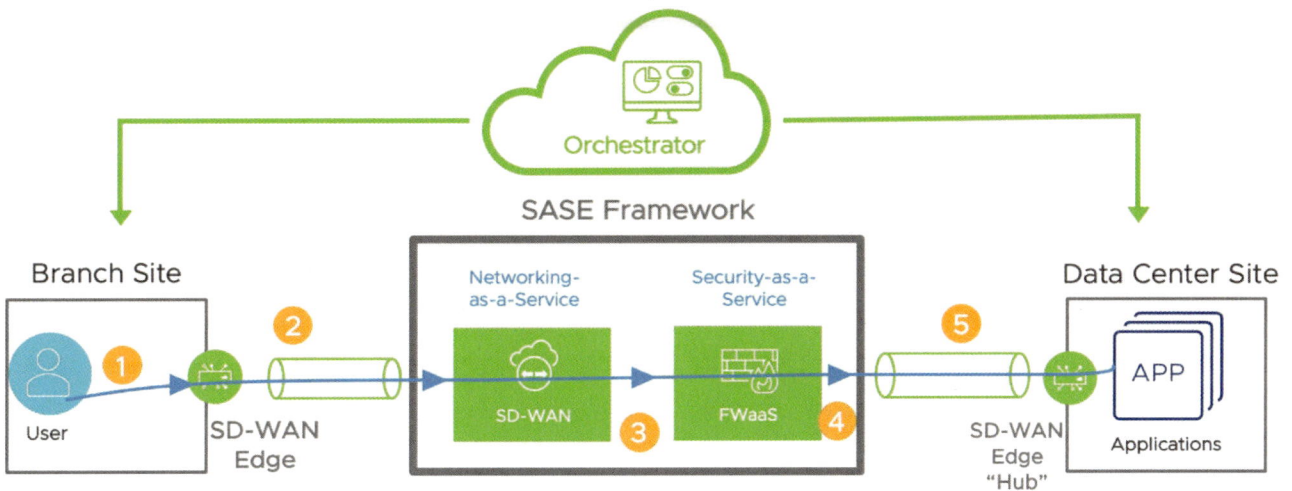

Figure 5.5 SD-WAN Core Component for SASE (Networking as a Service)

Figure 5.5 walks through the end-to-end traffic flow for a user connecting to On-Premises DC Application

1) Traffic from the endpoint device (e.g., user laptop) hits its local gateway. In this case, the local gateway is the SD-WAN Edge device.

2) The SD-WAN Edge uses Deep Packet Inspection (DPI) to recognize the traffic type. It forwards this connection to the appropriate, optimal WAN link. The user traffic goes over the SD-WAN overlay tunnel and reaches SASE PoP.

3) Based on pre-defined business policies from the cloud-based Orchestrator, traffic handoff happens from the SD-WAN component to the security component (e.g., Cloud Firewall FWaaS). Traffic is still inside the SASE PoP.

4) The traffic receives granular inspection by FWaaS based on security rules defined from the centralized Orchestrator.

5) The security service forwards the traffic toward the On-Premises DC SD-WAN device (Hub). This traffic goes over the SD-WAN overlay tunnel. The return traffic follows a similar traffic pattern.

Beyond just moving packets, SD-WAN systems offer application performance, operational simplicity, intrinsic security, and SaaS acceleration capabilities to enhance the SASE framework.

Global SASE PoP

A PoP (point of presence) is a location where a service provider or other network entity maintains equipment, services, or connectivity. It serves as an endpoint for a connection from an endpoint device/end-user network and entry point into a larger network environment.

Equipment at a traditional PoP implementation includes modem banks, WAN routers, and DSLAMs (digital subscriber line aggregation multiplexers). These devices are common connection points that bring together large volumes of individual links, allowing them to exchange traffic–both with each other and upstream systems–at a central location.

A PoP may exist in a provider's own environment (e.g., data center) or be co-located at a third-party location (e.g., Internet exchange) alongside PoPs from other providers. Service providers distribute PoPs across their service areas to ensure that customers can connect to their larger infrastructure with a minimum of cost and latency; larger providers may have hundreds of PoPs spread across multiple geographies. PoP availability and diversity is a key concern for solution providers looking to deliver responsive, available services. Cloud providers and as-a-service vendors often place their systems at the same exchanges as ISP PoPs to maximize these benefits.

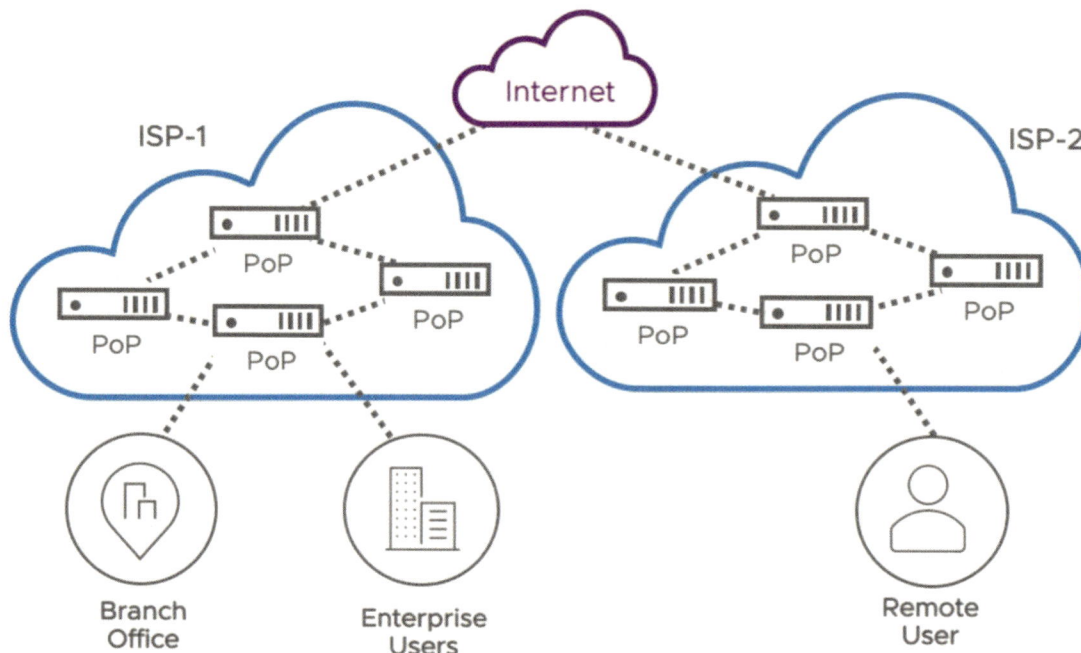

Figure: 5.6: Global Point of Presence (PoP)

PoPs bring together and connect the world. They streamline connectivity and communication between different networks, creating Internet exchange points (IEPs) crucial for minimizing the Internet's diameter. Multiple PoPs provide redundant connectivity points, increasing service reliability and helping connections route around individual outages. Their direct connectivity into end-user networks serves as a focal opportunity for traffic security and processing.

What role does the PoP Play in SASE?

A SASE PoP service distributes individual PoP sites across its service region. Optimal placement locates them logically near enterprise resources (e.g., data center, campus, branches, users) and cloud services (e.g., SaaS applications, platform providers). Individual users will automatically connect to their nearest PoP to minimize latency and improve performance. These PoPs serve as the initial point of security and processing for end-user traffic, protecting both the enterprise network from malicious attacks and the user from public Internet threats.

SaaS Acceleration

SD-WAN uses the global PoP infrastructure to provide SaaS acceleration. SD-WAN optimizes the traffic taken to SaaS providers and cloud applications, eliminating the need to backhaul traffic to the data center. This incorporates a distributed network of service gateways deployed at top-tier cloud data centers worldwide to optimize access to SaaS resources. It can assure application performance for applications and data hosted on a private and public cloud while simplifying the deployment and reduce cost.

For instance, VMware SD-WAN provides doorstep-delivered, secure, optimized access to SaaS cloud-based services. VMware SD-WAN incorporates a distributed network of gateways deployed at top-tier PoPs around the globe, providing high performance, scalability, redundancy, and on-demand flexibility.

Self-healing Architecture and AIOps

AIOps is short for artificial intelligence for IT operations. It provides automation and minimizes day-to-day operation through AI/ML (Artificial Intelligence/Machine Learning). AIOps is the notion of collecting information directly from the infrastructure and analyzing the data using AI/ML to assist IT operations. To automate actions and make them more efficient, the IT operations team needs to extract the correct information through analytics. Using data analytics, IT can recommend preventive and predictive maintenance tasks. Anomaly detection can also create alerts for ongoing issues and take action to automate the remediation process.

AI/ML plays a key role by providing near real-time monitoring of user performance, dynamic adaptation of network policies using self-healing and self-optimization, and constant security threat monitoring using real-time data streams. For instance, when a user experiences network connectivity issues or security behavior, it is important to know whether the issue is due to problems with the LAN, WAN, data center, security context, or posture.

Multi-Cloud Ready Architecture

SASE architecture simplifies cloud onboarding and multi-cloud interconnect by providing automatic discovery of IaaS routing domains (e.g., VPCs and VNETs) and connection to enterprise resources (e.g., user devices, branch sites, and data centers).

It delivers security for multi-cloud use cases with seamless connectivity, consistent policy, and rapid workload mobility. Automation of networking and security tasks ensures a fast, consistent operational environment, allowing IT staff to spend time adding value rather than performing low-level tasks.

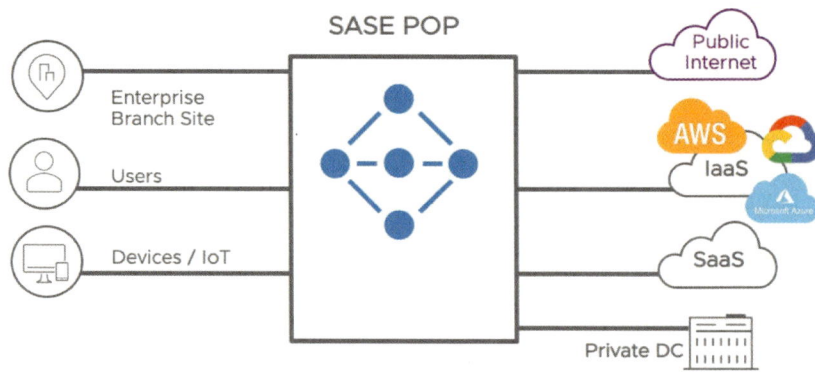

Figure: 5.7: SASE On-Ramp to Multi-Cloud

SASE should be a central part of an enterprise's multi-cloud optimization strategy. Its capabilities allow for:

- Automated deployment of SD-WAN Edges into IaaS.
- Auto-provisioning of tunnels from branch sites to multi-cloud environments.
- A seamless extension of network segmentation between data center, IaaS, branch, and ZTNA devices.
- Rapid cloud adoption and scaling of new operating models, interconnecting multiple clouds through SASE infrastructure.
- Natively supporting workloads in hybrid and multi-cloud.
- Discovery and audit of new multi-cloud instances for consistent network security.

Core Cloud Security Components

Core security components for SASE that protect the enterprise infrastructure are cloud-delivered and include ZTNA, SWG, CASB, and FWaaS.

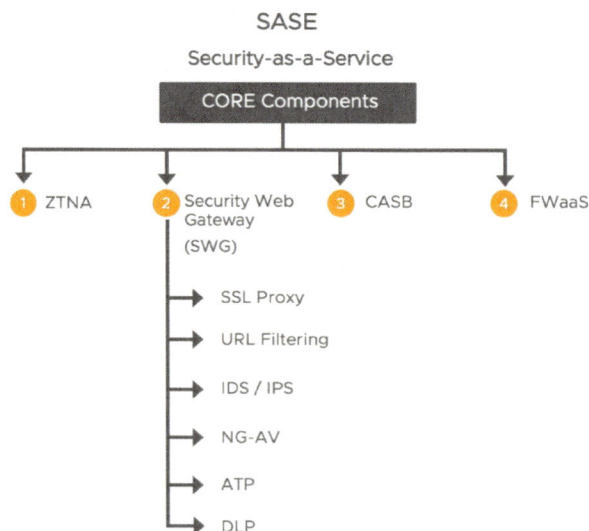

Figure 5.8 Core Security Component for SASE

ZTNA

Zero-trust network access (ZTNA) works from the foundational principle that no safe security perimeter/zone exists and that all access requests should be treated as suspect until verified (i.e., the least privilege principle). It hides the network location of resources while using user identity controls to limit access.

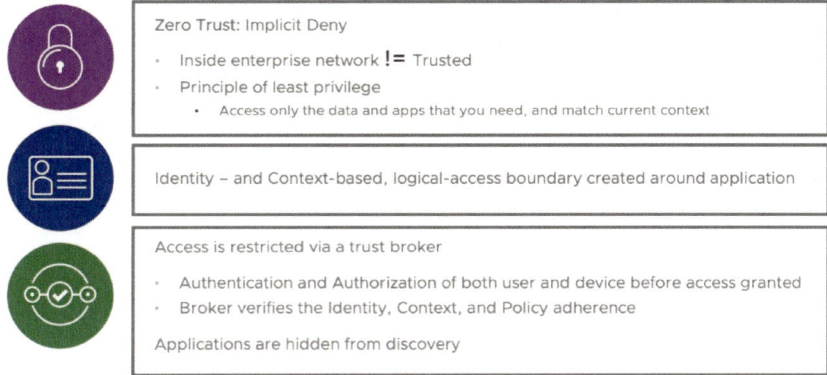

Figure 5.9: What is Zero Trust?

This Zero Trust architecture allows security teams to control access by user and location while applying the same policies regardless of where the application, data, or other resources reside. Centralized controls provide enforcement throughout the ecosystem with policies that follow users across devices.

In a ZTNA environment, every connection attempt is explicitly verified. Resources are not directly visible to users; connectivity is only possible through the architecture's controls. Both the individual user and accessing device must be verified. Users are authenticated using multi-factor systems (e.g., token, biometric) and authorized for access to individual network resources. Devices must be validated as running authorized hardware/OS and be properly patched to minimize the risk of bringing an untrusted device or compromised system onto the network.

A ZTNA environment is constantly evaluating the state of connections, users, and devices; it manages and coordinates the capabilities of the ecosystem's security tools to isolate and shut off access from invalid users and systems.

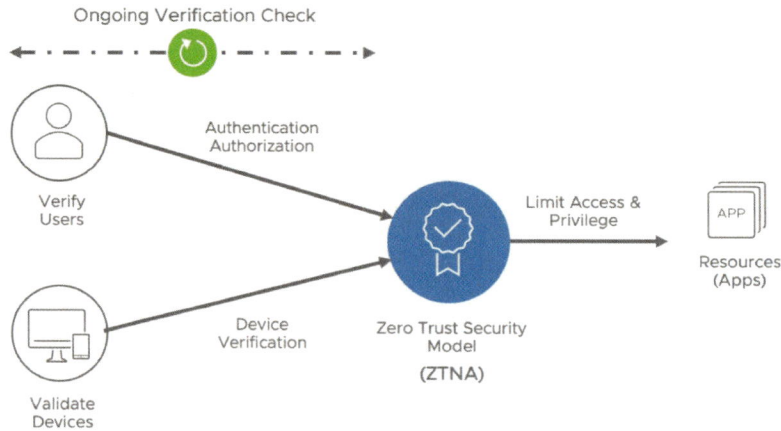

Figure 5.10: Zero Trust Security Model

ZTNA plays many roles in SASE:

- **Consistent, always-on, intrinsically secure access:** With ZTNA, a user will always be connected to enterprise applications. ZTNA vets and grants users and devices policy-based access centered on the user and device identity for each connection. If the user is within the branch or corporate network, the VPN service will automatically be paused. If the user works from home or goes on the road and tries to connect to their administrator-allowed applications, the network connectivity will transparently and automatically be applied with secure trust established with the device. Additional authentication (e.g., multi-factor authentication) can be applied as needed. Customizable per-client application policies can be fine-tuned to only bring what is needed to the remote access service, lowering user acceptance friction due to privacy concerns.

- **Productive work experience:** Users are working remotely from everywhere. ZTNA ensures that they have a fast and seamless user experience when accessing their applications. The remote access client will automatically connect to the closest SASE infrastructure. Based on enterprise policy, user traffic may be passed to a cloud firewall, a web security service, to another enterprise branch, a data center, or a specific application or service. Note that only enterprise traffic will go to the enterprise site, with personal traffic being forwarded directly to the Internet. The idea here is to avoid latency-inducing hair-pinned paths through an enterprise data center with strained VPN appliances.

- **Efficiency for IT teams:** The simplicity of ZTNA—all cloud-hosted, all software, no hardware—makes it easy to deploy without the need to hire new specialists. This simplicity allows IT to adopt technology that can secure access to applications moving to the cloud, including unmanaged mobile devices, while maximizing the productivity of the IT staff.

Routing Policy and security controls will remain in the hands of the enterprise while the SASE cloud service handles scaling, management, upgrading, and multi-region VPN service presence. It can be difficult and expensive to scale quickly, especially across multiple regions. Offloading this service allows IT teams to focus on more complex and critical tasks for the business.

- **Deliver agility and scale:** As the number of employees, devices, applications, and amount of traffic continues to grow, ZTNA delivered from the cloud ensures the increasing scale is not a concern of the IT team. The ZTNA service handles the additional load automatically without the need to deploy additional hardware appliances or virtualized firewalls, which cloud slow cloud adoption. Increased agility and scale are critical factors for IT success and are delivered through ZTNA.

- **Accelerate the adoption of public cloud and mobile devices:** Cloud and mobility are key priorities for the majority of enterprises. Today's traditional networks have complexities and security challenges when providing access to cloud apps from unmanaged user devices. ZTNA uses software to reduce this complexity, in turn reducing implementation time to just days or hours. With ZTNA, organizations can more quickly reap the benefits of cloud and mobility.

Simple policies and easy management are key for a SASE solution. ZTNA principles within a SASE solution allow for identifying and controlling users, devices, and applications; irrespective of where they are, organizations can benefit from using a single cloud solution for all of their connectivity and security needs.

Secure Web Gateway

Applications used to reside in the data center; now, more and more are moving to and reside in the cloud. Dedicated gateways were built with stacks of security appliances to allow secure Internet access. These gateways were centralized to minimize the cost and complexity of securing multiple locations. With the move to the cloud, user traffic is now bypassing the traditional enterprise security perimeter. The complexities of deploying and managing all the different dedicated security appliances—and their associated costs—are overwhelming IT team budgets. With applications in the cloud and the explosive use of mobility to access these applications, it makes sense to move security to the cloud. A secure web gateway (SWG) in the cloud is an essential and natural evolution of the enterprise security architecture and, combined with an SD-WAN network, provides the SASE framework.

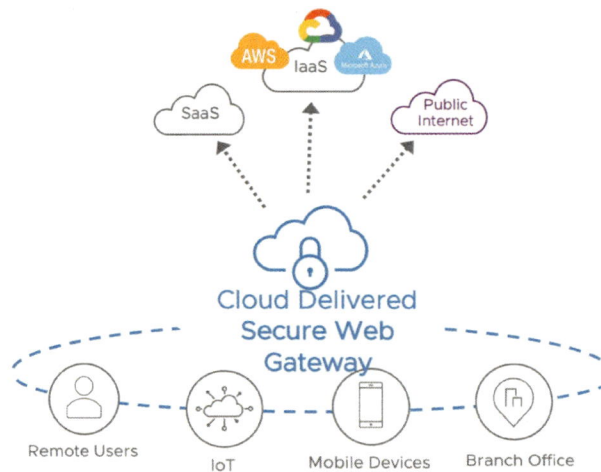

Figure 5.11: Secure Web Gateway Cloud Protection

A secure web gateway (SWG) protects an organization from online security threats and infections by filtering unwanted software/malware from user-initiated Internet traffic. It also enforces corporate and regulatory policy compliance. As a key component of SASE architecture, the SWG provides data context and granular policy controls for the cloud and web.

An SWG secures traffic passing between the two zones according to standard policies and pre-defined rules. These protections are bi-directional, preventing not only intrusion from malicious actors but also ensuring the safety of internal users accessing external sites.

In addition to controls for safety, an SWG may also enforce corporate policies for legal compliance, acceptable use, and intentional/accidental data transfer. Different from a traditional firewall, an SWG focuses on the application layer. It understands details of protocols and sessions rather than packets and headers.

The growth of both remote workers and cyber threats has greatly expanded the scope and complexity of securing the corporate perimeter. Secure web gateways serve as points of consolidation, funneling user sessions through a consolidated security environment, as shown in **Figure 5.11**.

Depending on the implementation, an SWG may be a point product operating independently or part of a larger security architecture (e.g., SASE).

An SWG will terminate sessions with web traffic and perform security inspections on their content. These checks can include anti-virus/anti-malware scans, URL filtering, and data infiltration/exfiltration. Problem sessions can be terminated immediately or sandboxed for further investigation. For valid traffic, it then proxies the session on to its final destination.

The following categories are essential to secure web gateway capabilities. They are explored in additional detail in the following sections:

- SSL Proxy

- URL filtering

- Intrusion Detection and Prevention

- Next-Generation Anti-Virus (NGAV)

- Advanced Threat Protection

- Data Loss Protection (DLP)

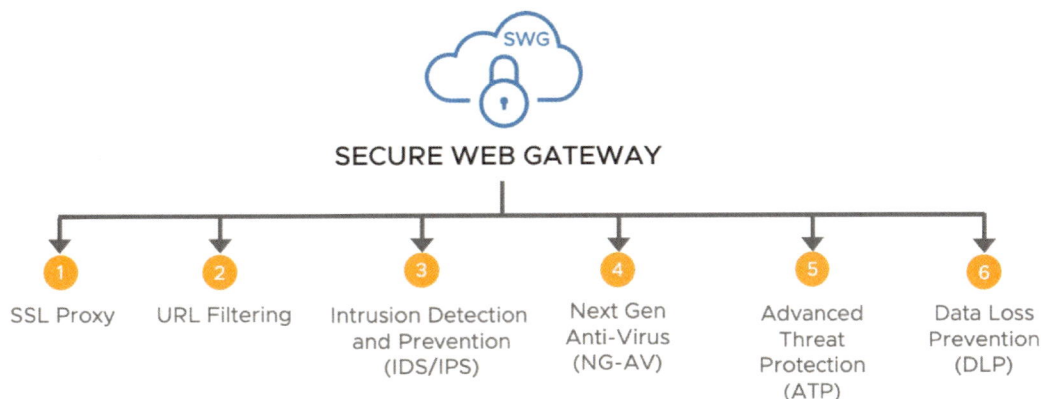

Figure 5.12: Secure Web Gateway Capabilities

SSL Proxy

What is an SSL Proxy?

An SSL proxy is a device that performs traffic inspection by terminating SSL sessions between two devices.

Sitting between the client and server, it transparently handles communication in both directions, encapsulating and decapsulating packets to allow access to their encrypted content. Rather than rely on more advanced techniques that attempt to divine the nature of a flow, an SSL proxy provides direct access to the data for processing.

How does an SSL Proxy Work?

The SSL protocol is secured through the use of server certificates that allow a user to trust the identity of the server they are connecting to. An SSL proxy emulates these certificates to provide a seamless end-to-end connection. An IT administrator configures endpoints to trust the SSL proxy. This is done by adding the root certificate authority (CA) certificate of the SSL proxy to the browser's trusted root CA list on the client system.

There are mainly two types of proxy, **Forward and Reverse proxy.** A forward proxy is used by the client (e.g., a web browser), and the reverse proxy is used by the server (e.g., web server). A reverse SSL proxy can perform additional tasks such as offloading HTTPS encryption/decryption functionality normally performed by the end server.

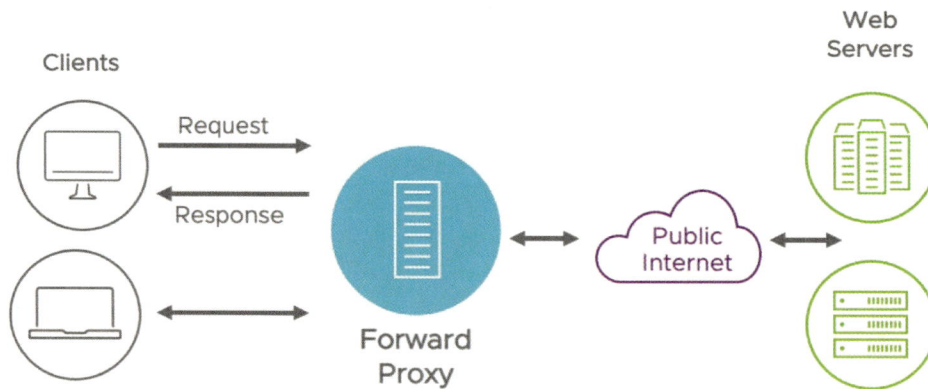

Figure 5.13: Forward SSL Proxy

In **Figure 5.13**, the forward proxy sends back its own public key, instead of the server public key, to the client. This signature is trusted by the client's browser as the SSL proxy was earlier added to the list of trusted root CAs. The client now perceives the connection to the proxy as a direct connection to the server.

What are the Benefits of SSL Proxy?

The decrypted access provided by SSL proxies permits granular inspection of data by security services. This level of visibility is essential for the accurate implementation of DLP and compliance-related tools. In addition to simple data inspection, it enhances the capabilities of anti-malware and advanced threat tools in detecting and identifying threats before they reach internal servers.

A web proxy allows IT teams to monitor and enforce the use of specific encryption protocols by both the client and server instead of trusting application developers to adhere to corporate standards or upgrade to newer algorithms.

This boundary layer offers an opportunity to scale resources and compute power independent of an individual server or application. Encryption can be a compute-intensive task that can be offloaded from the application server, allowing the proxy to perform this task while freeing up system resources for more productive uses.

URL Filtering

URL filtering is the most common and straightforward service in a secure web gateway. Filtering blocks known-bad URLs which encourage users to download malware or spoof legitimate sites with similar domain names or web pages. Additional layers (e.g., AML, AV) can augment security when this functionality is insufficient to protect a session on its own (e.g., compromise of a legitimate, allowed site).

URL filtering can operate on both DNS names and IP addresses. It implements this process using an access list approach which explicitly either permits good sites or blocks bad ones. In addition to classic static models, more advanced blocklist solutions can incorporate individual keywords or make real-time decisions based on on-site content (e.g., violence, gambling) to make an allow/block decision.

In **Figure 5.14**, traffic in red represents the IP address or URL site being blocked. This traffic is dropped and never goes out to the public Internet.

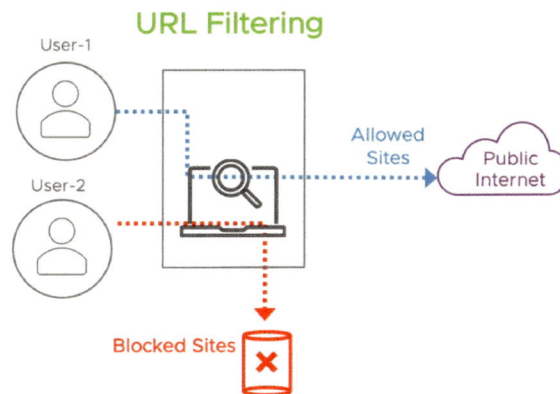

Figure 5.14: URL Filtering

As with traditional firewall-based access-list models, maintenance of these lists can be confusing and cumbersome. Blocklists are the more common implementation model due to the vast number of sites and services required in the modern enterprise. Many security companies offer curated blocklists that are centrally managed and regularly updated, helping remove the management burden from enterprise IT security teams. Cloud-based web filters further enhance these capabilities, moving the decision point from a local appliance updating its list on a periodic basis to a distributed platform that is always up to date with the latest threat awareness. These services remove the burden of local administration while increasing resiliency and visibility. They also offer greater AI/ML capabilities than could be achieved with limited on-premises compute resources, regularly parsing millions of individual web pages and URLs submitted from across their complete customer base. Optimally positioned by carriers to service their mobile clients, these platforms grow more relevant for distributed corporate customers exploring the SASE concept.

While cloud filtering services offer the potential for increased scalability and reduced costs, they bring the same concerns as 3rd party services. Compliance restrictions may limit a business's ability to use such services, and lack of visibility over rules or decisions can complicate operational workflows or troubleshooting.

Intrusion Detection and Prevention

As with on-premises systems, cloud-based IDS and IPS solutions monitor, alert and act on malicious activity. They support signature-based, policy, based, and anomaly-based approaches to ensure the greatest possible coverage. They leverage the scale and always-connected nature of the cloud to bring massive computing power along with the latest industry knowledge of ongoing attacks and threats.

Next-Generation Anti-Virus

Next-generation anti-virus (NGAV) solutions enhance the capabilities of traditional AV offerings with cloud-based platforms that use AI/ML capabilities to:

- Detect and prevent a standard malware attack.
- Recognize and respond to known threats and attacks.
- Identify unknown malicious behavior, tactics, techniques, and procedures.
- Collect and analyze comprehensive endpoint data for root-cause evaluation and reporting.
- Respond to novel and emerging threats that may otherwise go undetected.

NGAV is an evolution of endpoint protection beyond signatures and pattern-matching to deliver more comprehensive security than previously available.

Advanced Threat Protection

Advanced threat protection (ATP) enhances a company's security profile by focusing on sophisticated and novel malware concepts and hacking attacks. Instead of a single product or function, ATP services bring together different components (e.g., client agents, service gateways, data inspection) to provide early detection and rapid response against attacks on cloud infrastructure.

Data Loss Prevention (DLP)

Like on-premises capabilities, cloud-based DLP solutions focus on preventing modification, deletion, and exfiltration of data from the corporation. Systems work to enforce general best practices and corporate-specific requirements for compliance and governance. While traditional information theft is often the initial focus of these efforts, the increasing threat and impact of ransomware attacks highlight the importance of comprehensive solutions that protect the entire enterprise.

Common DLP use cases include:

- Protect information as required by governmental regulation (e.g., PII, HIPAA) or compliance controls (e.g., financial).
- Secure intellectual property from both internal and external threats.
- Partition company domains from personal environments on BYOD systems.
- Ensure proper control over data located in cloud environments.

Data loss is not only an issue of active, complex threats from insiders, cybercriminals, and nation-state actors; it also happens through simple negligence. Interfaces with default passwords and unprotected databases are often cited as the source of breaches. The basic theft of a laptop with an unencrypted hard drive can put a business at risk of substantial fines or regulatory action based on the potential exposure.

Users and access methods are increasingly mobile. The volume of applications and data outside the corporate perimeter continues to grow. A cloud DLP solution that protects users, devices, applications, and data is an essential component of comprehensive enterprise security.

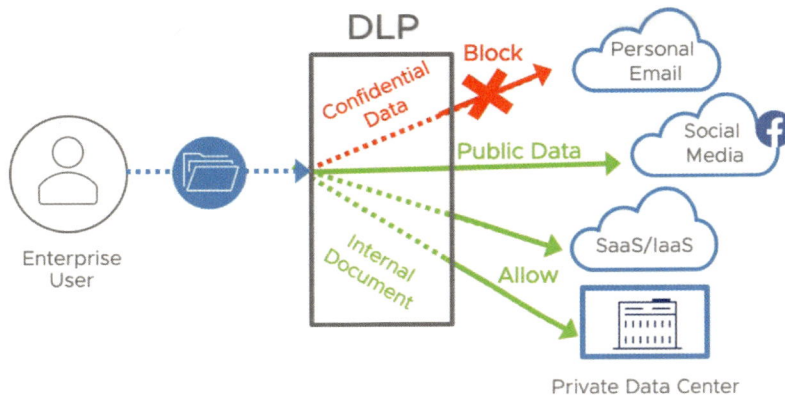

Figure 5.15: Data Loss Prevention (DLP)

Figure 5.15 shows an enterprise user is trying to send confidential or classified data to a personal email account. DLP detects and blocks this activity while allowing non-sensitive data to pass to other sites. DLP tracks user data as it moves In and out of the enterprise network and prevents unauthorized leak of data by creating and enforcing security policies.

CASB

A cloud access security broker (CASB) secures traffic between an enterprise and cloud providers. Located either on-premises or in the cloud, it monitors communication between users and cloud services, enforcing policies and securing traffic. CASBs provide a standardized user experience while enhancing control over session visibility and traffic management.

CASB systems centralize cloud provider access for both official IT offerings and shadow services. They provide insight into user access details, traffic patterns, and service utilization. Architecturally, a CASB is located directly in the data path and operates on traffic in real-time – detecting malware, encrypting information, and enforcing policy. It can operate independently or in conjunction with on-premises and cloud-based security systems. When integrated with cloud-provider APIs, it is part of the enterprise's cloud ecosystem that helps ensure consistent policy application and enforcement.

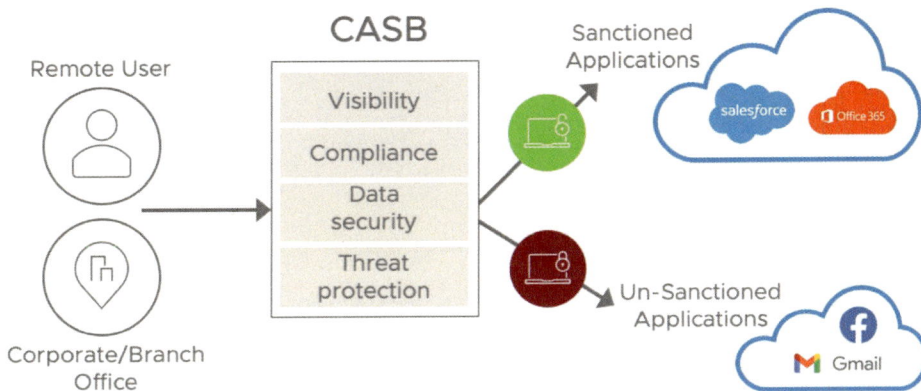

Figure 5.16: CASB

FWaaS

Firewall-as-a-service is another term for a cloud firewall, an application layer-service that protects cloud assets similar to how a physical firewall guards the corporate perimeter. With a significant volume of corporate traffic living its entire life in the cloud, providing the same degree of control as available for legacy systems is essential to securing intellectual property and preventing malicious access.

A cloud firewall is a provider-managed and maintained service. Customers are responsible for policy development and system configuration, but as with other as-a-service offerings, the burden of maintenance is owned by the vendor. In addition to the capabilities of traditional and next-generation firewall devices, FWaaS offerings also provide cloud IPS, advanced threat protection, DNS security, URL filtering, and proxy services.

In the SASE model, cloud firewalls help address the challenges presented by a disappearing network perimeter. They sit alongside other services (e.g., CASB, ZTNA) to protect a unified enterprise cloud and on-premises environment.

5.6.2 – SASE Recommended Components

Networking Recommended Components for SASE

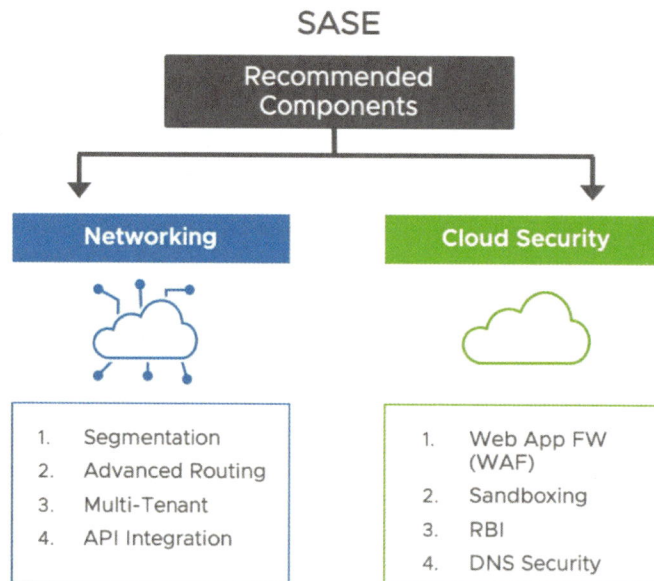

Figure 5.17: SASE Recommended Components

Segmentation

Segmentation is standard practice in LAN and data center design, but it is also important in the WAN. SASE infrastructure helps extend segmentation from the campus to the branch, allowing for greater control over workloads and implementing a Zero Trust model for user management. WAN segmentation helps separate traffic from individual lines of business and user groups, enables greater flexibility in network management and addressing (e.g., IP address reuse), and isolation of distinct traffic categorizations (e.g., PCI).

Advanced Routing

Advanced routing allows for prioritization of individual routes, assignment of specific subnets to preferred VPN exit points, and control over protocol global routing preferences. These controls help with the ongoing management of existing SD-WAN environments and migration to newer SASE models. Advanced routing can also be integrated with the SD-WAN overlay to join non-SD-WAN sites, allowing for frictionless migration using simple and automated scripts.

Multi-tenant

In addition to WAN segmentation, SASE provides controls to partition the networking and compute environment for multi-tenant use. It keeps configurations, data, and policies for each client distinct, ensuring they only have visibility and control over their individual environment. From the customer perspective, it is operationally indistinguishable from a dedicated infrastructure as, at the SD-WAN level, the management, data, and control planes only service local information.

API Integration

Automation is a crucial benefit of software-defined solutions; SASE offerings have been designed with a cloud API mindset. Their functionality can be directly connected with cloud processes and workloads, ensuring integration with security, alerting, and monitoring systems.

Cloud Security Recommended Component for SASE

Web Application Firewall

Web application firewalls can be positioned at the SASE tunnel exit point to efficiently process user sessions. They work in conjunction with other cloud security components to block unauthorized traffic and protect against secure data leakage.

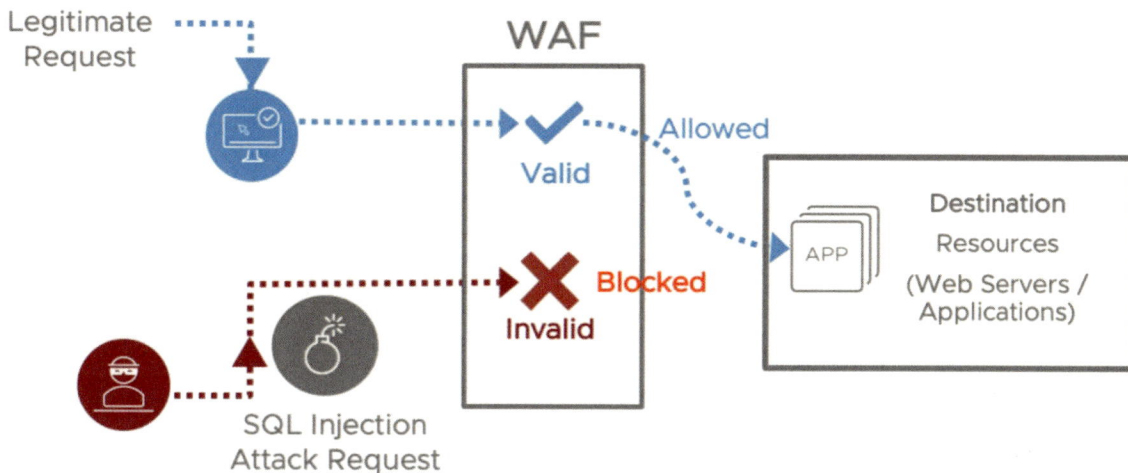

Figure 5.18: Web Application Firewall

Sandboxing

Sandboxing creates an isolated virtual machine environment to execute potentially unsafe software code without affecting local and network resources. When based in the cloud, it provides the opportunity to bring extensive compute resources to bear. Advanced malware detection systems can allow attacks to play out in virtual environments to understand how they work and track information flows back to attacking systems. The resources available in the cloud provide far greater capabilities than a single customer environment could provide, while the connected nature of the service allows information to be quickly shared by the broader security community.

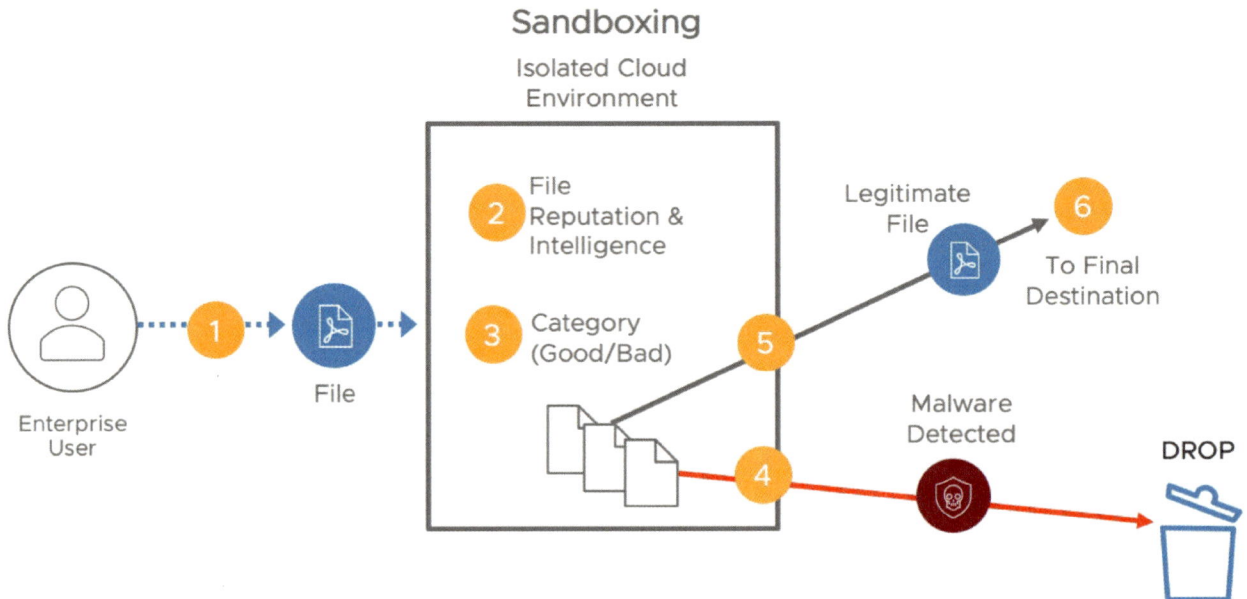

Figure 5.19: Sandboxing Isolated environment

Figure 5.19 walks through the sandboxing operational flow. While shown as an outbound process, it functions similarly for inbound traffic.

1. The user sends an email message with an attached document.

2. Cloud sandboxing analyzes the document in an isolated environment.

3. Based on analysis of any code identified in the file, it will be categorized as legitimate or malicious.

4. If malicious code is identified, then the file will be dropped.

5. Otherwise, the file is sent to the destination.

Remote Browser Isolation

Remote browser isolation (RBI) is a relatively recent virtualization solution that separates the execution of any code from the browsing device. This prevents infection of the endpoint while allowing the attack to be identified and isolated. After any attacks have been addressed and is content cleaned, it is passed along to the endpoint. From a user's perspective, the browsing process should not have appeared any different than a standard session.

DNS Security

Ensuring the safety and accuracy of domain name system (DNS) information is the goal of DNS security solutions. DNS is a decentralized directory system that provides the name-to-IP mapping of Internet systems along with other service-related information (e.g., mail routing records). Corruption of the service and modification of its data are common attack vectors by bad actors seeking to compromise corporate security.

The original DNS protocol was not designed with security in mind. Its data transfers were unencrypted, unauthenticated, and unsecured. DNS Security Extension (DNSSEC) introduced signed updates and key management concepts to enhance trust in the service's information. Queries may also be encrypted through TLS or HTTPS protocols, with such functionality being available by default in some modern browsers.

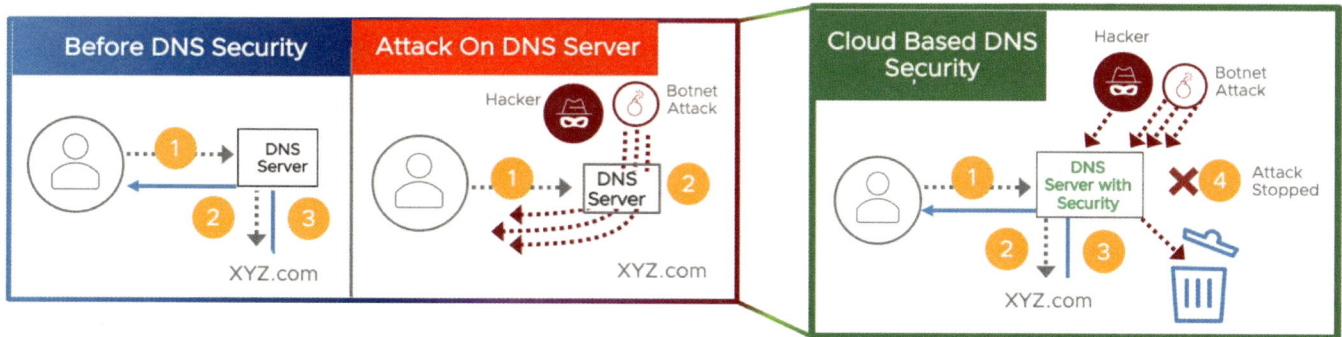

Figure 5.20: DNS Security

Figure 5.20 depicts multiple DNS transaction scenarios:

- Basic Request

  o   A user requests to access xyz.com. The client sends a request to a DNS server asking to translate the domain name to an IP address.

  o   Upon successful resolution, the DNS server returns the IP address of the destination server – xyz.com.

  o   The client can initiate a connection to xyz.com.

- Compromised Name Server

  o   A user requests to access xyz.com. The client sends a request to a DNS server asking to translate the domain name to an IP address.

  o   A hacker or botnet has successfully attacked the DNS server, changing its database information. Incorrect details about xyx.com are returned to the client.

- o   The client may attempt to connect to a malicious destination or suffer other effects from improper DNS information.

- With Cloud DNS Security

  - o   A user requests to access xyz.com. The client sends a request to a DNS server asking totranslate the domain name to an IP address.

  - o   A hacker or botnet attempted to attack the DNS server. Its attack was identified, scrubbed, and dropped by Cloud DNS security.

  - o   The server is still able to successfully resolve the request and returns the IP address of the destination server – xyz.com.

  - o   The client can initiate a connection to xyz.com.

Additional enhancements can add transaction and server protections to further secure this fundamental capability. DNS firewalls can rate-limit queries to blunt the impact of DDoS attacks while increasing resolution speed for valid queries. Resolvers may be configured to filter dangerous content or prevent communication with compromised sites. While such solutions may be deployed on-premises as independent offerings, their power increases dramatically when delivered as part of greater cloud-based service.

5.6.3 – SASE Optional Components

Additional components can be integrated into the SASE architecture to further enhance its capabilities and flexibility. Examples include:

- **5G Connectivity:** The availability of 5G as a programmable underlay allows the creation of networks on-demand and serves as a driving force for the deployment of low-latency applications (e.g., IoT aggregation, customer presence & loyalty systems).

- **VPN:** A remote user can initiate a VPN connection to access enterprise resources, creating a secure tunnel from the user to the data center. VPNs complement the SASE model by offering greater control over individual user sessions. Individual branch sites which have not yet been integrated into an enterprise SASE infrastructure can use VPNs to connect their users to data center resources.

5.7 – Technological Differences

A variety of technologies, products, and solutions can be combined to customize a company's SASE implantation. It is important to be aware of how the selection of specific components affects the infrastructure's overall functionality and security profile.

VPN vs. ZTNA

Virtual private networks create point-to-point encrypted tunnels between remote users/sites and data centers for resource access. With a VPN connection, the endpoints are protected along with the user traffic inside the tunnel. They do not provide any validation of users or protect against lateral movement in the network, so end users will have access to other resources in the data center. If the tunnel terminates inside the corporate perimeter, it will provide full access to all resources unless further security controls are employed.

A Zero Trust solution may incorporate VPNs as part of its connectivity but does not rely on them for its control of resources. ZTNA assumes that all traffic is untrusted until explicitly authenticated and authorized, whether it originated on the local network or arrived from the public Internet.

IPS vs. IDS

Intrusion prevention systems (IPS) evolved from the initial implementations of intrusion detection systems (IDS). An IDS traditionally sits out of the direct line of traffic instead of receiving details about flows or an actual copy of packets via a network tap. It inspects this information and reports/alerts on areas of concern but does not take any preventative action. It is more akin to a monitoring system than an active security device.

In contrast, an IPS was designed to intervene directly when an issue is detected. These systems usually sit in line with the packets they are monitoring, allowing them to filter, block, or drop traffic as required. This lets them prevent attacks from entering the network in the first place or blocking communication between the attacker and target if initial preventative efforts were insufficient. IPS systems align more with firewalls in the approach of taking an active role in the protection of corporate networks.

NAC vs. SDP

Network access control (NAC) allows or blocks connectivity to the network based on user and device profiles. It may validate physical parameters of the endpoint (e.g., device type, hardware address), operating system/patch levels, and installed security controls (e.g., anti-virus software, DLP agent). It may include additional controls to identify individual users and restrict access to only approved resources.

Software-defined perimeters (SDP) enhance the user-specific capabilities to control access not only to corporate resources but also cloud environments and data. SDP can further augment connectivity with secure tunnels, encryption, and enhanced security protections.

SWG vs. Firewall (On-Premises)

Secure web gateways (SWG) are proxy solutions tailored to identify and protect against attacks targeting web servers and services. Instead of inspecting individual packets and making low-level decisions, they operate at the application level to better understand high-level threats. They will decapsulate and examine payload data and bring an understanding of specific protocols and traffic flows.

Firewalls are extremely efficient at line-rate processing of packet traffic based on ruleset pattern matching. They do not provide in-depth knowledge of exchanges at higher layers of the OSI stack or have visibility of the full data exchange involved in protocol negotiation, allowing many threats to bypass their protection. This has led to the development of next-generation firewalls, which incorporate legacy packet filtering capabilities with technology from SWGs and other modern security solutions.

Secure Web Gateways vs. CASBs

Cloud access security brokers (CASB) share some capabilities with SWGs but focus more on securing the experience between users and cloud resources. Secure web gateways do not provide visibility of cloud data movement or validate user posture details. For a complete solution providing control and visibility, SWGs and CSABs should be deployed to complement each other rather than compete as a single source of security.

5.8 – Key Takeaways Checklist

✓ SASE is the cloud-native convergence of networking-as-a-service and security-as-a-service.

✓ SASE core essentials include SD-WAN, ZTNA, SWG, CASB, FWaaS, network optimization, and enhanced end-to-end security.

✓ The SASE architecture helps build a smarter, more secure enterprise network. It provides secure and consistent access for branch and remote users with a Zero Trust model.

✓ SASE simplifies the creation, configuration, and enforcement of uniform networking and security policy.

✓ SASE delivers greater visibility and control for users, devices, data, and applications.

✓ SASE eliminates the installation and management of point products from different vendors by integrating multiple network and security services as part of a unified solution.

✓ SASE optimizes application performance and overall user quality of experience.

✓ SASE speeds time to market, reduces deployment timelines, and minimizes the complexity of connecting new branches, temporary sites, and remote offices.

VMware SASE Spotlight

by Craig Connors

When I think about VMware and the origins of the company, my mind is naturally drawn to virtualizations and virtual machines. With vSphere and ESXi, VMware was able to build this amazing platform that could take any generic compute and run whatever applications I wanted on top of it. This VMware platform truly redefined computing as we knew it at the time.

Reflecting on the origins of VeloCloud Networks, an ambitious startup with a single-digit employee count when I joined in 2013, I think about increasing velocity to the cloud - both in terms of how quickly you could migrate (i.e., speed of adoption) and how quickly you could connect (i.e., application experience).

In 2017, these two worlds came together when VMware acquired VeloCloud and VMware SD-WAN was born. Since that day, we have continued to expand on that cloud-delivered SD-WAN platform as our users' requirements have evolved.

One of the requirements that we have seen is the Secure Access Services Edge (SASE). Prior to the COVID-19, the "work from anywhere" movement was already picking up steam and modern security techniques that required cloud-scale computing were gaining favor. With the pandemic, the SASE market took off like a rocket – a transition much more rapid than most of us thought we would ever see in networking.

We are incredibly fortunate to be operating at the convergence of VMware's and VeloCloud's achievements as the SASE market takes shape. To us, SASE is about a platform – a platform for delivering cloud applications at the near edge. It allows us to combine the great strengths of VMware and deliver them directly into our SD-WAN Edges and Gateways. While many folks think of SASE as being "firewall in the cloud", to us that is just one of many use cases that this platform will support.

Going forward, this SASE platform will not only deliver on the initial use cases that the authors of the book will demonstrate but will also set the stage for the future of networking. With a comprehensive SASE platform, when there is another transcendental shift in the way networks are operated, we will all be ready.

– Craig Connors

Craig Connors is currently VP and CTO for VMware SD-WAN and SASE. Craig was previously the Chief Architect for VMware SD-WAN, both before and after the acquisition. He came to VeloCloud from Cisco Systems, where he worked in the Corporate Development Technology Group's Advanced Development Team. Prior to Cisco, Craig spent time as a Principal Engineer and Software Development Manager for Talari Networks. His programming work prior to Talari Networks was centered in the online gaming space which is what led him to networking. Craig is a veteran of the United States Army and holds a BS in Computer Science from North Carolina State University.

Chapter 6

VMware SASE Platform

6.1 – The Case for VMware SASE

6.1.1 The Evolving Nature of Work

Enterprises are transforming their technology to realize increased agility. They are staying competitive by moving applications to the cloud. Their users increasing demand to access information from the anywhere – office, home, or away.

As they make this shift, enterprises must protect themselves against an ever-evolving set of security threats. IT must support this transformation by providing users the same application experience regardless of their location while ensuring the security of the network, application, and data. While this transformation was already in motion, the COVID-19 pandemic dramatically accelerated its importance; the near-immediate shift to remote work environments will heavily influence the new normal.

Current operational practices for many enterprises separate networking and security stacks, saddling both IT and end-users with multiple pain points:

- **User and Device Proliferation:** The way people work has dramatically shifted. From traditionally being deskbound 9-to-5, employees today are increasingly out of the office and off corporate networks. They expect the digital business experience to offer a familiar, easy-to-use, mobile-like simplicity across all their platforms. Consumerization is forcing IT to support an end-user compute experience where users have the choice to bring their own devices and apps to work, with personal and work data co-existing in the same environment.

- **Inefficient Cloud/SaaS Access:** Most enterprises run their applications across multiple public and private clouds. This puts an additional strain on operational resources, security, and quality of service. Cloud and SaaS applications require efficient, optimized access and infrastructure specifically architected to support them. A traditional hardware-heavy, transport-dependent network that relies on backhauling all cloud traffic through a single choke point in the data center cannot support the requirement for quick, efficient cloud access.

- **Poor Application Quality:** Corporate networks were engineered to provide reliable, optimal performance for mission-critical applications while supporting the day-to-day operations of the entire enterprise. This is true not just on the campus but also at branch sites and field offices. As workers move further from traditional corporate environments, enterprise IT must address the challenges posed by these home and remote locations. Employees must still be able to work efficiently when consuming bandwidth-intensive services, download image files, and collaborate with customers.

- **Compromised Security:** Enterprise IT is already faced with the challenges of separate networking and security stacks for their own networks. This problem will be compounded by the growth of remote and home workers. Employees accessing corporate networks from their home machines or home networks heighten the risk of compromise the organization's security through data breaches and attacks. IT needs a way to secure the users' home networks and devices while managing the risk of what data leaves the enterprise network.

- **Operational Complexity & Expenses:** Traditional hub-and-spoke networks are not designed for cloud access. Environments built around legacy hardware-centric architectures cannot scale rapidly or cost-effectively. Ensuring future corporate productivity will require increasing the size of the network to provide reliable connectivity to home and remote workers. Separate stacks for the branch network, remote access, network security, and content security is not only operationally inefficient; it creates support complexity.

Applications are moving from data centers to clouds. Device counts are growing with the adoption of IoT and the proliferation of mobile platforms. Users expect immediate, high-performance access to their preferred applications from any location. IT organizations must be ready to support these expectations and deliver a superior user experience while remaining focused on the imperative of ensuring corporate security. To be prepared for the new normal, enterprise IT needs to implement operationally efficient solutions for workers in the branch, home, or away. They must provide secure, reliable, consistent access to applications and services—from cloud, SaaS provider, or legacy data center—while also protecting against internal and external security threats.

The model for achieving all of this is what Gartner has branded the Secure Access Service Edge (SASE), the convergence of cloud-native networking and security. SASE can help make this vision into reality, bringing networking and security architecture to the cloud. It removes the complexity of heavy branch design, transforming it into a thin model focusing on cloud-delivered networking and security services.

6.1.2 The Solution

VMware SASE Platform is based on the idea that the cloud is the network. It is architected to leverage the power of the cloud while minimizing complexity at the edge, offering an easy to consume one-stop-shop for security and network services. It delivers a unified edge and cloud service model with a single place to manage business policy, security rules, configuration, monitoring, operations, and troubleshooting. VMware SASE Platform provides customers with the intrinsic security measures necessary to operate in the digital world effectively. Key benefits include:

- A multi-tenant platform that combines industry-leading VMware SD-WAN, Zero Trust Network Access (ZTNA), SWG, and firewall-as-a-service in a PoP for secure access to public and private cloud applications.

- Advanced analytics and intelligence on application performance, providing end-to-end visibility from the device to the PoP to the application.

- A single interface to manage business policies spanning multiple security and network services.

- Open connectivity for third-party services (e.g., security, analytics, mid-mile) in addition to integrated services that ensure efficient resource utilization.

The VMware SASE solution comprises **three primary tenets:** *consolidation of security and networking services, scale, and SD-WAN as a building block.*

The *first tenet* is a way to provide a complete set of **security and networking services** from the cloud. It necessitates that enterprises move away from what most have always done in the past – locating their IT infrastructure on their premises. To do this, services must be offered in the cloud. Since SASE is a cloud-oriented solution, the enterprise needs to embrace cloud access and cloud-delivered applications to realize the full value.

The *second tenet* is the element of **scale.** This has been elevated in importance given what has occurred in response to COVID-spread prevention – mass numbers of employees moving to a work-from-anywhere model. As employees shift to primarily working from home, they should retain the same level of experience and access that they had when in the traditional office. Accommodating hundreds or thousands of enterprise users who end up working away from the office is complex. Delivering them services swiftly and at scale is critical.

The *third tenet* is providing a platform that delivers all these requirements without starting from scratch. From day one, *VMware* **SD-WAN** has touted that the cloud is the network; it is all about delivering services directly from the cloud. SD-WAN is an edge-to-edge technology, and communication traditionally starts from a branch edge and goes to a data center edge. As usage patterns continue to shift, traffic is increasingly coming just from individual clients rather than just the branch edge. Business traffic is no longer only headed to the corporate data center; it is moving through the cloud to reach target applications, platforms, and even individual containers. Edge-to-edge has evolved to client-to-cloud-to-container.

These three tenets encapsulate the significance of SASE that enterprises must heed as they adapt to the new operational normal. This new paradigm's vital component is to ensure network security in a massively distributed workforce environment.

Cloud-delivered SD-WAN is the logical starting point for building a VMware SASE services portfolio. The SASE model brings together networking and security services in a consolidated, cloud-delivered service model.

VMware has assembled a suite of services that can scale with growing remote workforce requirements, addressing their need for business-grade application performance coupled with secure access. Whether working from home, a coffee shop, or a mobile hot spot, it delivers the same consistency of access and security on the corporate LAN or a traditional VPN connection. It also provides IT teams a consistent approach for managing all these workers, with a solution covering services both direct from VMware and service providers.

6.2 – VMware SASE Solution Components

The VMware SD-WAN architecture was purpose-built for the cloud. Now it is expanding to support the additional components of SASE, including Cloud Web Security, Cloud Firewall, and Zero Trust Network Access. VMware's service offering is already in place with over 100 global Points-Of-Presence.

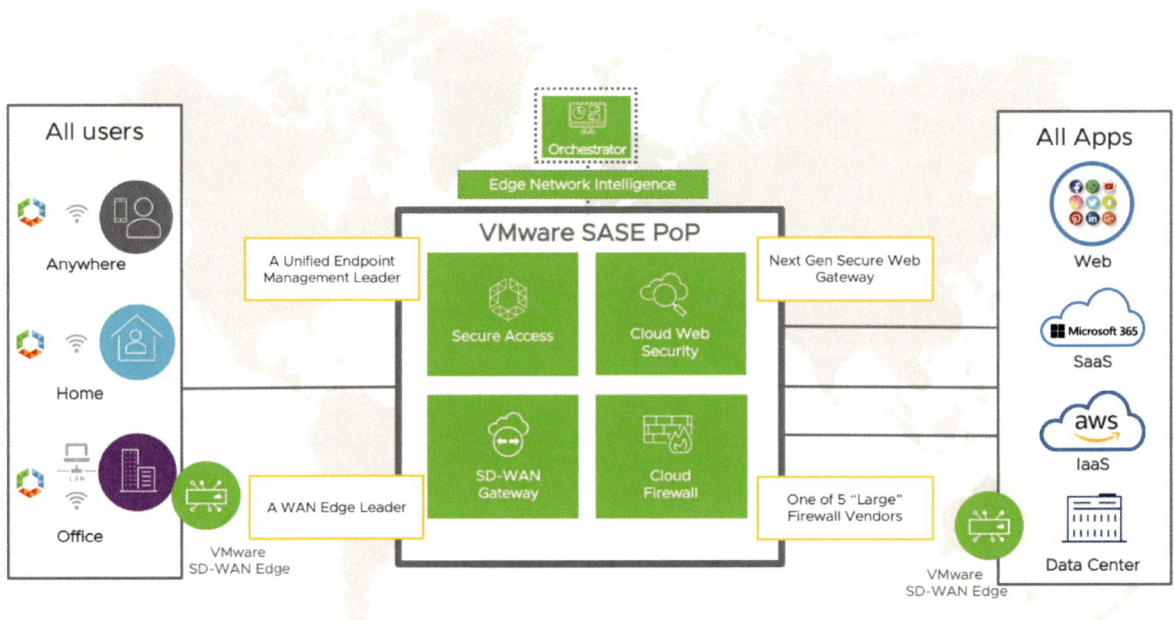

Figure 6.1: VMware SASE Platform: Cloud-Native Approach

Through the use of VMware SD-WAN, the SASE architecture provides:

- Branch connectivity to cloud services

- Reliable transport for all users

- Firewall services for local protection

6.2.1 – Architecting the Perfect SASE PoP Platform

VMware's unique approach to SASE includes PoPs around the globe to serve as an onramp to SaaS and cloud services. This global footprint provides VMware a presence to launch new networking and security services as well as integrations with best-of-breed security partners. This cloud-native architecture ensures integration with partner services provides optimal performance regardless of location (e.g., branch, mobile) or endpoint type (e.g., IoT device).

The following example details the steps taken in establishing a connection between a branch user and a SaaS application.

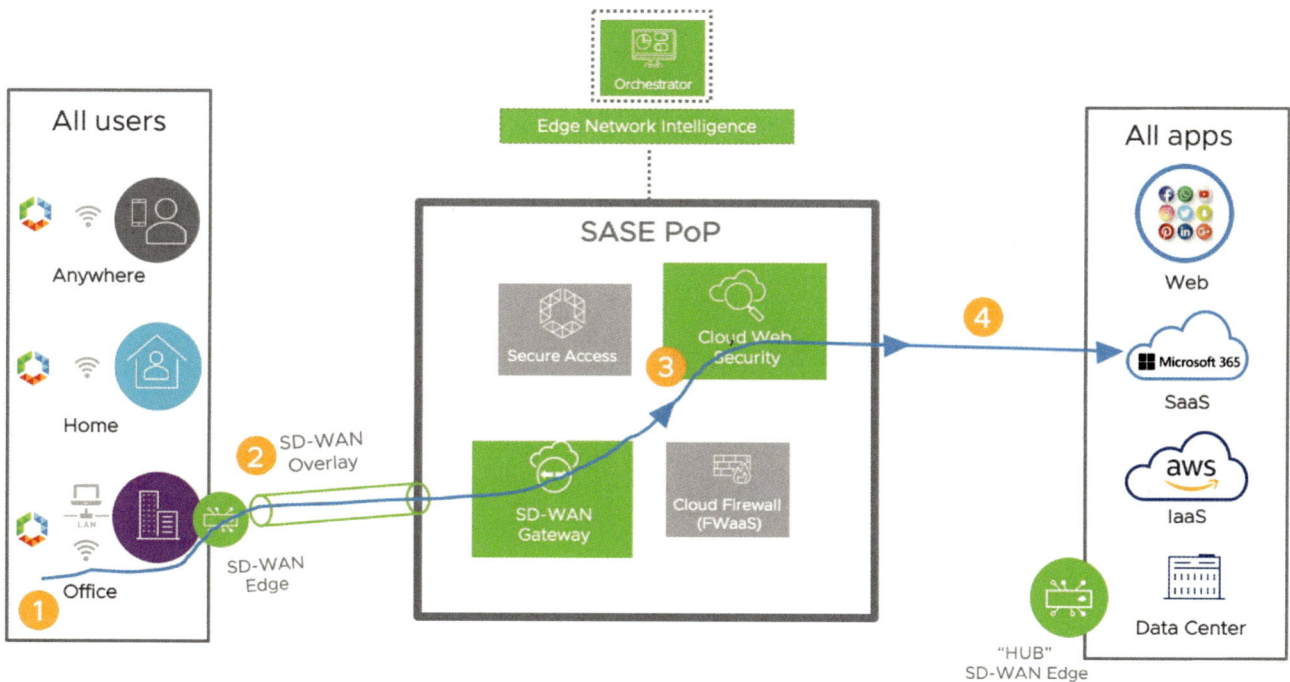

Figure 6.2: Network Flow: Branch User with SD-WAN to SaaS

1. The branch user attempts to connect to a SaaS application such as Microsoft Office365. Traffic is directed locally to the SD-WAN Edge. The SD-WAN Edge has connectivity and WAN link performance information for the SD-WAN Gateway component in the SASE PoP. These SASE PoPs have a global footprint and are at the doorstep of many SaaS applications.

2. A nearby SASE PoP is selected based on edge geographical location, and the traffic is directed to the SASE PoP via an SD-WAN overlay tunnel.

3. The traffic exits the SD-WAN overlay tunnel and is processed by Cloud Web Security services based on the security rules.

4. If there are no security implications, the traffic progresses out of the SASE PoP framework and is forwarded to the SaaS provider.

The VMware Orchestrator will be used for the configuration, operations, management, and continuous performance monitoring of networking and security services. Edge Network Intelligence, an advanced AIOps solution from VMware, provides fault isolation and actionable remediation for sessions across the branch, WAN, and more.

In another example of remote user access, this time from off corporate premises, the Secure Access component authenticates and authorizes both the remote user and device posture.

1. The remote user initiates a secure tunnel directly from their endpoint to the nearest SASE PoP.

2. VMware Secure Access in the SASE PoP authenticates and authorizes the user and device posture.

3. Secured traffic is forwarded to an SD-WAN Gateway component which will forward it to a cloud web gateway based on security policy and user context.

4. Cloud Web Security will apply security rules before forwarding the SaaS traffic.

These models demonstrate how the VMware SASE PoP platform brings together SD-WAN, Secure Access, Cloud Web Security, Cloud Firewall, ENI, and Orchestrator into a unified solution. The following section will examine these components and services in greater detail.

6.2.2 – Services offered by SASE POP Components

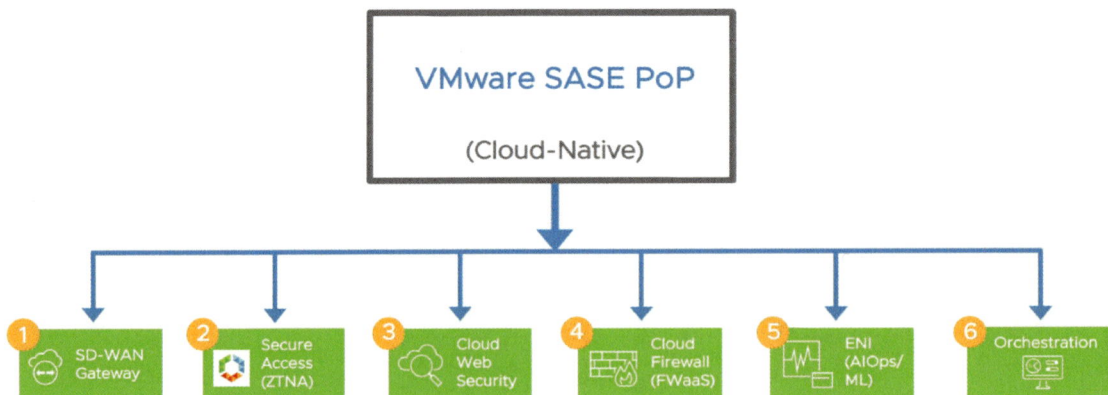

Figure 6.3: VMware SASE Platform Components

VMware SD-WAN Gateway

The first VMware SASE PoP component provides the basic building block of SD-WAN services. VMware SD-WAN Gateway provides assured, reliable application delivery to mobile clients, branches, and campuses – even under unfavorable network conditions.

Inside the SASE PoP, SD-WAN Gateways provide optimized cloud access directly to the doorstep of SaaS and IaaS offerings. VMware SASE PoP incorporates a distributed network of service gateways deployed at top-tier Internet exchange peering points (IXPs) around the world, providing SaaS acceleration, high performance, scalability, and on-demand redundancy. These fully automated systems are managed and operated by VMware, though they also support flexible consumption options and can run in partner or service provider networks.

VMware SD-WAN Gateway has both data plane and control plane functionality. VMware SD-WAN Gateways are stateless in nature and play an important role in day-0 and day-1 activity.

Day-0 starts with activation of the Edge devices by leveraging WAN IP discovery, assisting in bandwidth measurement and resolution. These are mandatory control plane functions for VMware SD-WAN Gateways. Day-1 activity includes route updates and distribution by the control plane. Additionally, IPSec tunnel can be used to extend SD-WAN connectivity from branches to legacy data centers.

VMware SD-WAN Gateway and SD-WAN Edge services include application steering, dynamic multi-path optimization, underlay visibility and reporting, on-demand mesh VPN, stateful firewall, and multi-cloud network orchestration.

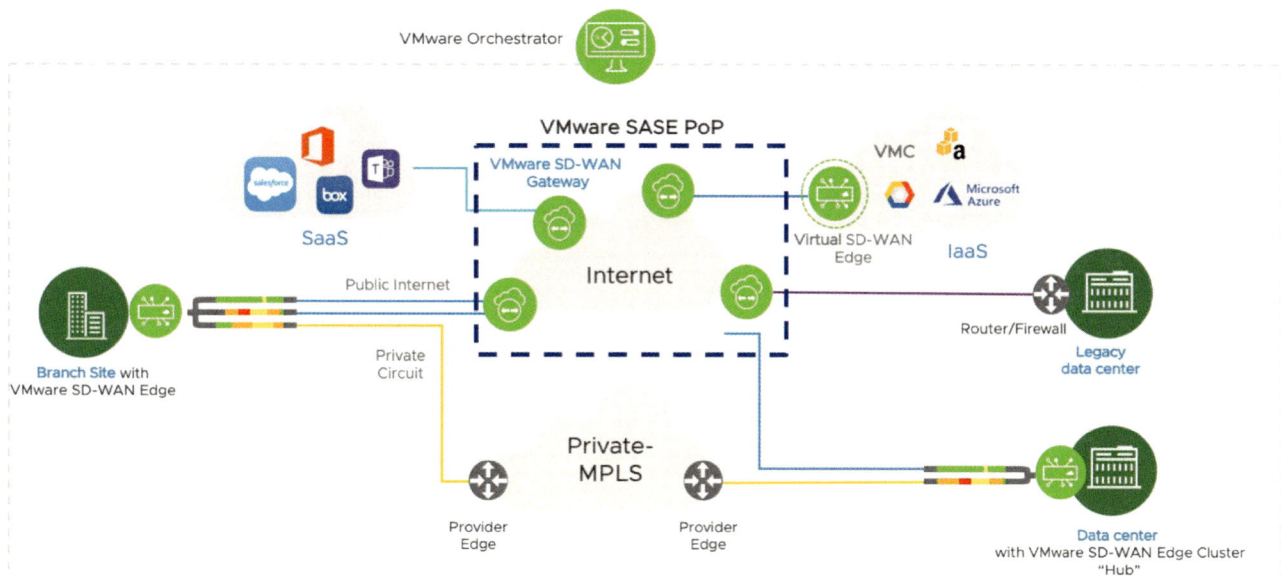

Figure 6.4: VMware SASE Component: SD-WAN Gateway

Branch sites equipped with a VMware SD-WAN Edge will extend an SD-WAN overlay connection to the VMware SD-WAN Gateway. The traffic originating in these branches will benefit from VMware's patented Dynamic Multipath Optimization (DMPO) protocol.

The SD-WAN Gateway component of the SASE PoP is stateless, horizontally scalable, and multi-tenant. They are hosted by VMware and technology partners.

VMware Secure Access (ZTNA)

VMware Secure Access allows enterprises to implement Zero Trust Network Access (ZTNA), an access model that allows only trusted devices and users access to enterprise applications and resources. Individual users are mapped to application policies—both for on-premises and SaaS/IaaS applications—that applies regardless of where they are located. This reduces the IT's policy management burden, helping to reduce operating costs.

> **DMPO employs unique Dynamic Multi-Path Optimization to boost the capacity and service capabilities of Internet as well as hybrid links. WAN circuits are continuously monitored for link and path quality, as well as available capacity. Applications are automatically recognized and steered to the optimal links based on business priority, built-in knowledge of application network requirements, real-time link performance, and capacity metrics. VMware SD-WAN applies remediation, including error correction, jitter buffering and local re-transmits, on-demand when only a single link is available or concurrent link degradations cannot be steered around. On-demand remediation is applied for priority applications that are network sensitive and when brownout link degradation occurs.**

Secure Access Framework

Secure Access policies are built from a ZTNA framework of three elements – identity types, context, and services. These pieces identify distinct aspects of users, systems, and resources, allowing the creation of policy that meets the dynamic and flexible nature of the modern workforce.

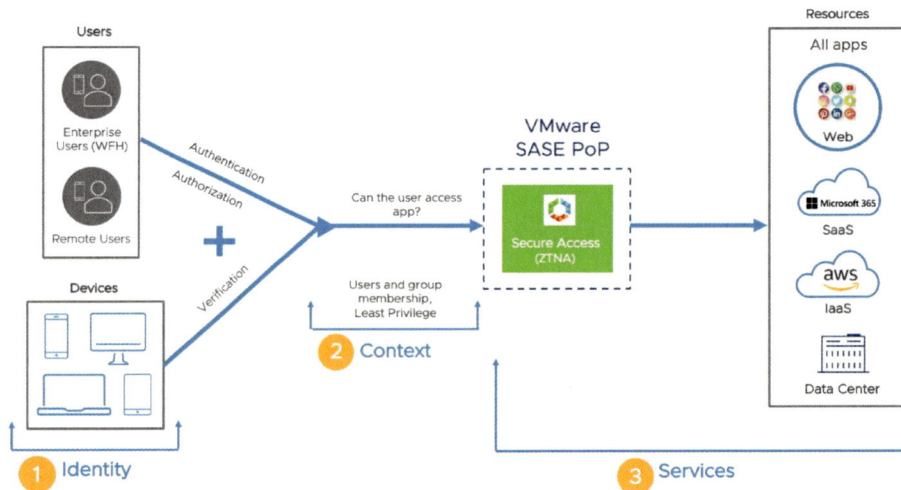

Figure 6.5: It's all about Identity, Context, and Services

Identity allows unique identification (i.e., authentication and authorization) of any user attempting to access enterprise resources, whether hosted within the enterprise data center or in the cloud. Both users and devices must be identified before being permitted access to enterprise resources.

For example, one user is an enterprise employee accessing a SaaS application from a coffee shop over a public Internet connection. A second user is a contractor accessing a data center-hosted enterprise application. Both are remote users, but their unique identities matter a great deal in determining how and what they can access.

After the network has established who the user is (i.e., identity), it analyzes the **context** for the access request. Context is about granting access to the right resources and applying the right services. The system needs some basic information to help determine context:

- How is the user connecting? What kind of device is the user using, and what is that device's security posture?
- Which resources is the user trying to access, and how sensitive are those resources?
- Where is the user accessing the network from, and over what kind of connection?

The answers to those questions dictate policy, allowing the network to apply the right network and security services automatically.

Services are the third component of contextual identity. These include both service components applied directly to the connection along with native application resources. VMware SASE PoP services include both networking and security services, all of which can be delivered from the cloud.

Identity + Context + Services = ZTNA

ZTNA changes the game for secure remote connectivity. It implements a Zero Trust model, where users have no visibility of corporate resources, much less access to them, without explicit permission. Users access each individual application, not the full enterprise network, via a secure, encrypted connection. The network automatically applies the right security (services), allowing only trusted devices (context) and users (identity) to access the application. The network does this for both on-premises and cloud-hosted applications.

ZTNA maps each user to the policy defined for that specific application, regardless of whether the user is inside or outside the office. This allows IT personnel to maintain a single set of policies per user, reducing operational complexity and costs. It also ensures a consistent application experience, no matter where users connect from (e.g., remote or branch) or where the application resides (e.g., branch, data center, cloud, or Internet).

Use Case for ZTNA

Remote and mobile users in legacy connectivity environments have a dramatically different experience accessing enterprise resources than users at office or branch sites. Users inside the defined perimeter are granted an assumed degree of trust and have free access to resources both within the corporate perimeter and the cloud. Remote users were granted this same degree of freedom once they successfully connected. To address these challenges, enterprise IT began deployment of VMware Secure Access, allowing replacement of VPN concentrators with a Zero Trust model.

In SASE networking, an intelligent software network overlay selects the best path for each packet based on real-time network conditions. To ensure a consistent application experience no matter where or how users connect, SD-WAN can prioritize applications, monitor links, and automatically remediate issues. Within a SASE framework, this networking intelligence can even extend to off-premises connections such as users' homes and remote endpoints.

On the security side, the network can apply services from the full security stack, such as the access control lists and key management (e.g., SSL/TLS). The network can also apply the many intrinsic security functions aggregated within SASE (e.g., ZTNA, Cloud Web Security, Cloud Firewall-as-a-Service) to protect users, devices, data, and applications in the cloud from internal and external threats.

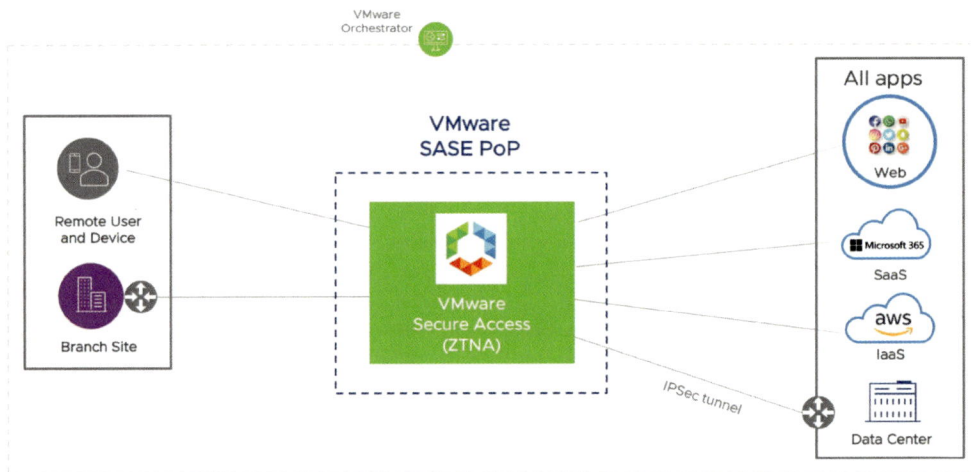

Figure 6.6: VMware SASE PoP Component: VMware Secure Access

VMware Secure Access is responsible for providing remote users with consistent, optimal, and secure access to enterprise applications. This is offered as a service and is an essential component to VMware SASE PoP.

VMware Cloud Web Security

Cloud Web Security brings together best-of-breed security capabilities: *SSL proxy, URL filtering, anti-malware, Cloud Access Security Broker (CASB), data loss prevention (DLP), remote browser isolation (RBI), and more.* Incorporating these services into the VMware SASE PoP, Cloud Web Security provides secure, direct, and optimal access to SaaS and public Internet access.

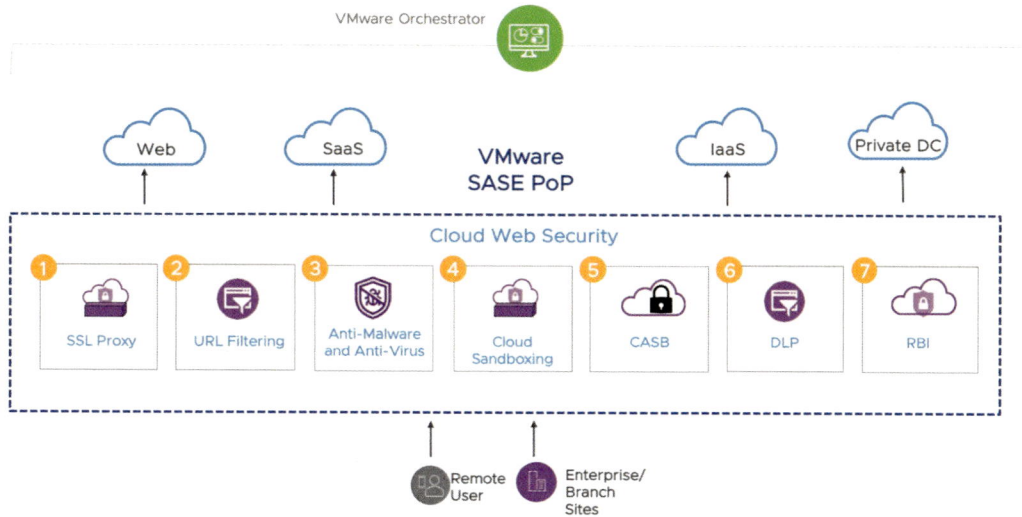

Figure 6.7: VMware SASE PoP Cloud Web Security Component

When traffic arrives at a SASE PoP, the SD-WAN gateway component redirects it to the applicable services. These services implement policies assigned by the SASE orchestration engine, a management component responsible for global organization and distribution of enterprise policy. A common security services traffic flow begins with SSL proxy services, then URL filtering, followed by anti-malware processing. Further granular inspection can be performed by doing cloud sandboxing. Other services may also be employed based on policy specifics, such as Cloud Firewall (FWaaS), if the traffic is ultimately destined for an on-premises data center. The following sections explore the purposes and capabilities of individual Cloud Web Security (CWS) services.

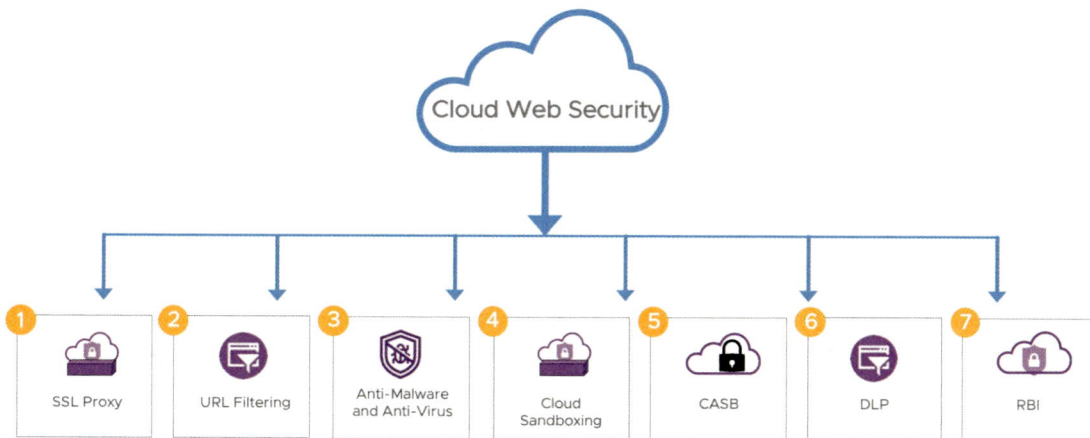

Figure 6.8: VMware SASE Cloud Web Security

SSL Proxy

SSL Proxy
Encrypt and Decrypt Traffic for Granular Inspection

Figure 6.9: SSL Proxy

Like other proxy services, SSL proxy sits between the client and server. A key function of the SSL proxy is to emulate server certificates. This allows a web browser to use a trusted certificate to validate the identity of the webserver. SSL encrypts data to ensure that communications are private and the content has not been tampered with.

Figure 6.10: VMware CWS Security Services: SSL Proxy

In **Figure 6.10**, the SSL proxy does the following:

- Acts as a client for the server by determining the keys to encrypt and decrypt.

- Acts as a server for the client by authenticating the original server certificate and issuing a new certificate along with a replacement key.

- Encrypts and decrypts in each direction (i.e., client and server). Keys are different for both encryption and decryption.

- Hands off HTTPS traffic to the HTTP proxy for protocol optimization and other acceleration techniques.

In a VMware SASE Secure Web Gateway, traffic is decrypted by an SSL proxy, directed for inspection by enterprise security policies, then re-encrypted before leaving the SASE PoP.

URL Filtering

URL Filtering
Delivered via cloud-based gateways using VMware hosted URL categorization database

Figure 6.11: URL Filtering

The VMware SASE PoP cloud-delivered URL filtering service follows category-based classification. It supports wildcard-based URL permit and deny lists for HTTP and HTTPS traffic. Policy configuration and management are accomplished through the VMware Orchestrator. URL policies are part of the security rules distributed by the VMware Orchestrator.

While the most common reason for the restriction is user safety (e.g., malware propagation, phishing), businesses may choose to block content they find inappropriate (e.g., violence, shopping) or that violates compliance regulations. They may also restrict sites that can impact overall network performance (e.g., bandwidth consumption from streaming media, gambling sites).

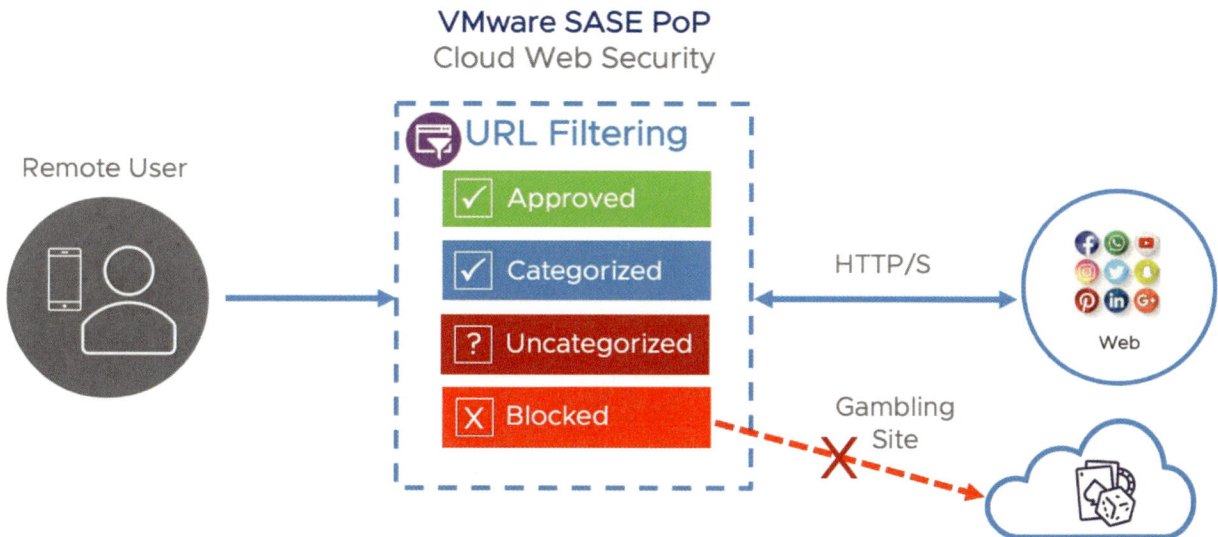

Figure 6.12: Cloud Web Security Services: URL Filtering use case

Anti-Malware & Anti-Virus

Advanced Anti-Malware
Advanced Anti-Malware and Anti-virus protection delivered via cloud-based gateways

Figure 6.13: Anti-Malware and Anti-Virus

Anti-malware solutions protect endpoints from threats such as malware, spyware, adware, and worms, securing corporate data from corruption or theft. Modern offerings often combine advanced malware protection capabilities and sandboxing technology. Cloud Web Security (CWS) provides next-general anti-malware protection along with anti-virus, web isolation, and e-mail protection services. All these services are configurable directly from the VMware Orchestrator and delivered by VMware SASE PoP Cloud Web Security services.

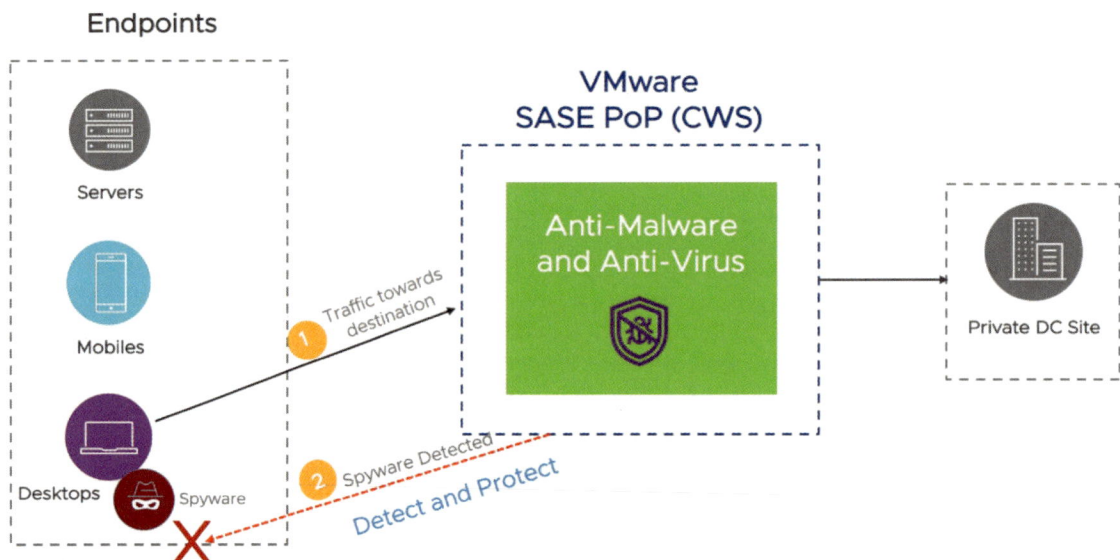

Figure 6.14: Cloud Web Security Services: Anti-Malware use case

In **Figure 6.14**, a user is opening an attachment e-mail with spyware on their laptop. VMware SASE PoP Cloud Web Security anti-malware services can detect this action and prevent both infections of the end-user device and propagation of the malware to the broader corporate network.

Cloud Sandboxing

Cloud Sandboxing
Allows isolate in a safe, cloud-based environment to detect
Malicious or altered Payload

Figure 6.15: Cloud Sandboxing

Cloud sandboxing is used by many enterprises to protect against web-based threats caused by the downloading, installation, and execution of unknown software code, which could otherwise allow hackers to access personal data or get access into the enterprise network.

It protects users, networks, and data by detecting and quarantining threats before they can gain a foothold on or spread from an endpoint. A cloud sandbox provides a safe environment for opening suspicious files, running untrusted programs, or downloading URLs without affecting the devices they are on. Malware is prevented from ever reaching the endpoint, whether it has been properly detected or not. It can be used anytime, for any situation, to safely examine a file or code that could be malicious before passing it on in full to the end user — all the while keeping it isolated from an endpoint and the enterprise network.

Sandboxing assesses a given file and categorizes content as safe or unsafe. If malware is detected, it blocks or drops the malicious file. If the file is safe, users will be allowed access.

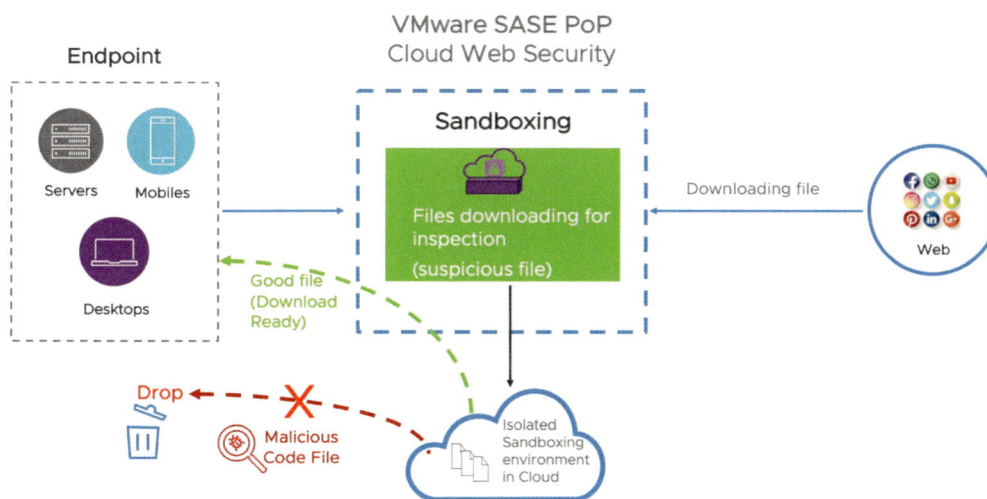

Figure 6.16: Cloud Sandboxing Use Case

In **Figure 6.16**, a user is downloading an e-mail with an attachment file from their personal inbox. The SWG component of SASE PoP will use the sandboxing capability for additional security. The cloud sandboxing initially categorizes it as an unsafe file and creates an isolated virtual cloud sandboxing environment for file analysis and intelligent threat detection. If the file is determined to contain malicious code, it is dropped. Otherwise, the good file can be downloaded and open safely by the end-user.

Cloud Access Security Broker

Cloud Access Security Broker (CASB)
Visibility into web traffic and compliance, threat protection and data leak prevention

Figure 6.17: CASB

Cloud Access Security Broker (CASB) functionality is used to protect end users when accessing sanctioned and unsanctioned applications. It provides real-time visibility and control for all incoming and outgoing traffic. Sanctioned applications reside in the public SaaS cloud (e.g., Office365, Salesforce), while un-sanctioned applications are on the public Internet (e.g., personal e-mail).

The cloud-delivered CASB provides visibility and control into web traffic, policy compliance, threat protection, and data leak prevention.

As part of VMware SASE PoP Cloud Web Security services, the CASB solution offers a fully functional API that controls the lateral movement of data within the SaaS environment. It operates according to defined enterprise security policies, enforcing malware prevention and encryption.

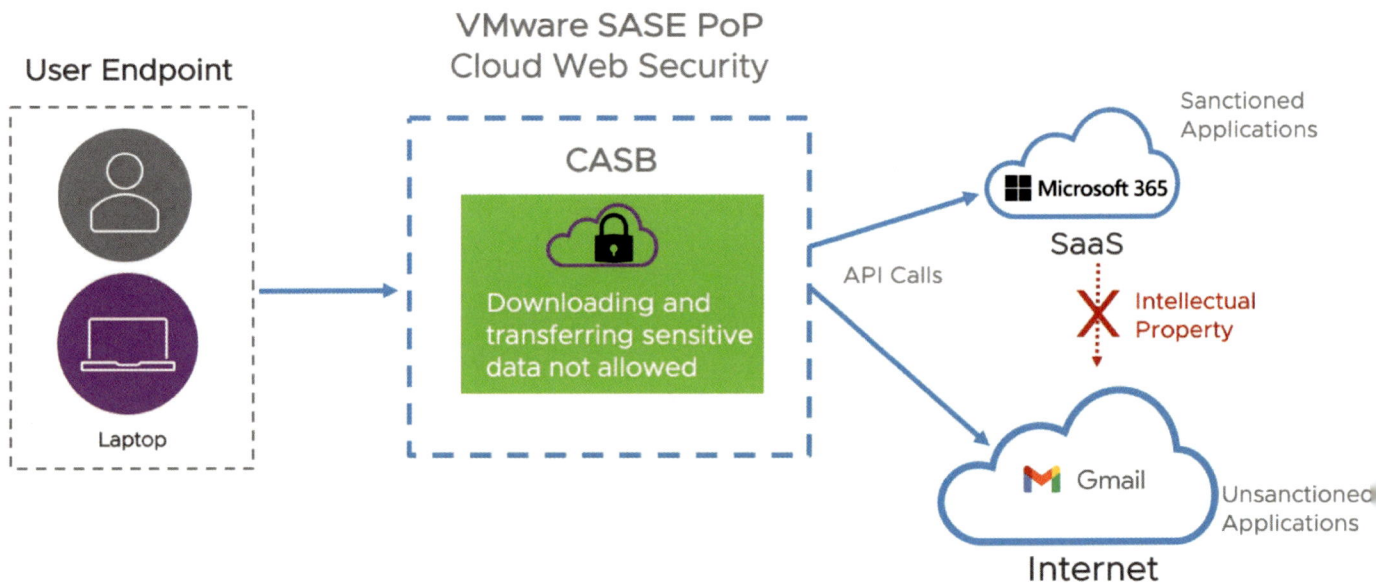

Figure 6.18: Cloud Web Security Services: CASB Use Case

In **Figure 6.18**, a user is accessing an enterprise-sanctioned application and transferring sensitive data to their personal e-mail folder on the public Internet. This operation is detected by the CASB, and the transfer of intellectual property is blocked.

Data Leak Prevention

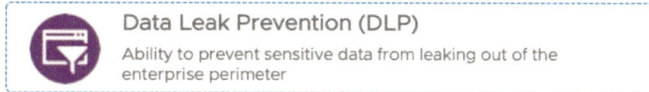

Data Leak Prevention (DLP)
Ability to prevent sensitive data from leaking out of the enterprise perimeter

Figure 6.19: Data Leak Prevention

Data leak protection (DLP) systems traditionally prevent sensitive corporate information from leaking out from the perimeter. As the nature of the enterprise perimeter has evolved, so too must the capabilities and coverage of DLP solutions; they must grow to address the demands of cloud services, web traffic, and highly mobile users.

Data leak prevention uses digital markers, file fingerprinting, document filtering, and pattern matching techniques to identify and block unauthorized communication of sensitive data (e.g., credit card information, Social Security numbers, personal health information) outside the network. DLP, also known as data loss prevention, differs from other security inspections as it primarily focuses on the internal network data rather than threats from the outside enterprise networks.

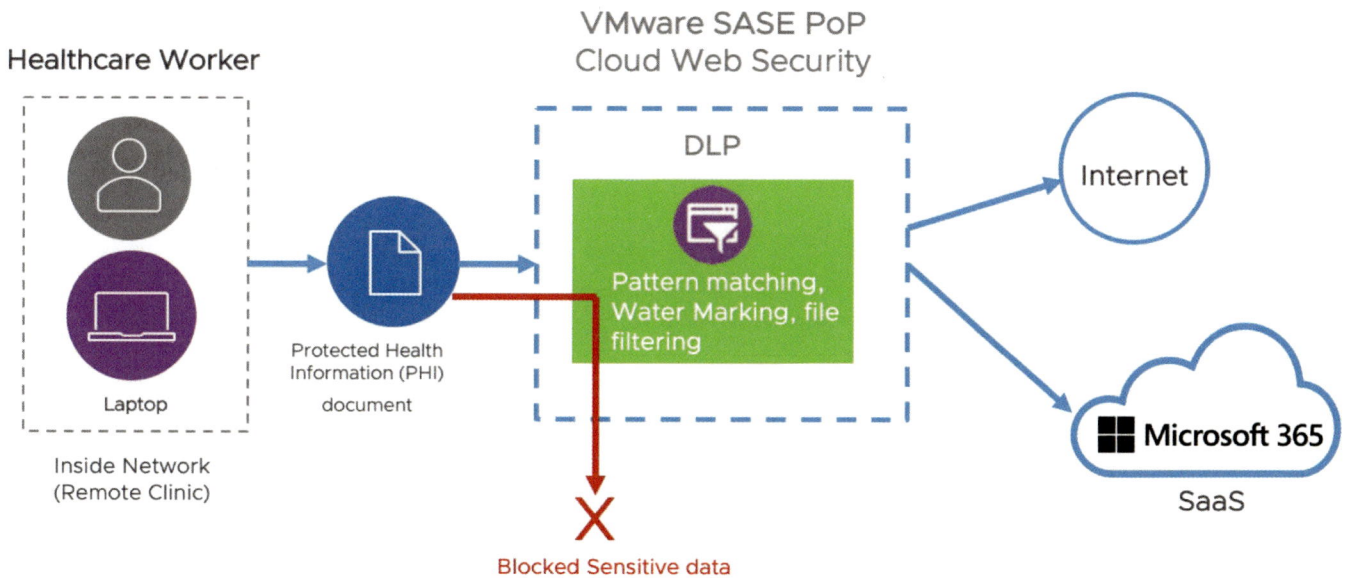

Figure 6.20: Cloud Web Security Services: DLP Use Case

In **Figure 6.20**, the remote user from the healthcare clinic is sending the protected health information to the public Internet. The PHI document is watermarked as sensitive information in the DLP. The traffic is identified as sensitive by DLP security services and is protected by blocking the sensitive data.

Remote Browser Isolation

Remote Browser Isolation for Safe Browsing Experience
Ability to isolate web browser content in the SASE PoP and only render the
User Interface to the end device

Figure 6.21: RBI

Remote browser isolation (RBI) creates a lightweight sandbox environment for evaluation and viewing of content. Web browser sessions are isolated from the network and executed remotely in a cloud-based platform. Only safely rendered information is returned to the actual browser, providing a secure browsing experience to the end-user. This technology can also enhance the overall user experience by abstracting performance from specific endpoint hardware, allowing a higher degree of security processing regardless of endpoint capabilities. RBI can be performed server-side, which eliminates the need for a user to install additional agents to receive advanced web protection.

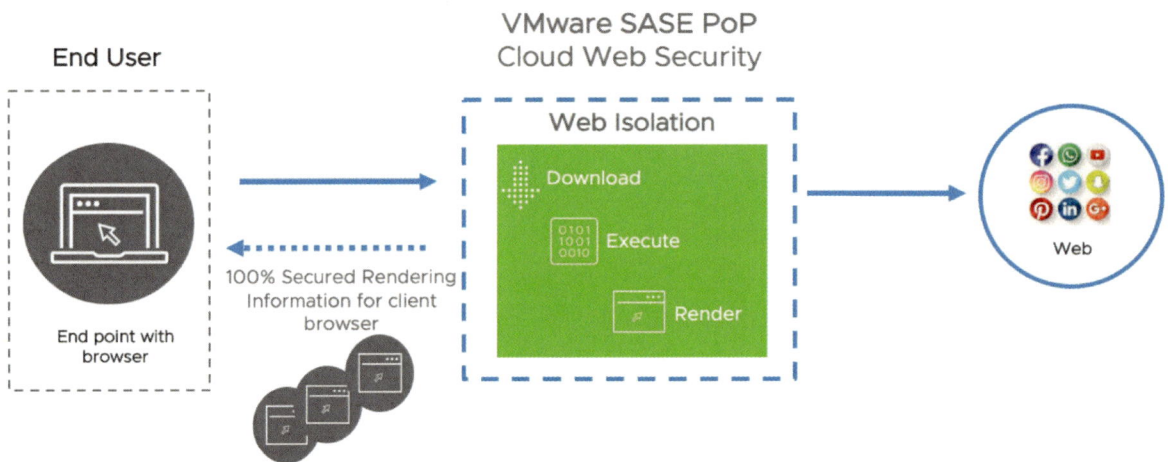

Figure 6.22: RBI Use Case

In **Figure 6.22**, the user is trying to access a website to complete a web form. This website is identified by RBI as containing a suspicious web form. This webform is isolated by downloading its code and executing its functions in a remote cloud-based sandboxing environment. Only sanitized, nonexecutable content is rendered safely in the end user's device.

VMware SASE Cloud Firewall (FWaaS)

VMware's SASE PoP Cloud Firewall component integrates next-generation firewall and advanced security functionalities such as IPS, ATD, Anti-Malware, and URL Filtering. It is a core part of the SASE solution, providing complete security coverage at layers 2 through 7. These capabilities help protect enterprise applications and data by offering visibility of and control over traffic moving between branches and private data centers.

SASE PoP Cloud Firewall component protects traffic types of web/non-web/TLS and clear traffic between enterprise branch sites, remote users, IaaS, and private DC applications.

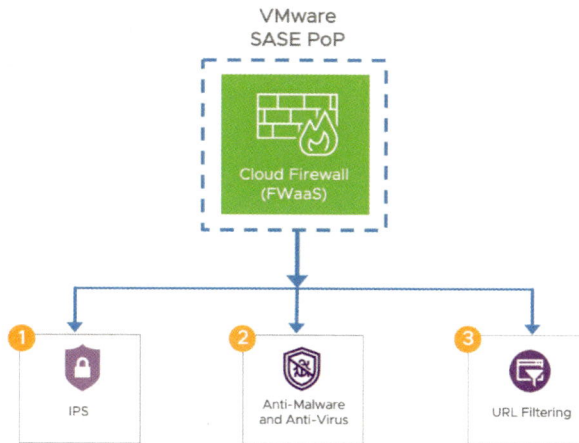

Figure 6.23: VMware SASE PoP Cloud Firewall capabilities

1. Intrusion Prevention System

Intrusion Detection and Prevention
High performance IPS engine and file reputation checks built into the SASE PoP in the Cloud Firewall

Figure 6.24: IPS

An Intrusion Prevention System (IPS) is a network security prevention solution that inspects network traffic flows to detect and prevent vulnerability exploits. IDS/IPS compare network packets to a cyber threat database containing known signatures of cyberattacks — and flag any matching packets. IPS requires the database to be updated on a regular basis with the new threat information.

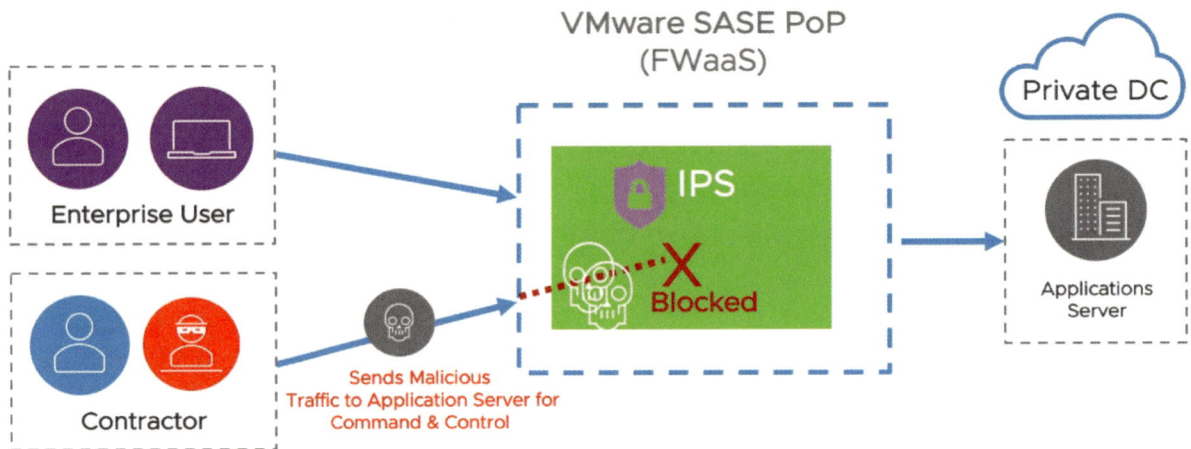

Figure 6.25: Cloud Firewall Services: IPS Use Case.

In **Figure 6.25**, The contractor is sending malicious traffic to take command and control (C2) on the application server in the private DC site to steal enterprise data. IPS blocks malicious traffic and protects the application server.

Anti-Malware and URL Filtering is discussed in the previous section of Cloud Web security.

VMware Edge Network Intelligence

Edge Network Intelligence (ENI) leverages multiple sources of data to provide a coherent and correlated set of actionable insights. It examines the network experience from the perspective of end-users and IoT devices, bringing together visibility and performance information about networks (e.g., LAN, SD-WAN, Wi-Fi), services (e.g., DHCP, DNS, RADIUS), and applications (e.g., Zoom, Microsoft 365, Workday).

Application Assurance	Wireless & Wired End Client Experience	Business Continuity & WFH
What is the baseline for my enterprise application performance per client?	What is my Wi-Fi experience and how does it compare to other sites and to my peers?	What is my remote worker's experience accessing enterprise applications?
Change Verification & ROI	Fault Isolation & Recommendations	IoT Operational Assurance
Did my infrastructure change result in desirable or undesirable outcome over time, and why?	Is my perceived application problem due to Wi-Fi, DHCP, WAN, VPN, Internet or the app?	Is my IOT device talking to an undesirable host? Is the device behavior impacted by network performance?

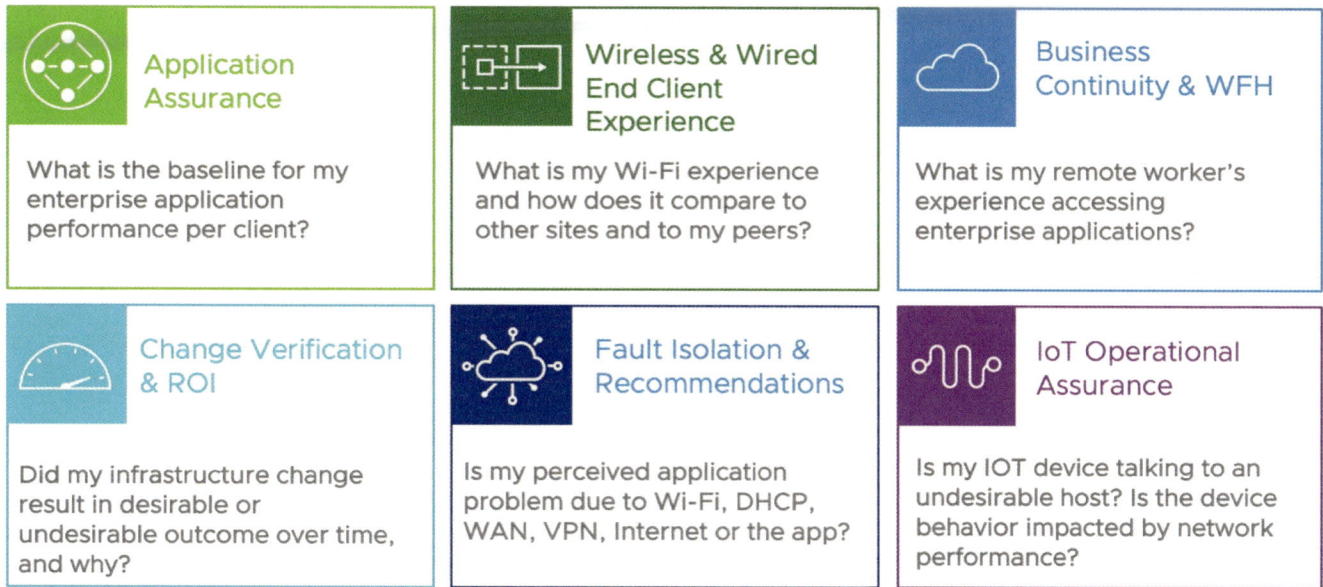

Figure 6.26: ENI AIOps Use Cases

VMware ENI focuses on the enterprise edge with a vendor-agnostic approach to optimize end-user and device performance and security. VMware ENI AIOps use cases span endpoint devices, LAN, Wi-Fi, IoT devices, WAN, application performance, SD-WAN, and VMware SASE components and environments. **Figure 6.26** presents a variety of different use cases for AIOps.

ENI capabilities are deployed in multiple areas of a VMware SASE PoP environment. They are used to monitor the overall quality of the SASE service, tracking resource utilization and component degradation. Issues can be resolved proactively to avoid service disruption and maintain an optimal network state.

ENI also monitors application performance and user experience at the flow level. It tracks the latency between individual hops (e.g., user to SASE PoP) to understand when performance varies against the baseline. The system not only can report a problem but also pinpoint a component or link for corrective action. The VMware SASE solution brings security information into this environment to further expand visibility into potential root causes. The tools and techniques ENI uses to deliver these capabilities, along with common use cases, are explored in an upcoming section.

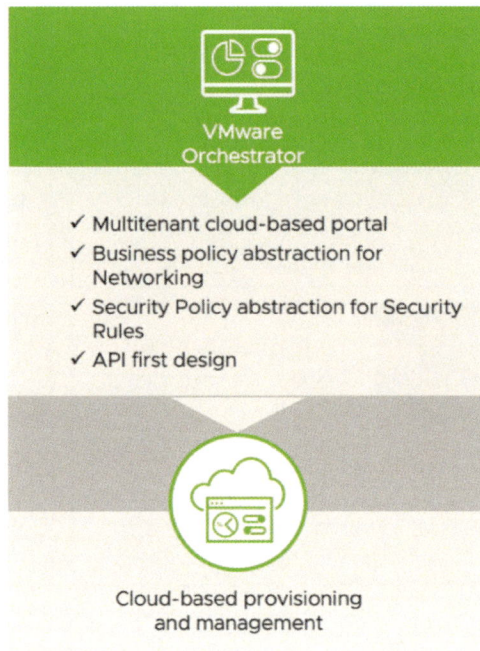

Figure 6.27: VMware Orchestrator

VMware Orchestrator

The VMware Orchestrator for SASE is a unified cloud-hosted management platform that centralizes policy creation, distribution, automation and control. It simplifies day-0 to day-2 operations to alleviate installation, deployment, monitoring, and troubleshooting challenges through automation. VMware Orchestrator provides a single-pane-of-glass view along with global end-to-end network and application performance visibility.

This orchestration layer is failsafe, highly resilient and simplifies end user deployments — meaning no IT administrator-dependent branch office installation is required.

6.3 – VMware SASE Global Point of Presence (PoP)

The VMware SASE Platform is the secure access service edge (SASE) platform that converges industry-leading cloud networking and cloud security to deliver flexibility, agility, security, and scale for enterprises of all sizes. The VMware SASE service presents enterprise IT with a significant set of capabilities and benefits. Its as-a-service model simplifies adoption and ongoing operation. Consolidation of VMware services and integration with a familiar environment streamlines integration with existing processes and provides an immediate opportunity to demonstrate return on investment.

VMware SASE PoP is a hyper-scale global network of multi-tenant cloud gateways and orchestrators. VMware SASE PoPs have a global presence reaching 85% of the world's major metropolitan areas with a sub-10ms response. These SASE PoPs are placed at strategic cloud locations to establish direct peering connections with all major SaaS/IaaS providers, providing sub-5ms latency between the PoPs and cloud applications. This proximity translates to a fast onramp to cloud between user requests, packet steering, content inspection, and application access. With over 100 PoPs around the world, VMware has the global presence to deliver new networking and security services as well as integrations with best-of-breed security partners.

VMware SASE PoP allows businesses to realize their digital transformation strategies through greater agility, operational simplicity, and comprehensive security.

Massive Gateway Scale
100+ PoPs
- Productivity gain with secure and optimal access to applications
- Eliminates cost of managing the life cycle of routers in the DC for SaaS and Cloud connectivity

Integrated Networking & Security services
All Services in same PoP with low latency
- Increased productivity due to latency reduction from single processing for access, security and networking
- Future proofed for new service additions

Secure Access
Cloud Web Security
SD-WAN Gateway
Cloud Firewall (FWaaS)

VMware SASE PoP

SASE Platform
Demonstrated cloud scale Metadata exchange
- Increased productivity with better resiliency and uptime with less points of failure
- Faster on-ramp with automation to accelerate cloud migration and reduce operational costs

Figure 6.28: VMware SASE PoP

6.4 – VMware SASE Partnership

While cloud-delivered applications offer a myriad of benefits, including agility, accessibility, the economy of scale, and ease of use, they multiply the risk of cyberattacks and performance degradation due to the very benefits of the delivery model. Security and networking are particularly challenging to manage with distributed applications and usually limited IT resources. With the accelerated rise of the hybrid workplace, where users can connect from anywhere, it has become imperative to deliver an integrated solution and support services that address a wider set of customer use cases.

VMware SASE Platform provides the integration with third-party security services vendors like Zscaler. This offers flexibility to the customer with the best-of-breed solution for networking and security.

6.4.1 VMware SASE with Zscaler Partnership

Zscaler delivers comprehensive cloud security and enables inspection of all traffic at scale—all ports and protocols, including native SSL inspection, URL filtering, full proxy content inspection, and access control, advanced firewall, intrusion prevention, advanced threat prevention, sandboxing cloud access security broker (CASB), and data loss prevention (DLP).

6.4.2 Benefits for VMware and Zscaler Integration

Together, VMware SD-WAN and Zscaler deliver the best application performance and security with:

- **Low Latency Connectivity:** Direct-to-cloud connectivity to eliminate backhauling and reduce latency

- **Cloud delivered Security Services:** users in all locations get identical protection—including native SSL inspection, access controls, advanced threat protection, and DLP

- **Simplification:** Flexible deployment to simplify branch IT operations while enabling centralized policy and WAN management

- **Faster Deployment:** Zero-touch provisioning to enable rapid deployment at scale, ensuring security and performance from day one

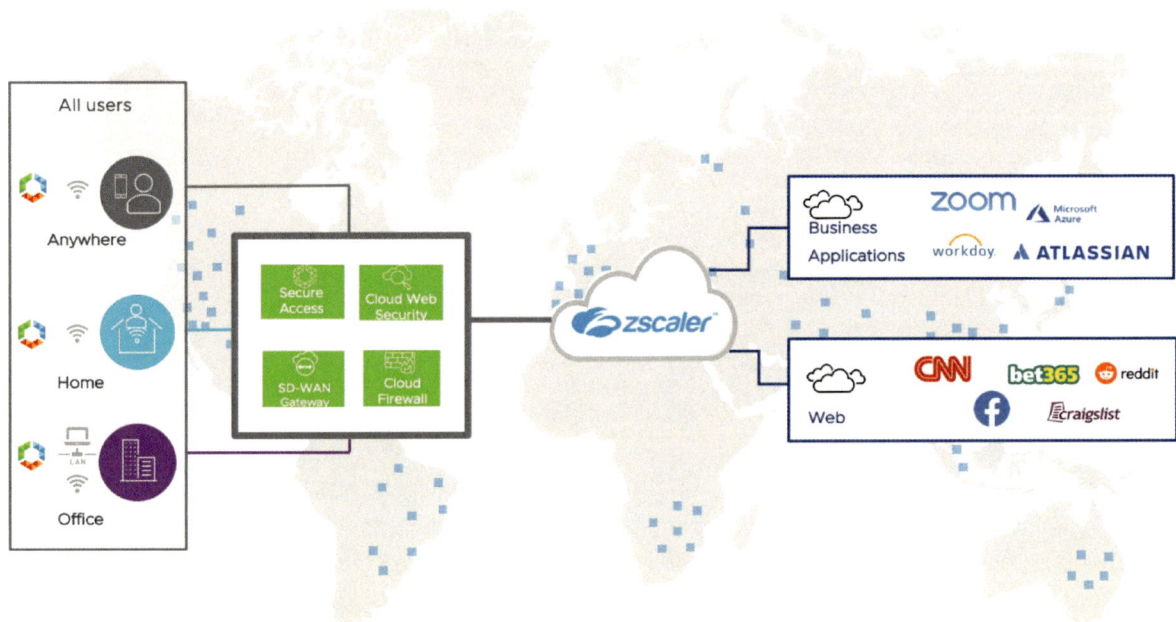

Figure 6.29: Protect users and workloads at all level with Zscaler and VMware

With Zscaler and VMware SD-WAN as an integrated solution, it becomes much easier to migrate from hub-and-spoke to an optimized direct-to-cloud architecture without compromising performance and security. With VMware Orchestrator, administrators have the option to steer traffic from VMware SD-WAN Edges at branch site directly to Zscaler Cloud Security Service or via VMware SD-WAN Gateways. Both routes are provisioned with IPsec tunnels in a centralized manner.

The strategically deployed VMware SD-WAN Gateways component of VMware SASE PoP offers the added benefit of real-time monitoring, packet steering, and remediation on the link between user location and these gateways, which then hand-off the traffic to either Zscaler tenant locations or to cloud service locations.

While VMware SD-WAN offers a WAN-agnostic overlay to simplify and optimize site connectivity to applications, Zscaler offers comprehensive security to user traffic. The joint VMware SD-WAN and Zscaler integration enable organizations to easily scale and deploy access and security policies across a large number of locations from a single console with a few clicks.

Together Zscaler and VMware deliver an integrated, secure SD-WAN solution that optimizes performance for cloud applications while providing assured security, scalability, and flexibility to meet the needs of today's enterprises.

6.5 – Key Takeaways Checklist

VMware's SASE platform is truly a differentiator. This chapter explored both its capabilities and business benefits, detailing an extensive checklist of motivations for adoption and areas of impact.

✓ The SD-WAN gateway serves as the key building block for the VMware SASE platform and is the enabler of multi-cloud interconnect.

✓ All SASE services are cloud-based, driving their ease for consumption, scaling, and maintenance.

✓ Functionality is directly built into the SASE PoP – ZTNA, SWG, CASB, DLP, and NGFW. Security teams do not have to piece together custom solutions from a wide variety of manufacturers.

✓ VMware offers a comprehensive suite of features that provide contextual analysis, network security, application protection, and data encryption. Working together, these tools effectively protect the entire organization from attacks at all levels.

✓ SASE ensures both the availability and performance of mission-critical applications in the event of link failure or network degradation.

✓ Aggregate different types of circuits with application-aware per-packet link steering and on-demand remediation to achieve optimal performance for demanding, real-time voice and video over any transport.

✓ Day-0 through Day-N operations are streamlined using zero-touch provisioning, deployment automation, active fault monitoring and isolation, proactive remediation recommendations, and network self-healing.

Chapter 7

Network Flow for VMware SASE PoP

7.1 – Chapter Objective

VMware SASE PoPs connect users to the closest regional point of presence with secured access to enterprise resources. This model is consistent whether those resources are hosted in a private or public cloud, and it supports a variety of device connectivity options. SASE PoPs rely on a number of components and protocols to operate reliably and securely, and this chapter discusses the technical and logical flows of these sessions. It provides examples and step-by-step processes for use cases applicable to various business environments.

7.2 – Definitions

The examples in this chapter rely on specific meanings for certain terms and concepts. Definitions are provided to help place context around their use in this environment.

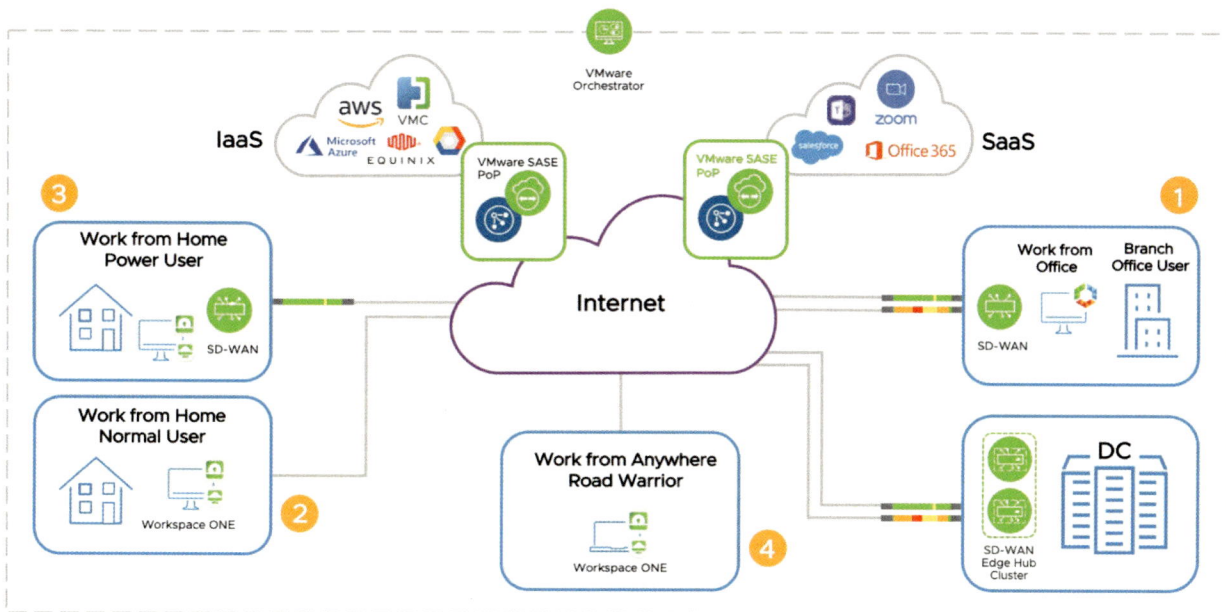

Figure 7.1: Different User Types

User Types

- **Work from Office – Branch Office Users:** Users working from enterprise office. These users are directly connected to the branch office network and have access to private Data Centers. Logically they are located inside of the enterprise security perimeter and protected by Internet-boundary firewalls, SD-WAN Edge devices, and Workspace ONE for ZTNA.

- **Work from Home – Normal User:** An enterprise user working from home and remotely accessing the enterprise network. This user is typically an engineer or developer accessing an application in a private Data Center. They may also connect to public cloud resources, such as publishing to GitHub or leveraging a SaaS service. This user type does not require full SD-WAN capabilities because their workloads do not involve significant volumes of real-time traffic, video, or graphics-intensive sessions.

- **Work from Home – Power User:** An enterprise user working from home and remotely accessing both internal enterprise resources and cloud SaaS applications. An example is a financial analyst accessing secure information in the corporate Data Center while working in a SaaS application (e.g., Office365). Users in this category typically have enterprise-grade WAN links managed by SD-WAN Edge devices that can deliver higher bandwidth and privacy.

- **Work from Anywhere –** Road Warrior: Users in this category combine the needs of other categories with a more mobile work experience. A sales rep may frequently change their work environment between a branch office, home office, and on the road while still requiring access to the same set of enterprise resources. These road warrior users share resource requirements with the normal remote user category, expecting secure and reliable connectivity to both cloud-based and on-premises systems. These users are connected to enterprise resources using ZTNA.

Device Types

- **Managed devices:** A managed device is one entirely controlled by enterprise IT, whether it is owned by the company or end-user. A company-issued laptop managed by a mobile device management (MDM) system is an example of a managed device. A managed device model allows IT to control all aspects of the environment, including operating system revision, patch levels, configuration/settings, application installation, data controls, and security compliance.

- **Unmanaged devices:** An unmanaged device provides the opposite extreme; the end-user is in complete control of the system, and IT has little to no visibility of its environment. Bring your own device (BYOD) systems—phones, tablets, personal laptops—are typical examples of unmanaged devices connected to enterprise systems. For these, the user is responsible for understanding enterprise compliance mandates and security threats, then updating and patching software as necessary.

Application Types

- **Sanctioned Apps:** Sanctioned applications are defined as business services that have been validated by corporate IT to adhere to security standards and are approved for enterprise use. These applications may take many forms – cloud-based SaaS/IaaS/PaaS (e.g., office365, Salesforce, Box), on-premises software (e.g., Oracle), or internally developed solutions. Management and control of these environments may vary, but they are confirmed to align with regulatory requirements, such as HIPAA or PCI, while providing controls to log and audit activity.

- **Unsanctioned Apps:** Unsanctioned apps are all other applications that have not received approval from IT. This lack of approval may be active or passive, but sanctioning is performed on a permit list model; any application which has not been explicitly approved falls into the unsanctioned category. For those actively placed onto the unapproved list, concerns may involve lack of access control, insecure data storage, or incomplete logging/auditing facilities. Unsanctioned applications may be in use throughout the enterprise. They may even be necessary for regular tasks, so care must be taken to restrict access to sensitive data and environments to only properly vetted solutions.

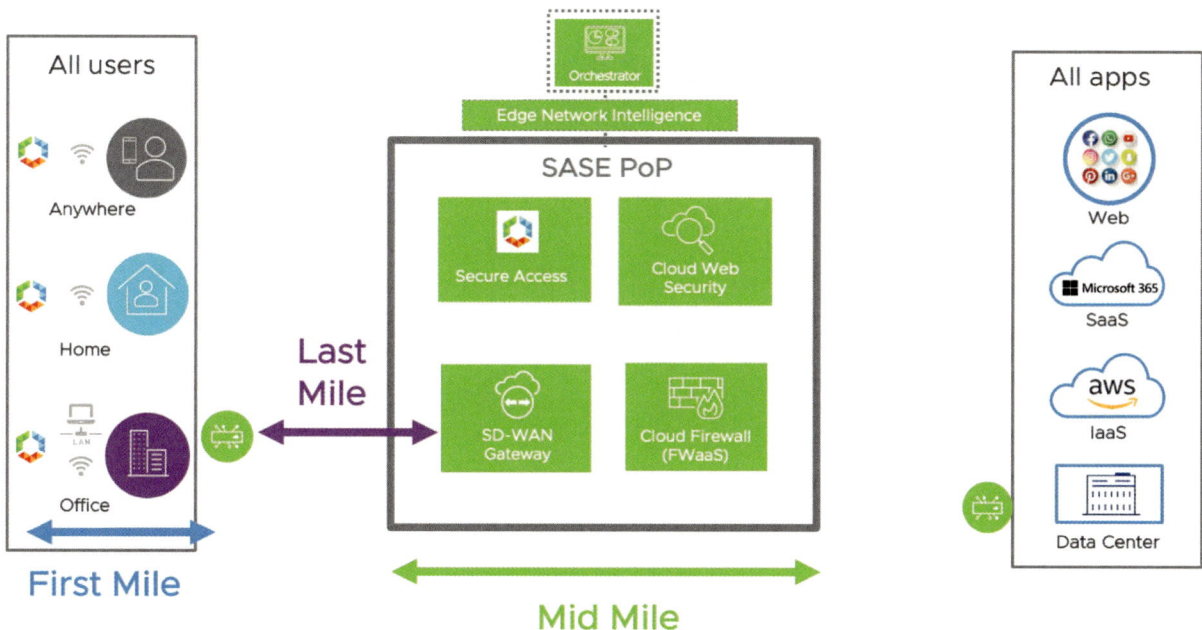

Figure 7.2: First Mile, Last Mile, and Mid Mile

Connection Types

- **First Mile:** The first mile refers to the initial path of a session's traffic – starting with its creation on the endpoint and progressing to the network edge. Regardless of user location—branch, home, or cloud—packets are created and begin their journey across a local network.

- **Mid Mile:** The mid mile is the Internet core – an Internet exchange point is a physical infrastructure through which Internet service providers and content delivery networks exchange Internet traffic among their networks. These Internet exchange points (IXPs) serve as centralized connection points for providers to interconnect their infrastructure and are convenient locations for cloud provider services and SASE PoPs.

- **Last Mile:** The last mile is the link between the ISP and a branch office site. This is a public Internet or a DSL connection link for a home user. For an enterprise branch office, the last mile connection is the private MPLS link and the public Internet.

7.3 – VMware SASE Network Traffic Flows

7.3.1 VMware SASE Management, Control, and Data Planes

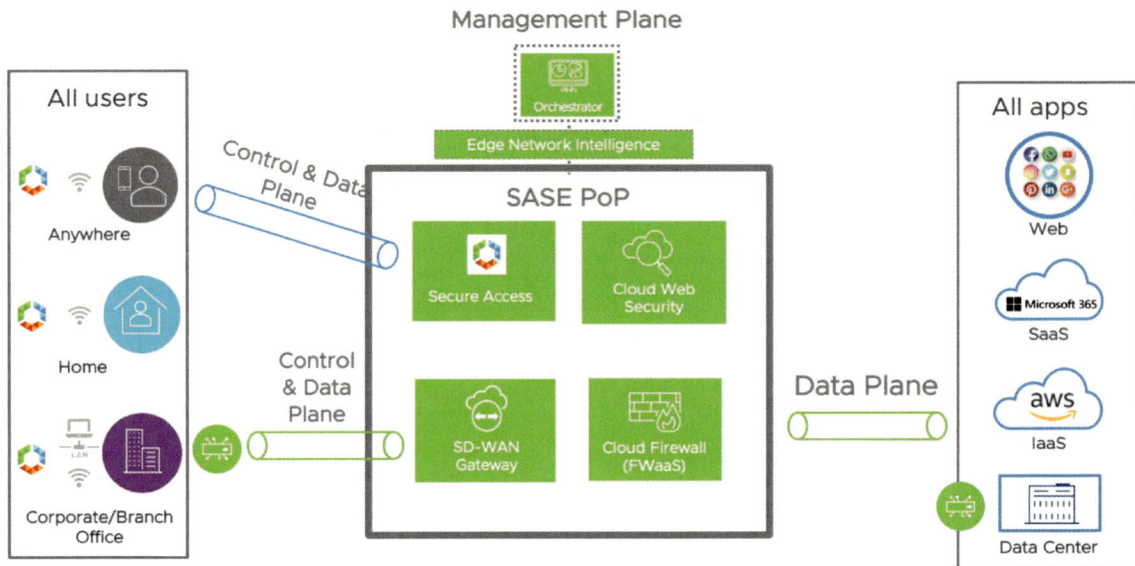

Figure 7.3: SDN: Management, Control and Data Plane for VMware SASE

The VMware SASE PoP architecture is based on software-defined networking. It has separate management, control, and data planes. The VMware SD-WAN, Secure Access, and Cloud Web Security components of VMware SASE PoP also adopt the same SDN principles with separate management, control, and data plane services.

Management Plane

All networking and security services hosted in the VMware SASE PoP—SD-WAN, Secure Access, Cloud Web Security, FWaaS—are managed and monitored by a central cloud-hosted orchestrator. The VMware Orchestrator provides the management plane used to operate all aspects of the services, including device configurations, network-wide business policy, security policy creation, network and security rules enforcement, and application-aware network optimization. A single profile or multiple sets of configuration attributes can easily be applied to devices and users at scale.

Control Plane and Data Plane

The control plane resides within each service of the SASE PoP. Policies for network and security are exchanged between different services via metadata exchanges. These provide detailed information of the traffic carried and which network and security policies must be enforced based on configured rules.

The control and data planes are created based on the defined user and application policies. For example, if an application is defined as requiring on-ramp to cloud optimization and URL inspection, the control plane and data plane will be set up between SD-WAN Edge, SD-WAN Gateway, and Cloud Web Security (CWS) components. If a remote access user was accessing an application located in a private datacenter and hosted with IPS inspection requirement, the control plane and data plane will be set up between SD-WAN Edge, SD-WAN Gateway, Cloud Firewall (FWaaS) component of VMware SASE PoP.

The data plane is the user traffic traversing from user location through the SASE PoP across each essential service defined by the network policies and security rules. The data plane is secured via HTTPS between the SASE PoP and the cloud provider.

7.3.2 Branch Office Traffic Flows

Branch users require access to many locations – public Internet sites, enterprise SaaS/IaaS providers, and corporate resources. These sessions will flow through the SASE PoP infrastructure but will be processed and forwarded in different ways by different components. The following examples examine the specific constraints and requirements that ensure secure connectivity.

Use Case 1: Branch User Accessing Public Internet Web Site

This first use case examines a branch user accessing a public Internet website such as a social media page. The details of this scenario include:

- End-user accessing social media site with a company-issued managed endpoint device.

- The SD-WAN Edge at the branch has an integrated stateful firewall.

- A networking business policy template directs traffic for the public Internet site to use VMware SD-WAN DMPO capabilities. Dynamic Multi-Path Optimization (DMPO) is used for application performance which includes capabilities like continuous link monitoring, dynamic path selection, and on-demand remediation.

- A security policy is created by the SD-WAN Orchestrator for Cloud Web Security and mapped to an unsanctioned application for social media apps.

- Security rules are set for further inspection by Cloud Web Security URL filtering, anti-malware, anti-Virus, and sandboxing before going to the public Internet site.

- These networking and security policies are pushed by the VMware SD-WAN Orchestrator.

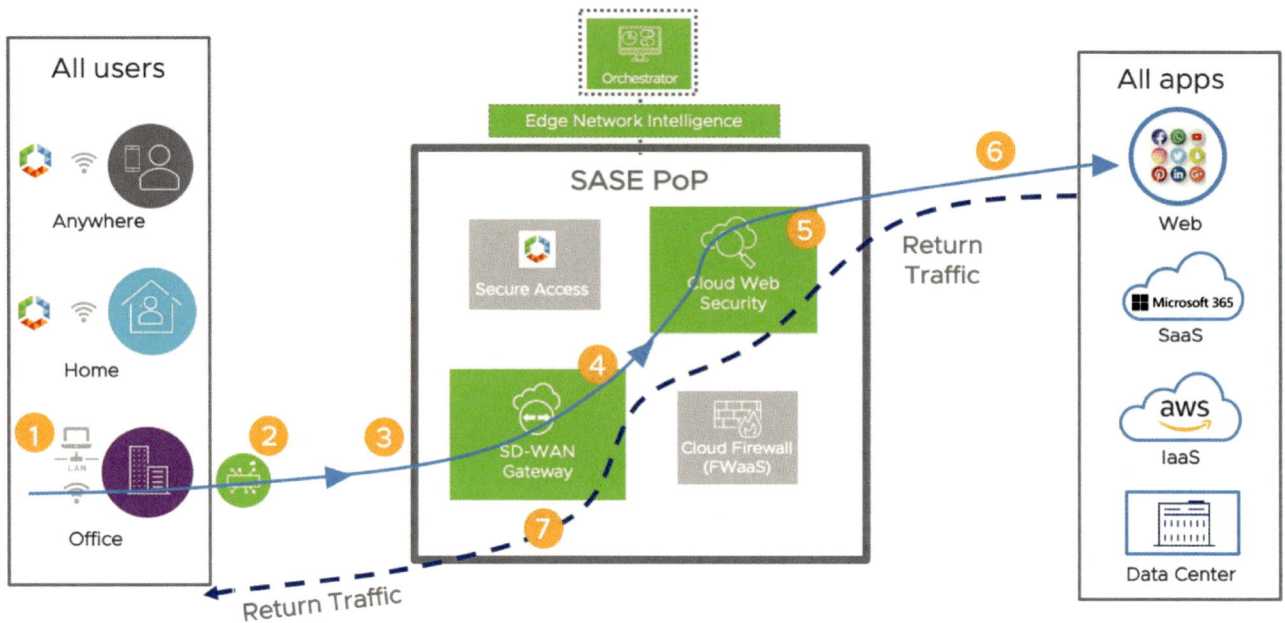

Figure 7.4: Network Flow: Branch user with SD-WAN

The following descriptions detail the actions taken at each step in the traffic flow diagram.

1. The branch user opens a browser on their device to access the social media site. Traffic moves from the LAN to the SD-WAN Edge, which processes it with its deep packet inspection engine.

2. Edge device DPI recognizes the traffic as social media and assigns it to the low priority/best effort category. The SD-WAN Edge's stateful firewall creates an entry for this outbound traffic, ensuring that only traffic for this specific connection is allowed to return.

3. Based on networking business policy, social media traffic is sent across the SD-WAN overlay tunnel to the nearest SD-WAN Gateway, arriving at a VMware SASE PoP.

4. The SD-WAN Gateway hands off the traffic to the Cloud Web Security services for granular security inspection. All the security service inspection happens using the inline proxy.

5. In Cloud Web Security services, SSL decryption is applied. Using the metadata information along with traffic destination details, Cloud Web Security enforces the use of URL filtering, anti-malware, anti-virus, and sandboxing.

6. With security processing completed, the traffic is encrypted at the SASE PoP by Cloud Web Security and sent to its final destination – the social media site requested by the branch user.

7. Return traffic comes back to the same path from the public Internet site to SASE PoP and then over the SD-WAN overlay tunnel to the end user's laptop.

Use Case 2: Branch User Accessing SaaS Application

In this example, the branch user is using a SaaS application such as Office365. Environmental details are similar to the public Internet setup:

- Enterprise user accessing SaaS application Office365 with a company-issued managed endpoint device.

- The SD-WAN Edge at the branch has an integrated stateful firewall.

- A networking business policy template defines traffic for the SaaS application to use VMware SD-WAN DMPO capabilities.

- A security policy is created by SD-WAN Orchestrator for Cloud Web Security and mapped to sanctioned application for Office365.

- Security rules are set for further inspection by Cloud Web Security, CASB, anti-malware, anti-virus, sand-boxing, and DLP before going to the SaaS application.

- These networking and security policies are pushed by the VMware SD-WAN Orchestrator.

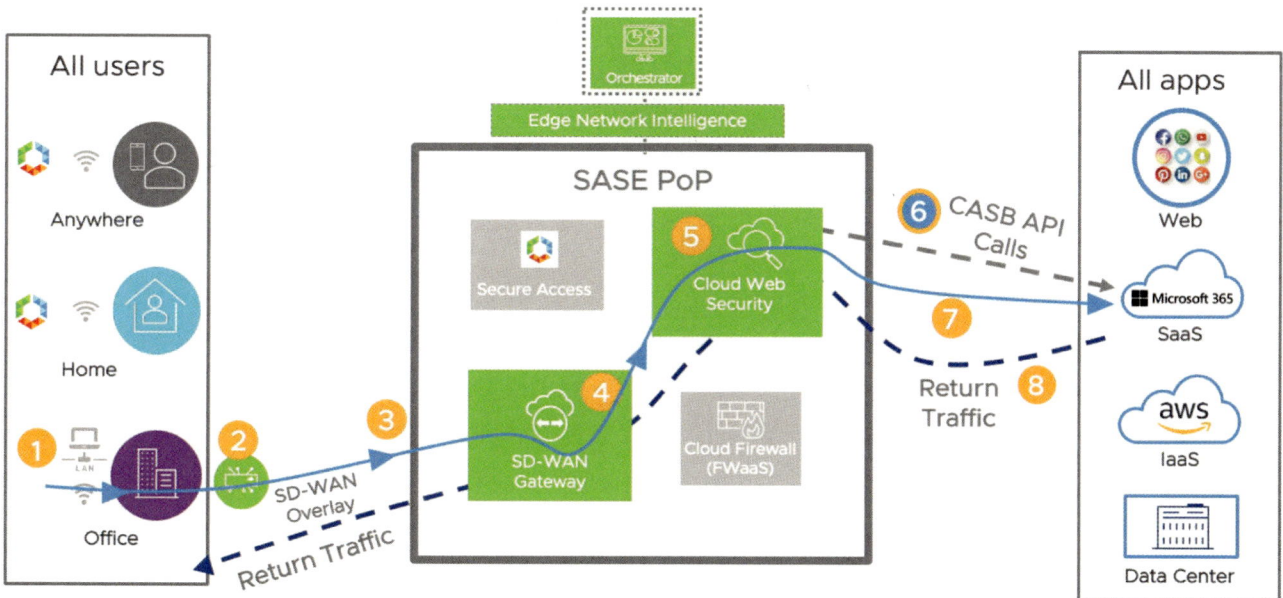

Figure 7.5: Network Flow: Branch user with SD-WAN

Steps of this flow are processed as follows:

1. The branch user opens a browser on their device to access the SaaS application, Office365. Traffic moves from the LAN to the SD-WAN Edge, which processes it with its deep packet inspection engine.

2. Edge device DPI recognizes the traffic as a business application and assigns it to the high priority. The SD-WAN Edge's stateful firewall creates an entry for this outbound traffic, ensuring that only traffic for this specific connection is allowed to return.

3. Based on networking business policy, Office365 traffic is sent across the SD-WAN overlay tunnel to the nearest SD-WAN Gateway, arriving at the VMware SASE PoP.

4. The SD-WAN Gateway hands off the traffic to the Cloud Web Security services for granular security inspection. All the security service inspection happens using the inline proxy.

5. In Cloud Web Security services, SSL decryption is applied. Using the metadata information along with traffic destination details, Cloud Web Security enforces the use of CASB, anti-malware, anti-virus, sandboxing, and DLP before going to SaaS application Office365.

6. CASB initiates API calls for visibility, control, policy enforcement, and threat detection. CASB interfaces via API calls with other security components to protect content against downloading, transferring, or sharing of sensitive data (i.e., lateral movement) to another folder or outside the enterprise. It provides visibility and control of information to only the authorized/sanctioned application and connects additional services (e.g., DLP) for ongoing protections.

7. With security processing completed, the traffic is encrypted at the SASE PoP by the Cloud Web Security component and sent to its final destination, Office365, requested by the branch user.

8. Return traffic comes back to the same path from the SaaS application to the SASE PoP and then over the SD-WAN overlay tunnel to the end-user laptop.

Use Case 3: Branch User Accessing IaaS Platform

This use case details branch access outside of the corporate perimeter where the user is connecting to a public cloud infrastructure-as-a-service (IaaS) platform.

- Enterprise user accessing IaaS (e.g., GitHub) using a company-issued, managed endpoint device.

- The SD-WAN Edge at the branch has an integrated stateful firewall.

- A networking business policy template defines traffic for the IaaS to use VMware SD-WAN DMPO capabilities. An SD-WAN business policy template defines the quality of service, resource allocation, link/path steering, and error correction details for this platform.

- A security policy is created by SD-WAN Orchestrator for Cloud Web Security and mapped to IaaS.

- Security rules are set for further inspection by Cloud Web Security capabilities like IDS/IPS, anti-malware, anti-virus, and sandboxing before going to IaaS.

- These networking and security policies are pushed by VMware SD-WAN Orchestrator.

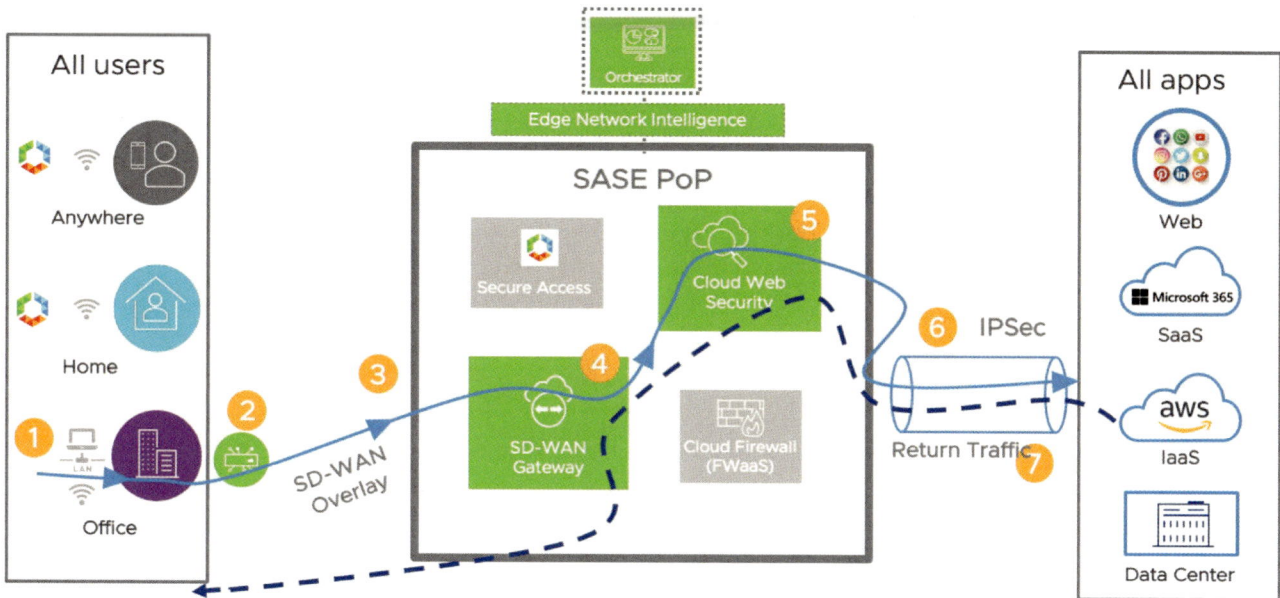

Figure 7.6: Network Flow: Branch user with SD-WAN

In this example, as shown in **Figure 7.6**, steps of this flow are processed as follows:

1. The branch user initiates a connection to the IaaS environment on their managed device. Traffic moves from the LAN to the SD-WAN Edge, which processes it with its deep packet inspection engine.

2. Edge device DPI recognizes the traffic as a business application and assigns it to the high priority as per enterprise requirement. The SD-WAN Edge's stateful firewall creates an entry for this outbound traffic, ensuring that only traffic for this specific connection is allowed to return.

3. Based on networking business policy, IaaS traffic is sent across the SD-WAN overlay tunnel to the nearest SD-WAN Gateway, arriving at the VMware SASE PoP.

4. The SD-WAN Gateway hands off the traffic to the Cloud Web Security services for granular security inspection. All the security service inspection happens using the inline proxy.

5. In Cloud Web Security services, SSL decryption is applied. Using the metadata information along with traffic destination details, Cloud Web Security enforces IDS/IPS, anti-malware, anti-virus, and sandboxing before going to the IaaS platform.

6. With security processing completed, the traffic is encrypted at the SASE PoP by Cloud Web Security component and sent to its final destination over an automated IPSec tunnel to the cloud provider IaaS. This automation configuration of the IPSec tunnel is done from the VMware SD-WAN Orchestrator to the IaaS.

7. Return traffic comes back to the same path from IaaS to SASE PoP and then over the SD-WAN overlay tunnel to the end-user device.

Use Case 4: Branch User Accessing Private Data Center Application

This traffic flow follows access from a branch user to an on-premises application in the corporate Data Center. Environmental conditions include:

- Enterprise user accessing enterprise on-premises applications (e.g., ERP) at a private Data Center. The user has a company-issued, managed endpoint device.

- The SD-WAN Edge at the branch has an integrated stateful firewall.

- The SD-WAN Edge at the Data Center site is configured as a hub device.

- A networking business policy template defines traffic for the enterprise on-premises application to use VMware SD-WAN DMPO capabilities. VMware SD-WAN DMPO defines the traffic rule as part of the business policy framework, the quality of service, resource allocation, link/path steering, and error correction details for this platform.

- A security policy is created by the SD-WAN Orchestrator for Cloud Firewall.

- Security rules are set for further inspection by Cloud Firewall capabilities like IDS/IPS, anti-malware, and advanced threat detection before going to the on-premises application.

- These networking and security policies are pushed by the VMware SD-WAN Orchestrator.

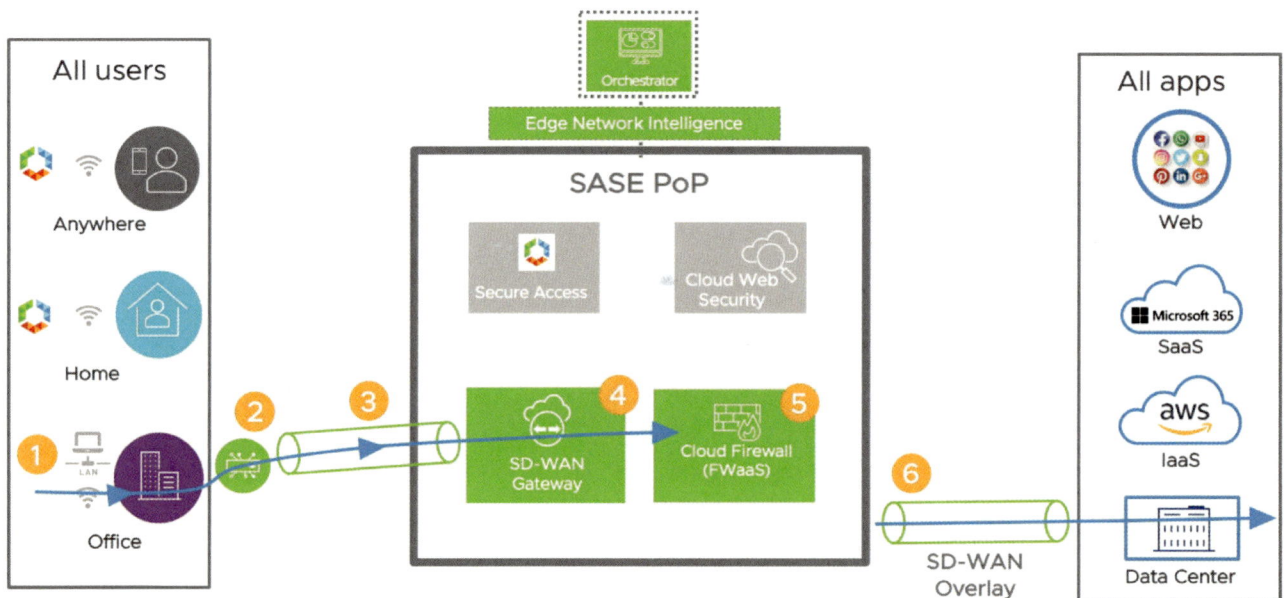

Figure 7.7: Enterprise user accessing DC Application

This example flows in the following manner:

1. The branch user initiates a connection to an on-premises application from their managed device. Traffic moves from the LAN to the SD-WAN Edge, which processes it with its deep packet inspection engine.

2. Edge device DPI recognizes the traffic as a business application and assigns it to the high priority as per enterprise requirement. The SD-WAN Edge's stateful firewall creates an entry for this outbound traffic, ensuring that only traffic for this specific connection is allowed to return.

3. Based on networking business policy, traffic to the on-premises enterprise ERP application is sent across the SD-WAN overlay tunnel to the nearest SD-WAN Gateway, arriving at the VMware SASE PoP.

4. The SD-WAN Gateway hands off the traffic to the Cloud Firewall for granular security inspection. All the security service inspection happens using the inline proxy.

5. In Cloud Firewall services, SSL decryption is applied. Using the metadata information along with traffic destination details, Cloud Firewall enforces IDS/IPS, anti-malware, and advanced threat detection before going to the on-premises Data Center for application access.

6. User traffic from the SASE PoP leverages the SD-WAN overlay tunnel and goes to the private Data Center SD-WAN Hub device. SD-WAN application performance is applied on the SD-WAN overlay tunnels. Return traffic comes back the same path, from the Data Center to the SASE PoP and then to the branch.

Use Case 5: Guest User at Branch accessing Public Internet

This final example from the enterprise branch site involves a guest user or temporary contractor rather than a corporate employee. This user is accessing a site on the public Internet with a personal device instead of a corporate-managed system.

- The guest is using the personal device/laptop and accessing the public Internet.

- The SD-WAN Edge at the branch has an integrated stateful firewall. SD-WAN at the branch site is configured with the segmentation feature. Guest segments and enterprise segments are configured.

- A global business policy dictates non-business critical applications have direct Internet access (DIA).

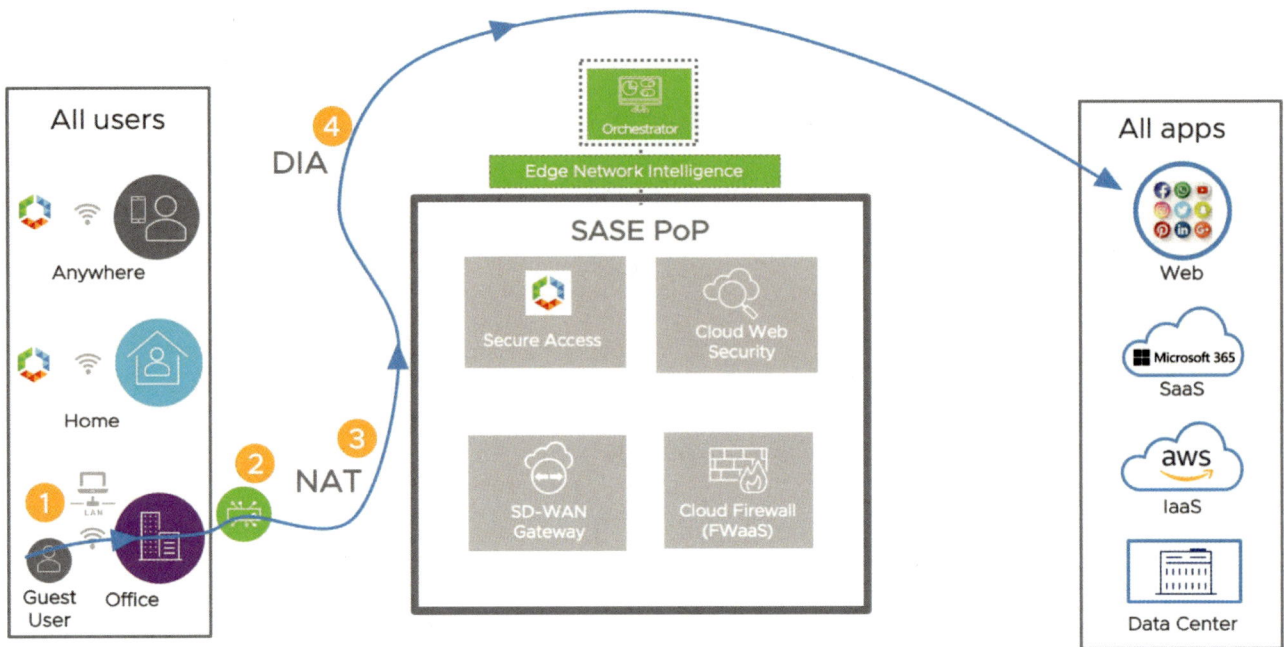

Figure 7.8: Network Flow: Branch user with SD-WAN

The network flow for this user is simpler than in previous examples.

1. The guest user's device obtains an IP address from the guest segment. This segment uses a distinct set of IP addresses than those assigned to enterprise networks, and its traffic is treated differently.

2. The guest user attempts to browse to a public Internet site. The traffic is routed to the SD-WAN Edge. The SD-WAN Edge provides a guest traffic segment where it performs deep packet inspection that recognizes the traffic as a non-business application. It tags it as a low priority with best-effort delivery.

3. The SD-WAN Edge performs network address translation (NAT), changing the source IP from the LAN to a global IP for Internet routing. The stateful firewall on the Edge creates an entry for the outbound traffic to restrict any non-associated flow returning connections.

4. Traffic is routed directly to the Internet across the WAN link. Because of this direct Internet access, it is not sent to the VMware SASE PoP.

5. The return traffic from the Internet website comes back to the branch site and then to the guest's laptop.

Benefits of SASE PoP

The SASE PoP architecture offers many benefits to the branch.

- **Application Quality Assurance:** The SASE PoP architecture provides assured, reliable application delivery to mobile, branch, and campus connections – even under unfavorable network conditions. VMware SD-WAN overly tunnels protect and optimize performance between any two individual SD-WAN devices. VMware DMPO ensures optimal application performance on any transport WAN links with per-packet steering, sub-second failover, continuous monitoring, on-demand remediation, and overlay quality-of-service.

- **Global Points of Presence:** VMware SASE PoPs have a global presence, reaching 85% of the world's major metropolitan areas within 10ms. These PoPs have been placed within strategic cloud locations to establish direct peering connections to all major SaaS/IaaS providers, providing sub-5ms latency between the SASE PoP and cloud applications. This proximity translates to the fast on-ramp to cloud between user request, packet steering, security inspection, and access to the application.

- **Operational Simplicity and ROI:** Configuration and policy management are performed from a single, centralized cloud-based orchestrator. The SASE PoP Orchestrator is responsible for both networking and security components to minimize configuration complexity and tool sprawl. The centralized platform offers visibility across the complete ecosystem while ensuring consistency of policy on all devices.

- **Cloud-Native Solution:** The cloud-based management model removes the burden of infrastructure management and allows the platform to take advantage of advanced scalability and resiliency capabilities.

- **Intrinsic Security:** Integrated capabilities protect distributed users and applications against internal and external threats at all levels. SASE PoPs offer ZTNA, Secure Web Gateways, CASB functionality, and FWaaS.

7.3.3 Work-from-Home Traffic Flows

Similar to branch users, employees working from home need to access a variety of sites and resources. The following scenarios examine the flow and processing differences when remote users are not on corporate premises.

Use Case 6: Remote User Accessing SaaS Application

This example looks at a user at home accessing a SaaS application such as Office365, similar to the workflow depicted in-branch use case #2. Specific details include:

- Remote user accessing SaaS application Office 365 with a company-issued, managed endpoint device.

- A security policy is created by the SD-WAN Orchestrator for Secure Access (ZTNA) and Cloud Web Security.

- Security rules are set for further inspection by Cloud Web Security capabilities like CASB, anti-malware, anti-virus, sandboxing, and DLP before going to the SaaS application.

- Networking and security policies are pushed by the VMware Orchestrator.

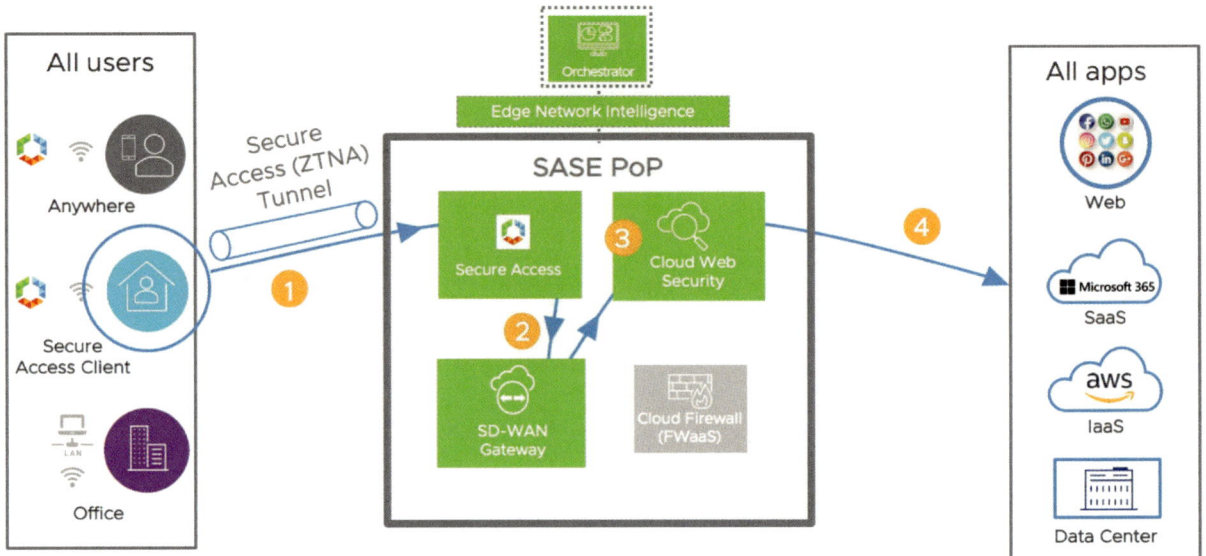

Figure 7.9: Use Case 6: Remote User accessing SaaS application

The traffic flow and processing actions include:

1. The remote user from the home location opens the Office365 application from the endpoint device. Upon connecting to the network, the endpoint sets up a session with the Secure Access service, which manages the ZTNA at the SASE PoP. Secure access authenticates and authorizes the remote user and device context. When successful, a secure tunnel is established between the endpoint and the SASE PoP.

2. The user attempts to connect to the SaaS application. Secure access steers the traffic to the SD-WAN Gateway, which examines the flow to identify its source and destination. It applies global security policies based on the user's identity, group membership, and application authorization access level.

3. Per the security policy, the SD-WAN component of SASE PoP routes traffic to Cloud Web Security, where it receives granular inspection by additional security services (e.g., CASB, DLP, sandboxing).

4. The traffic is then routed out of the SASE PoP and toward its final SaaS destination, Office365.

In this example, the remote user had only a personal Internet connection and associated hardware. If they had an SD-WAN Edge device, the traffic flow pattern would be similar to the branch site user model.

Use Case 7: Remote User Accessing Private Data Center Application

The final example follows the connection process when this same user accesses an application located in an on-premises corporate Data Center.

Environmental details include:

- Remote user accessing an on-premises application at a private Data Center using an enterprise-owned managed endpoint.

- A security policy is created by the VMware Orchestrator for Secure Access and Cloud Firewall.

- Security rules are set for further inspection by Cloud Firewall capabilities like IDS/IPS, anti-malware, and advanced threat detection before going to the on-premises application.

- Networking and security policies are pushed by VMware Orchestrator.

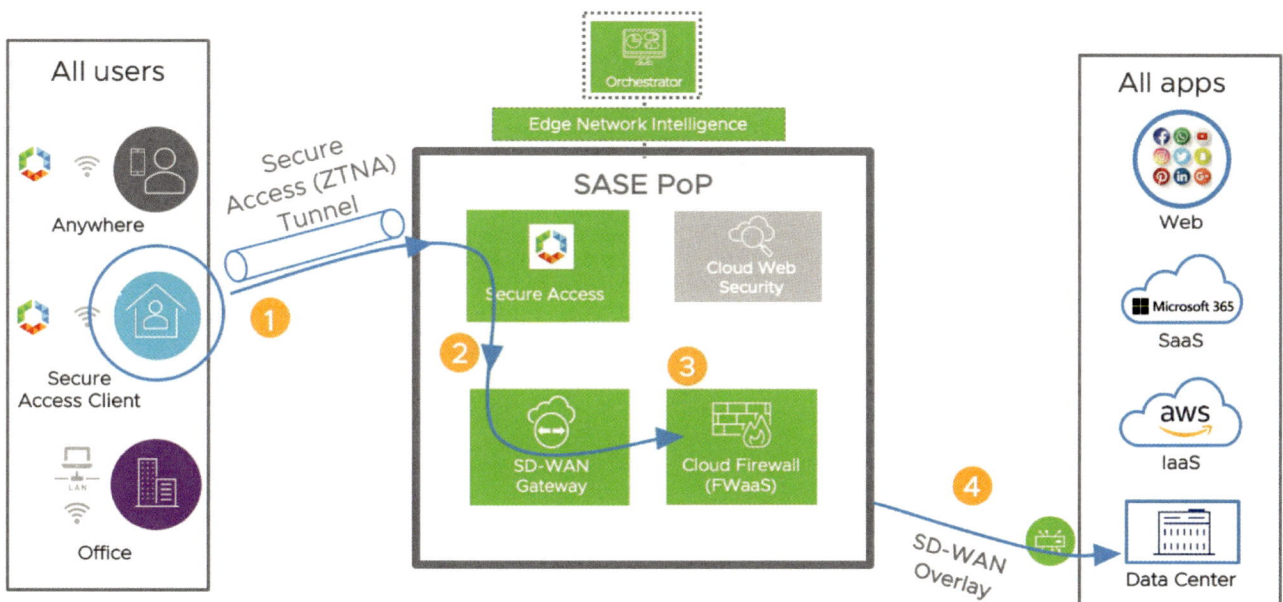

Figure 7.10: Use Case 7: Remote User from Home Accessing Private DC application

As before, the application flow and traffic processing follow a similar path:

1. Upon connecting to the home network, the endpoint sets up a session with the Secure Access service at the SASE PoP. Secure access authenticates and authorizes the user and device context. When successful, a secure access tunnel is established between the endpoint and the SASE PoP.

2. The user attempts to connect to the Data Center legacy application. The Secure Access component of SASE PoP steers the traffic to the SD-WAN gateway component, which examines the flow to identify its source and destination. It applies networking and security policies based on the user's identity, group membership, and authorization access level.

3. As per the security policy, the SD-WAN gateway component of SASE PoP then routes traffic to the Cloud Firewall, where it applies individual security rules (e.g., IDS/IPS, anti-malware, advanced threat detection) to the session.

4. The traffic leaves the SASE PoP, headed toward the final destination using the SD-WAN overlay tunnel to the hub device at the Data Center site hosting the application. The return path is the same traffic flow towards the remote user.

7.4 – Key Takeaway Checklist

These use cases presented in this chapter demonstrate both the consistency of SASE PoP access as well as flexible potential based on individual components.

✓ Regardless of a user's location or connection goal, their traffic flow will be optimized and secured.

✓ The policy is applied automatically based on corporate standards to protect both enterprise users, devices, data, and applications.

✓ Users are not required to work with cumbersome software or perform extensive authentication.

✓ The entire process is designed to provide a simple, secure, automated, optimized user experience regardless of the physical environment or work profile.

✓ Branch, remote, and mobile users all operate on a common infrastructure, simplifying user management and minimizing platform investment.

✓ The cloud-based platform provides scale and flexibility without the burdens of hardware management and resource capacity planning.

✓ Centralized management allows administrators to consistently create policy from a unified orchestrator and push it across the enterprise network.

✓ The platform provides unified, end-to-end visibility of users, connections, and policy applications.

✓ SASE PoPs bring together software-defined networking and intrinsic security in a compelling use case, simplifying IT's challenge of supporting seamless user mobility in a Zero Trust environment.

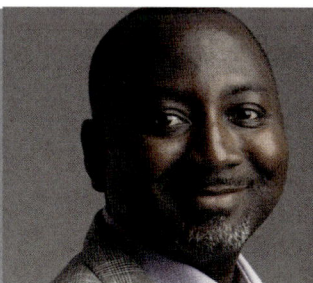

AIOps Spotlight
by Abe Ankumah

The rise of the distributed enterprise created the need for software-defined networking by providing a central and automated way to manage network connectivity across distributed locations. The need for SASE has been a result of multiple transformations, including the increasing adoption of SaaS applications, exponential use of BYOD and IoT, and acceleration of work-from-anywhere due to COVID-19.

SASE enables IT and security teams to invert the networking and security design pattern, shifting focus for security enforcement away from the data center and toward the user/device. While SASE brings ease of deployment and setup for networking and security as a converged solution, IT and security teams need to focus on day-2 operations within the SASE construct and understand the operating paradigm.

New operating models are required for SASE adoption, ones that leverage self-healing to identify and mitigate networking and application issues that impact user experience. Additionally, AI/ML can drive the access security requirements and policies required for users and connected devices to identify business policy violations, helping to recommend and verify appropriate security policies.

With software-defined and cloud-delivered networking and security in place, AIOps can help IT teams undertake the journey to accelerate the adoption of SASE by enterprise and service providers. As the volume and velocity of data from networking devices explode, AIOps will help tame operational complexity. AI/ML has been employed in transforming industries, including self-driving cars, manufacturing, and healthcare. While embracing AIOps involves a cultural shift, SASE will require IT and security teams to adopt the transformation in how networking and security are delivered and consumed. In this transformation, AIOps will be a critical enabler.

Digital transformation is changing the way users interact with their applications. These changes also require a transformation in how operations can manage a dynamic and distributed workforce. The new way to manage user experience requires solutions that harness the power of AI and ML to help IT stay ahead and focus more time on managing business expectations than fixing user downtime.

In the VMware Edge Network Intelligence (ENI) chapter, the authors will focus on the key aspects of AIOps that are imperative for IT and security teams to help transform their operations and manage the adoption of SASE. The benefits of AI and ML applied to operations will equip the team to drive efficiency and address essential business needs.

– Abe Ankumah

Abe Ankumah joined VMware via the Nyansa acquisition in February 2020. Prior to joining VMWare, Abe was CEO and Co-Founder of Nyansa, Inc., a fast-growing innovator of AI-based network analytics based in Palo Alto, CA. Before Nyansa, Abe was Director of Products and Alliances at Meraki (acquired by Cisco). Abe also held multiple roles at Aruba Networks in product management and business operations. Earlier in his career, Abe was part of the founding engineering team at the fabless semiconductor company Fulcrum Microsystems (acquired by Intel), a leader in the low latency switching market. Abe holds a BS degree from Caltech and an MBA from the Harvard Business School.

Chapter 8

Edge Network Intelligence and AIOps

Objective

Digital transformation is changing the way users interact with their applications. In response, these changes demand an operational transformation in managing a dynamic and distributed workforce. This new way to manage end-user and IoT device performance requires solutions that harness the power of AI and ML to help IT stay ahead. As a result, IT can spend more time managing business expectations, less addressing user downtime.

8.1 – Introduction

With their digital transformation underway, most enterprises have moved to wireless-first networks at branch sites, campuses, and remote locations. Device heterogeneity spans a spectrum ranging from end-user devices like laptops, phones, and tablets to IoT devices like robots, handheld scanners, infusion pumps, and bedside monitors. The number of devices that access the network has increased exponentially, and the volume of data has grown astronomically. IT administrators require meaningful insight into network behavior from a client context in this dynamic environment. They want a complete view across multiple domains—from access to applications—to understand where, when, and why a client device may have issues. This cohesive view must include all of the factors that affect performance, including device behavior, network performance, application performance, and other concurrent clients' impact.

Legacy operations tools focus on specific infrastructure domains and services. If a user has a problem accessing applications in the cloud, enterprise IT has to invest time looking across multiple tools to determine if the problem is related to user access, DHCP or DNS, SD-WAN, or the application itself. IT teams are forced to adopt a reactive posture, troubleshooting issues from the past using the present-day infrastructure. Often the infrastructure has changed over time, or the problem is intermittent and unpredictable, and as a result, cannot be reproduced. This leaves a pervasive blind spot in the infrastructure and a growing list of unknowns weighing on IT administrators' shoulders.

In the post-COVID environment, the enterprise perimeter extends to employees working from home or a coffee shop. This distributed nature of the enterprise workforce requires IT to ensure users are productively accessing their applications. The limitations of legacy tools are further exposed as the IT team needs to determine whether a problem is related to enterprise issues, local Wi-Fi, broadband provider, or the VPN.

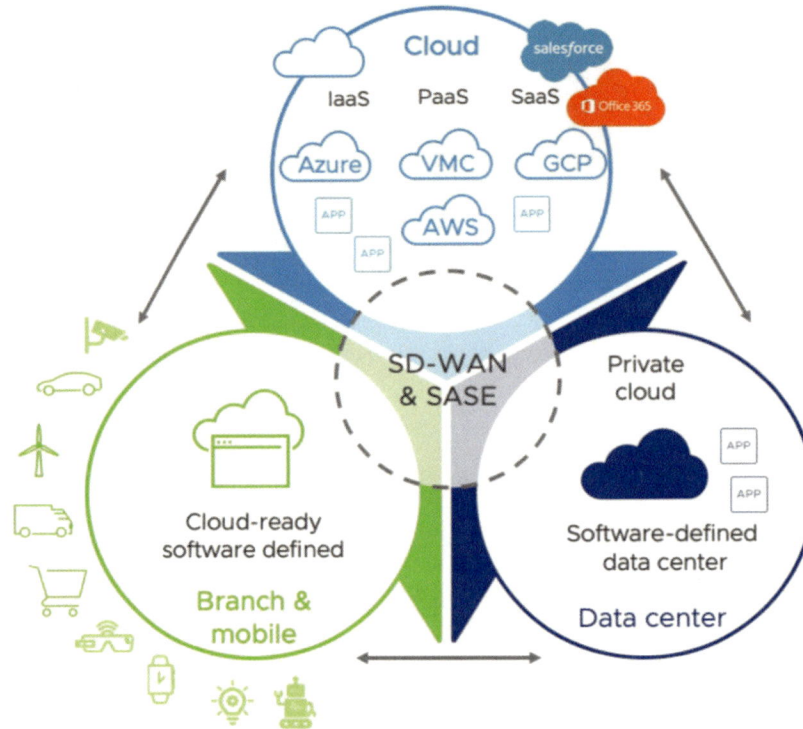

Figure 8.1: Enterprise Edge is getting increasingly complex

In this new era of digital transformation, shown in **Figure 8.1**, IT teams need a solution that can simplify the complex ecosystem of applications, clients, and infrastructure to manage client experience during normal and impaired conditions. IT needs insights into every end-user and IoT device experience when these devices access each enterprise application. They need a solution that offers automation and simplicity to shift the operating paradigm from a reactive mode to a proactive mode and on toward a path to self-healing. This starts with the ability to detect devices automatically, classify them, and establish a baseline for their performance. This expedites months of manually tracking performance and establishing thresholds for normal vs. abnormal behavior. It enables automated monitoring against the baseline and notifying operations teams only when deviations occur, often also providing steps for proactive remediation. This capability will significantly reduce alert fatigue and help IT focus on resolution. Apart from reactive use cases, it is important for the solution to analyze historical behavior and performance. This allows the system to take proactive steps and automated actions for self-healing before a problem fully manifests and impacts a large number of clients. When the problems escape the realm of human understanding, it is time for technology to intervene.

8.2 – ENI: AIOps for the network edge

8.2.1 – What is Artificial Intelligence/ Machine Learning?

Artificial Intelligence/Machine Learning (AI/ML) is a mathematical technique of using data to build mathematical models that generate insights and provide inferences about the system being modeled. Though the terms are often used together, it is crucial to understand their different meanings. Machine learning is a general term used for mathematical modeling. Artificial intelligence is a specific type of mathematical modeling where the goal is to automate tasks associated with human intelligence, such as detecting objects in images.

For an example of how AI/ML can benefit IT, consider an enterprise environment where there is a need to detect WAN link congestion. This condition will depend on the number of users in the enterprise at that branch and the types of applications they are using. Using data captured from the network and the correct mathematical model, it is possible to build such a prediction mechanism.

In AI/ML jargon, data relevant to this problem is referred to as features, and the mathematical equation governing the prediction is called the ML model or AI model. Using historical data, the model is trained; this means using historical data to determine the correct parameters of the model. Once a model is prepared, it can be used to make inferences.

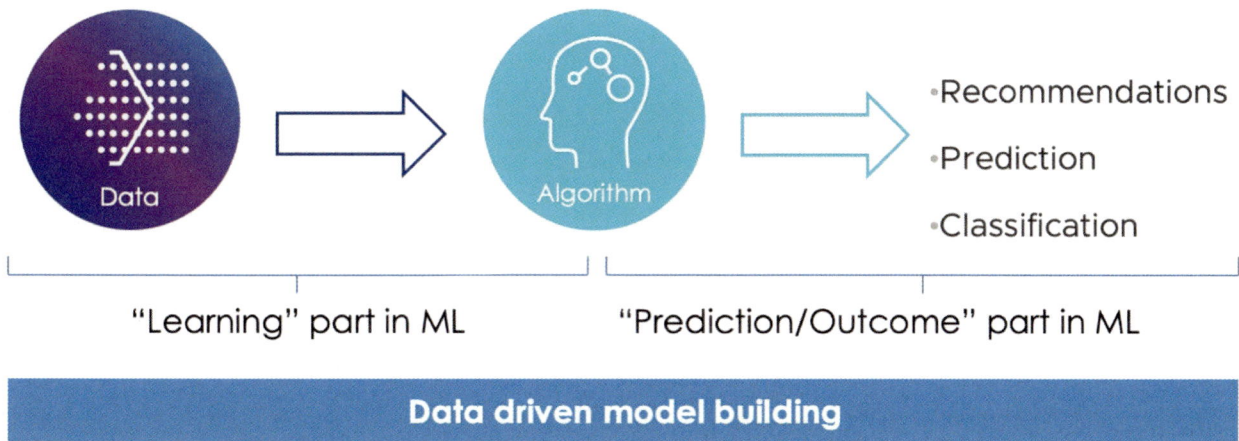

Figure 8.2: High-Level AI/ML Model

For the example in **Figure 8.2**, one such inference would be, "What will WAN congestion be when there is a sales conference two days from today?" The answer to this question will help the conference's IT team plan ahead.

Recent advances in data collection and compute have put AI/ML within reach of every enterprise. Modern computing systems enable the efficient collection, processing, transformation, and storage of large volumes of data. Modern, scalable computing systems enable cost-effective computation to build large-scale mathematical models.

8.2.2 – What is AIOps?

AIOps is the notion of collecting information directly from the infrastructure and analyzing the data using AI/ML to assist IT operations. To automate actions and make them more efficient, the IT operations team needs to extract the correct information through analytics. Using data analytics, IT can recommend preventive and predictive maintenance tasks. Anomaly detection can also create alerts for ongoing issues and take action to automate the remediation process.

AIOps is not explicitly linked to LAN, WAN, or other systems; it merely collects data and responds to events from all infrastructure elements (e.g., routers, switches, application servers, etc.) All data is fed into a common platform for analysis and remediation efforts. This process improves operational efficiency through surfacing insights for manual review or automated remediation through self-healing.

AIOps enters the picture at what is traditionally known as day 2 of the operations lifecycle. On day 0, IT assesses the requirements, deployment, and inventory. This involves identifying and selecting the proper infrastructure, applications, security, and other systems. Day 1 puts the infrastructure in place, installing hardware and configuring the components. The monitoring and maintenance lifecycle begins with day 2, and it is here that AIOps delivers on its promise of efficiency.

AIOps begins with collecting data from the modern networking, application, and security infrastructure then progresses to feeding it into a big data analytics platform and using AI/ML. This is the AI part of the operations; it takes this data, surfacing insights and actions to make the operational environment more efficient.

8.2.3 – Architecture of Edge Network Intelligence (ENI)

VMware Edge Network Intelligence is the AIOps solution for the network edge. The key component of the solution include: **data collection, analytics engine, visibility, and control.**

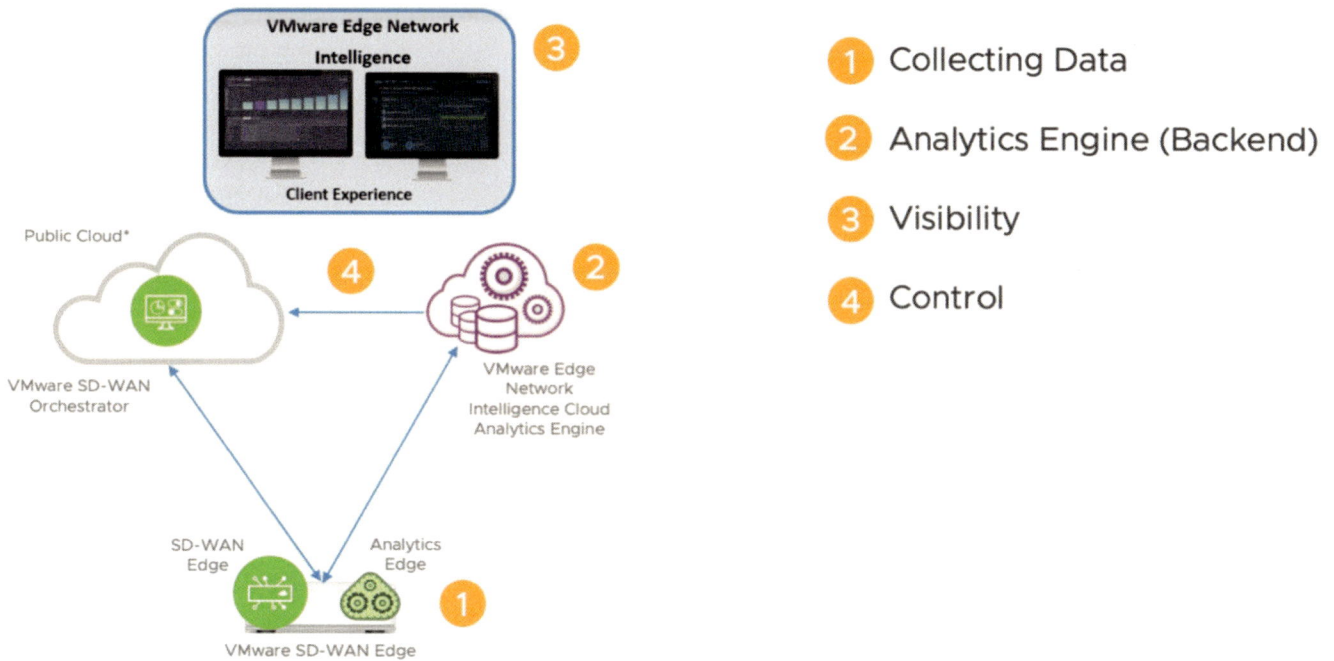

Figure 8.3: Architecture and Components

Data Collection

ENI collects data from various sources such as SD-WAN Edges, Wi-Fi access points, client applications, and data packets. It gathers application data from different vantage points and across multiple layers of networking, computes, and application stacks. This information is obtained via the management plane, so production traffic is not touched. Furthermore, only metadata per flow is collected, which reduces the data collection traffic to a small fraction of the original traffic. The entire process can be enabled directly in existing VMware SD-WAN deployments without installing additional software.

ENI focuses on the client's experience, behavior, and security. It examines all packets transmitted from every managed client at the edge, collecting data from infrastructure elements across the LAN, WAN, and application compute environments. It can also use application APIs to gather additional data specific to application performance. For example, leveraging Zoom's APIs permits extraction of MOS score, stream quality, and frame rate resolution – a level of insight that is not possible to obtain by simply examining raw packet data.

ENI also supports data collection via client software installed on servers and endpoint devices, ensuring full coverage in multi-vendor environments. It is essential for AIOps processes and tools to collect data from a wide array of manufacturers and protocols; the broader the scope of coverage, the more complete the resulting insights.

Analytics Engine

After the collection process has brought data into the system, backend analytics perform a series of tasks to organize and understand the information. The first step takes the data and connects it to a single entity, recognizing devices by identifiers like MAC addresses and classifying them according to endpoint types. Next, the system creates a time series of data to tell the story of what each device does over that period. This paints the picture of what applications the device uses, destinations it communicates with, protocols used for messaging, SSID/VLANs it belongs to, etc. This establishes an operational and performance baseline.

With these baseline standards in place, the engine can review ongoing streaming analytics to watch for patterns such as end-to-end performance, secure communications, or new traffic connections. End-to-end performance is an issue most likely to be seen by and directly impact an end-user. Performance problems are often transient and can be tough to troubleshoot or isolate; ongoing monitoring with streaming analytics ensures information is gathered at the time of any given incident. Secure communication involves not simply encrypted protocols but also assurance that systems are only passing data back-and-forth with expected destinations. While new traffic flow details—ports, protocols, source/ destination pairs—are not necessarily indicators of a problem, they can be an immediate indicator that something has changed in the environment and merits a closer look. This level of insight also lets IT move backward in time to identify the moment that something changed and wherein the environment the change occurred.

The final process is batch pattern analysis, where the system looks for patterns over a longer duration. Where streaming analytics works on a time frame of seconds, minutes, or hours, batch pattern analysis looks at trends over weeks, months, or longer. It can identify issues that happen every day at midnight, the first Monday of each month, or under less regular conditions. It can also use this analysis of historical data across thousands of different customer environments to make predictions and recommendations about which actions will yield the biggest benefits for improved user experience and security.

As the impact of these issues may not be immediately visible, the ability to identify patterns related to the root cause can save IT a significant amount of time and effort. As with other analytical aspects of ENI, this does not impact production data traffic as it is performed out-of-band across the management and control planes.

Visibility and Control

An essential aspect of any solution powered by machine learning is to deliver the results in a layout that is easy to understand and act on. Edge Network Intelligence UI provides information that can be used by all levels of IT staff, from the Service Desk to the CIO. The results are tied back to the end client experience with each enterprise application with a clear breakdown of fault domains when there is an incident. The UI offers visibility into historical trends compared to the enterprise or across the industry with an easy switch. The UI also displays recommendations in plain text for IT teams to address systemic issues in the network. Each recommendation provides details about the issue that the analytics engine surfaced from the data, along with a quantifiable benefit to end-user experience when that issue is addressed.

Issues surfaced by the machine learning system can be addressed by the IT through manual intervention based on alerts generated by the ENI system, or the ENI system can automatically take control actions by programming various controllers and network elements, e.g., VMware SD-WAN Orchestrator, Network Access Controller, etc. For example, when ENI identifies a misbehaving end-user device, it can program the Network Access Controller to take remedial actions that may include applying security rules or isolating that device to a quarantine network segment. Similarly, when ENI identifies performance issues on the network, it can access APIs on the VMware SD-WAN Orchestrator to apply policies on the remote SD-WAN edges.

8.3 – ENI For SD-WAN

AIOps plays a central role in ENI's success, allowing companies to make sense of massive amounts of SD-WAN data. This data is a potential goldmine of information just waiting for the right tools. This section looks at how IT can use AIOps as part of its overall SD-WAN approach to networking.

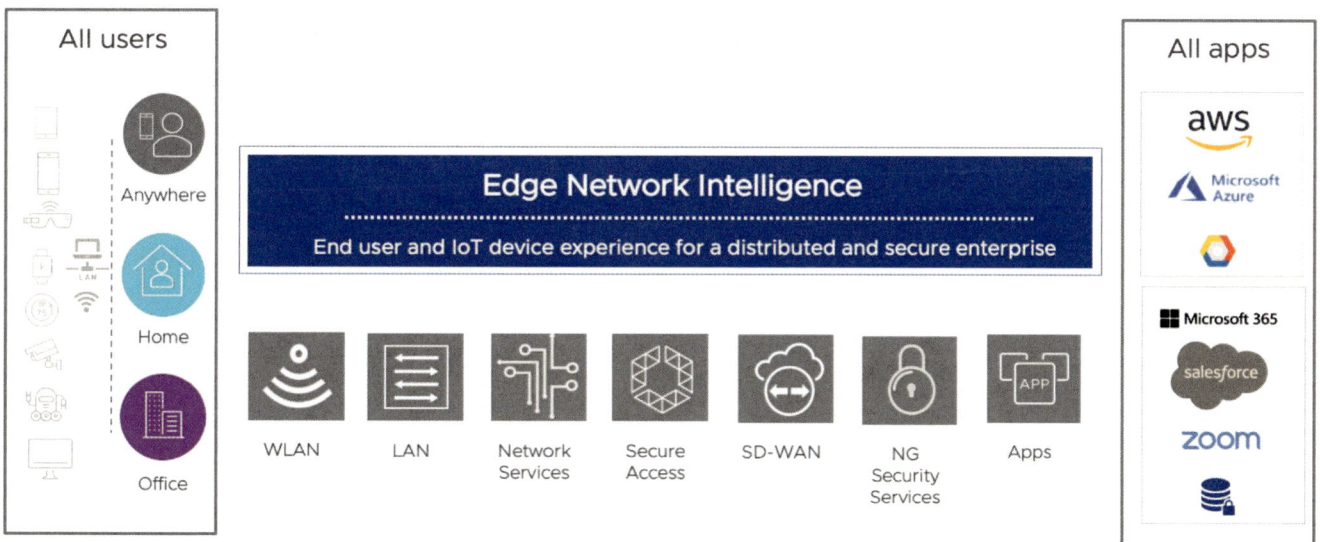

Figure 8.4: AI Ops Solution to deliver the rich client experience

Globally, VMware SD-WAN generates around 10 billion application flow records each day. All of this information is collected by orchestrators as it traverses SD-WAN networks. This data includes potentially valuable information on application performance throughout the entire network. These flows document details about each application, each device using that application, and those devices' experience.

Advantages of Automation and Big Data

This raw data can be explored and visualized but not manually analyzed to glean actionable insights; this is simply not practical with the magnitude of data coming into the system. Even where a VMware SD-WAN customer manually explores some data, there is only so much insight possible.

A unique advantage of this giant data set is that it encompasses traffic from many customers across all vertical markets, from single users to international corporations. This data is sourced from different types of networks all over the world. An analytics platform can gain valuable insights by looking at this anonymized data and its context, analyzing it in an intelligent way to provide meaningful benefits.

The VMware SD-WAN platform collects data from multiple vantage points. This allows the same application flow to be viewed from the perspective of the VMware SD-WAN Edge, the VMware SD-WAN Gateway, and/or the SD-WAN hub. With the right analytics, this data allows the system to identify faulty segments between the client LAN, the enterprise WAN, the Internet, and the data center LAN. It is another way of analyzing data in order to gain insights into network problems.

Managing a Complex SD-WAN Infrastructure Requires a New Approach

The modern network continues to grow in complexity as cloud-based IaaS providers, such as AWS and Azure, and third-party SaaS applications, such as Salesforce and Microsoft 365, enter the equation. SD-WAN helps the enterprise interconnect heterogeneous devices— end-user devices such as laptops and phones, and increasingly IoT devices such as point-of-sale and medical devices—with applications deployed anywhere and over different types of cloud services.

Locating Problems, Determining Patterns

In this environment, enterprise IT needs to understand many data points when application problems occur. Are problems related to the devices accessing these applications? Where is the problem located? Is it something going on the campus or branch? Is there a problem with the network? Perhaps the issue resides in the data center, cloud, or even with the application itself?

Determining high-level patterns affecting application performance is also critical. For example, does a service provider suffer regular outages, or is there a fault in the enterprise's network that local IT staff can fix? Successfully analyzing network data requires context and an understanding of how applications are performing over complex SD-WAN networks. Network data analysis can also provide valuable general knowledge about the trends of application adoption and usage.

Learning "Normal," Automatically

An automated AIOps process, fueled by machine learning, is key to making sense of the massive amounts of data generated by that SD-WAN. ENI begins by using data to automatically determine baselines—to define the normal behavior—for network activity and application performance. For example, what is a normal user experience for Microsoft 365? What is the normal percentage of devices that fail to connect? What is the normal number of users for a given enterprise?

Baselines also need to incorporate time and network activity. These conditions can vary based on the regular business hours and time zone for each enterprise and the location of any individual branch site. The system will also learn the norms for each entity's type of WAN link (e.g., satellite, cellular, MPLS) and vertical; a hospital network will look very different from a retail network. Importantly, VMware ENI performs these tasks automatically instead of relying on manual and inefficient processes. The ultimate result is an extensive catalog of baseline information that helps determine the typical application experience for each user.

Establishing Baselines and Thresholds

The VMware Edge Network Intelligence platform uses a Bayesian machine learning approach to data analysis. The system analyzes time series application performance data for each device on a network, combining it with other factors, including service provider, WAN link type, and business vertical. Once baselines are established for the enterprise network, the next step involves determining the thresholds for any degradation of a specific baseline.

Traditionally, administrators of legacy enterprise networks set performance thresholds manually. This is time-consuming, involves a lot of guesswork, and can lead to alert fatigue. VMware Edge Network Intelligence takes advantage of AIOps to automate this process, including alerting network engineers of real potential issues. It is no longer simply an assumption that a change was successful because it did not generate any alerts. The machine learning routines provide both the ability to detect the root cause of faults and the proof to show whether the mitigation strategy worked.

Shows Root Causes and How to Fix Them

The insight provided by analyzing application performance at different vantage points yields enough data for AIOps to determine the problem's location. ENI uses a nearest-neighbor style analysis to identify any correlating symptoms and determine the likely fault area: perhaps it is a poor WAN link at a branch, a problem in the data center, an issue with the application itself, or even routing in the WAN. In the end, the system automatically identifies the problem using application flow data from multiple vantage points.

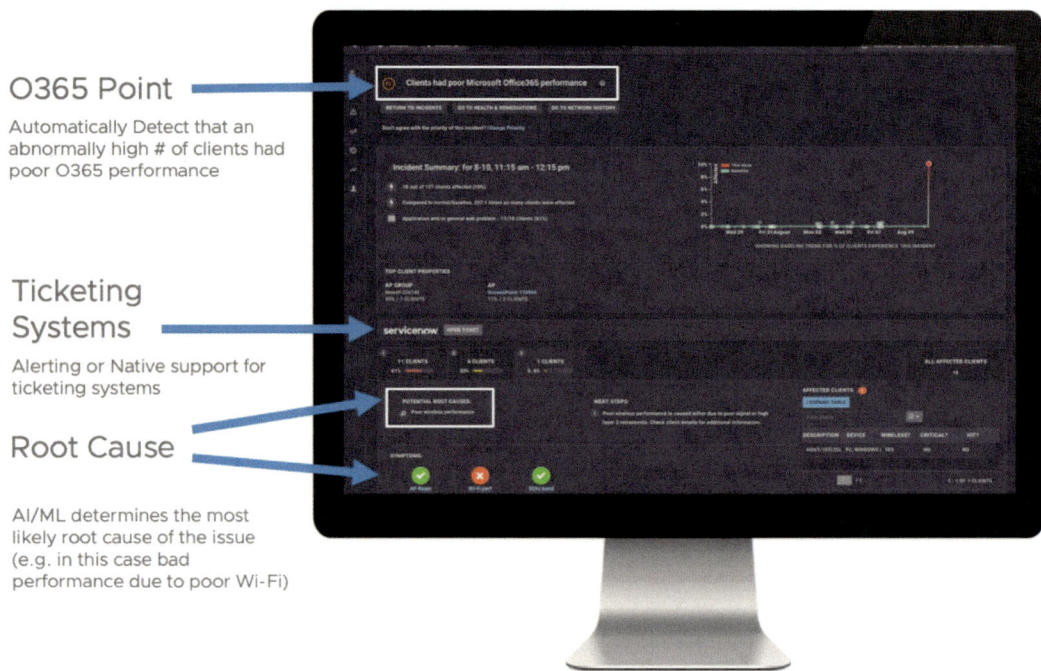

O365 Point

Automatically Detect that an
abnormally high # of clients had
poor O365 performance

Ticketing Systems

Alerting or Native support for
ticketing systems

Root Cause

AI/ML determines the most
likely root cause of the issue
(e.g. in this case bad
performance due to poor Wi-Fi)

Figure 8.5: Example screenshot from VMware Edge Network Intelligence shows how applications are performing against a normal baseline and suggests ways to fix them

Figure 8.5 offers an example of these capabilities. VMware Edge Network Intelligence has automatically detected that an abnormally high number of clients had poor Microsoft 365 performance, indicated by the graph's spike at the top right. The bottom left shows that Edge Network Intelligence is integrated with this organization's ticketing system. It determined that the most likely root cause is poor Wi-Fi.

AIOps Helps Determine If Network Changes Worked

Because VMware Edge Network Intelligence uses machine learning to determine enterprise network baselines and performance thresholds, it is useful to track the efficacy of any configuration, architectural, or device changes to the network. Once normal baselines are established, it becomes easy to determine if any network change had a positive, negative, or negligible effect on network performance.

Implementing a network change, updating the baselines, and analyzing the before and after performance data provide a more accurate picture of the result. It is a better approach than the legacy model, where network engineers relied on anecdotal reports and imperfect manual analysis. Ultimately, the VMware ENI automated AIOps approach provides a more objective view of the effect of any configuration change.

Edge Network Intelligence data analysis can show the ROI provided by the SD-WAN platform – after both the initial implementation as well as any subsequent configuration changes. It goes beyond simply learning baselines, identifying deviations in performance, and alerting IT staff. Edge Network Intelligence enables IT to be proactive about the enterprise's network environment, fix problems before they happen, and predict where issues might occur so that they are handled ahead of time.

Analyzing Historical Data for Proactive Network Management

Using ENI machine learning algorithms to analyze historical network data create models to help understand where problems typically occur and their potential impact. The platform actively makes recommendations and predictions to the enterprise IT team about the effects of any network changes. ENI might predict that prioritizing a billing application hosted in the data center would improve client experience on devices using the application over the network. This prediction is based on historical analysis, noting poor experience with this particular application during various usage scenarios. Machine learning routines can cluster this historical data, aggregating the data by their similarities. Identifying common issues drives the platform's recommendation engine. VMware Edge Network Intelligence uses data across customers for this analysis, tying back into the concept were learning from all customers benefits every customer.

The Time is Right for AIOps in SD-WAN

AIOps is an essential ingredient in any SD-WAN implementation. The power of machine learning helps enterprises make sense of the massive amounts of data generated by any network on a daily basis. Predictive insights make it easier for network engineers to ensure higher network performance while end-users and IoT devices gain higher productivity.

8.4 – ENI for SASE

User performance management and security analytics are important ingredients for SASE. When services are deployed and operationalized at the secure edge, IT needs to ensure that users experience these services with both the best performance and security.

AI/ML plays a key role by providing near real-time monitoring of user performance, dynamic adaptation of network policies using self-healing and self-optimization, and constant security threat monitoring using real-time data streams. AI/ML is key here for two reasons. First, it works on large streaming data providing near real-time ingestion and analysis. Second, it can enable fast response and action to self-heal/self-optimize as well as quickly address security threats.

User performance and security analytics in SASE require analyzing data on a per-client/device level. The data sources to be managed and analyzed are large and varied. Network data comes from a variety of sources, including network controllers, servers, switches/routers, and packet flow collectors. Security data is available from a wide range of perspectives such as device posture, device network behavior, and device type (e.g., IoT).

SASE service baselining is the collection of relevant data to build a baseline of how the user experience for a particular service is. It has two dimensions:

- Baselining of a user over time builds a time-based historical view of the user experience for that service. Such a baseline helps answer the question of how the current user experience compares with its other experiences over time. Historical service baselining helps identify and isolate user experience issues associated with device or network changes that affected the user/device. This could include changing the software version on the device, making a policy change on the network, or changing the ACL/security filter for the device.

- Baselining across other users in the same enterprise builds a comparative view of a user's experience against other users in a similar environment. Service baselining across users helps identify and isolate user experience issues peculiar to a device or a group of devices. A problem could result from a mismatch of network policy applied to this group of devices versus other similar devices in the network. A single device might be impacted by a network routing when it connects to the SASE POP from home while no issues are seen by similar devices.

Anomaly detection is the key mathematical technique used to analyze service baselines and detect deviations across both time and devices. The main principle behind anomaly detection is to create a model for an average user performance, then detect users that deviate significantly from the average performance. For historical baselines, the average is computed across time, and a user's current experience is compared with this average. For baselines across users, the average is computed across users. A simple example is the total volume of traffic sent and received by a user over time. A historical baseline would provide average traffic values in the morning, afternoon, and evening for this user. Anomaly detection would compare the current traffic volume to these baselines to compute the deviation and flag it if the deviation is significant.

ENI takes this to the next level by comparing it across other enterprises. It provides anonymized service baseline comparisons not only in time and across users but also across similar enterprise network environments. This can help an enterprise make important architecture decisions in terms of best practices in the industry on enabling SASE services.

Fault Isolation and Self-healing with Reinforcement Learning

When a user experiences issues with a SASE service, it is important to know whether the issue is due to problems with the LAN, WAN, or data center. The technique of fault isolation involves using AI/ML to correlate data across different network stacks and across different parts of the network to determine which segments are causing the issue.

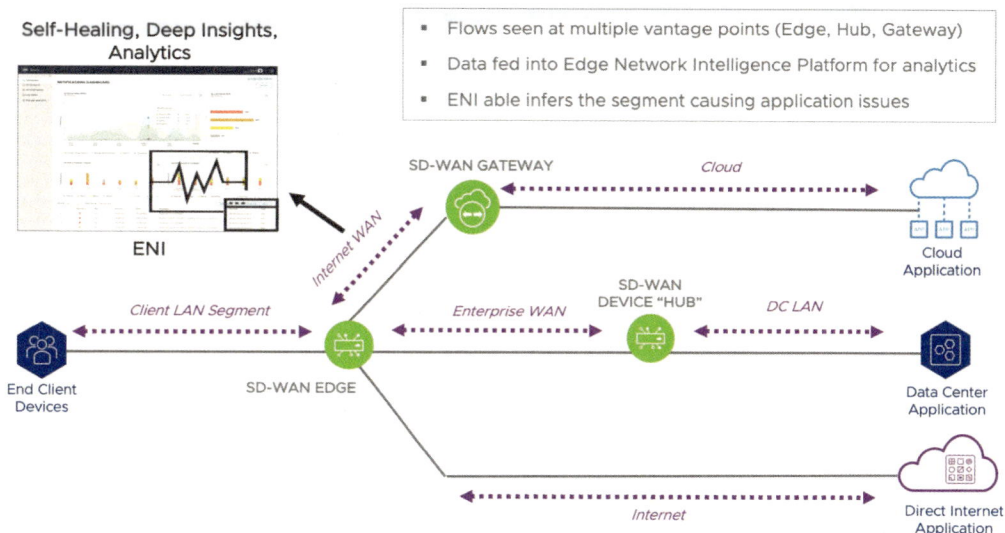

Figure 8.6: Isolating the most likely faulty segment

Figure 8.6 highlights the ability to isolate the faults by gathering the data about the flow. This information is collected from multiple vantage points, including the SD-WAN Edge at the branch site, SD-WAN Edge at the data center, and the SASE PoP (SD-WAN gateway component). The data gathered is processed by the SD-WAN Edge and sent to the analytics engine as metadata.

Root cause analysis is the next important component of AIOps. It is not sufficient to simply know that a user is experiencing issues with a SASE service. It is also essential to identify the issue's root cause. This can be achieved by collecting data and metrics from various system components—user devices, remote SD-WAN Edges, gateway PoPs, data center hubs, application server APIs—and correlating this data across the network stack to determine the root cause of a service issue. ENI systems use ML techniques of time-series analysis, vector correlation, and nearest-neighbor matching to determine the root cause.

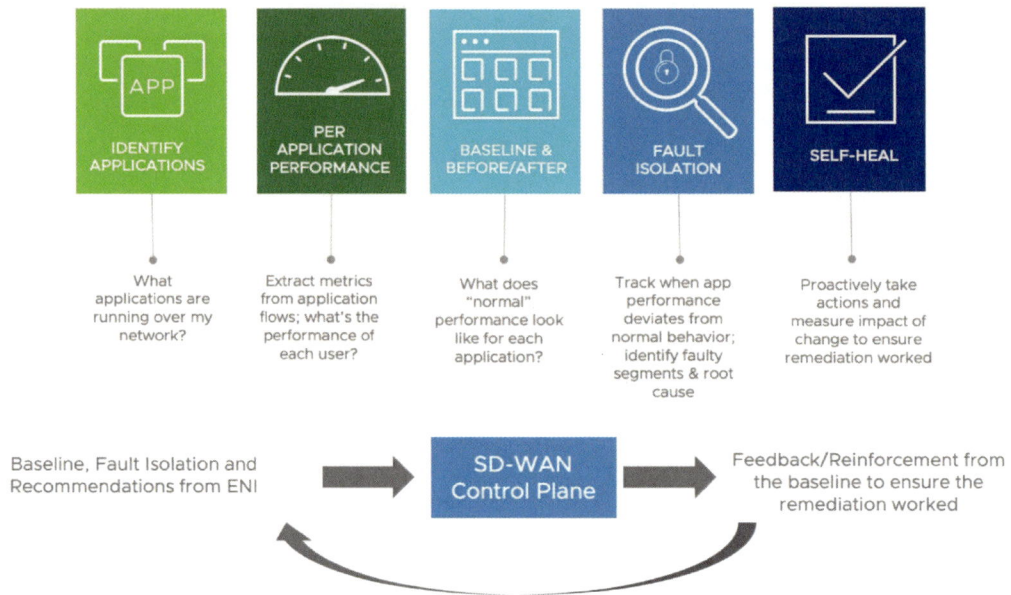

Figure 8.7: Self-Healing Networks

Finally, it is possible to close the loop by taking a corrective action based on input from fault isolation and root cause analysis. This process is referred to as self-healing. The AI/ML system takes corrective action by reprogramming the SASE environment to correct service issues, as detailed in **Figure 8.7.** This can involve static changes such as altering default policies or configurations but can also apply dynamic changes in terms of traffic re-routing, changing service gateways, and finding optimal service points in the SASE cloud. Reinforcement learning is a powerful AI/ML technique used to achieve this. Through reinforcement learning, the ML system learns on the fly as it makes decisions. This ensures that the model is always fresh, learning, and relevant to the ever-changing network environment. Each decision builds on learnings from the past decisions in real-time, allowing the ML system to quickly adapt to network and service disruptions.

8.5 – ENI Use Cases

8.5.1 – Data Analytics Makes Network Branch Sites More Secure and Efficient

Any technical infrastructure using SD-WAN generates a massive amount of data. Artificial intelligence and machine learning help companies glean actionable information from it.

This use case details how data analytics makes network branch sites, including home offices, more secure and efficient. Analytics supply the essential real-time data that lets network administrators ensure optimal performance at every point accessing the SD-WAN platform.

Devices Connected to SD-WAN Platforms Provide Useful Data Sources

AIOps platforms can analyze more than one source of data. SD-WAN systems generate information about application flows across an entire network; however, they do not provide any insight into the other parts of the client-to-container-to-application journey.

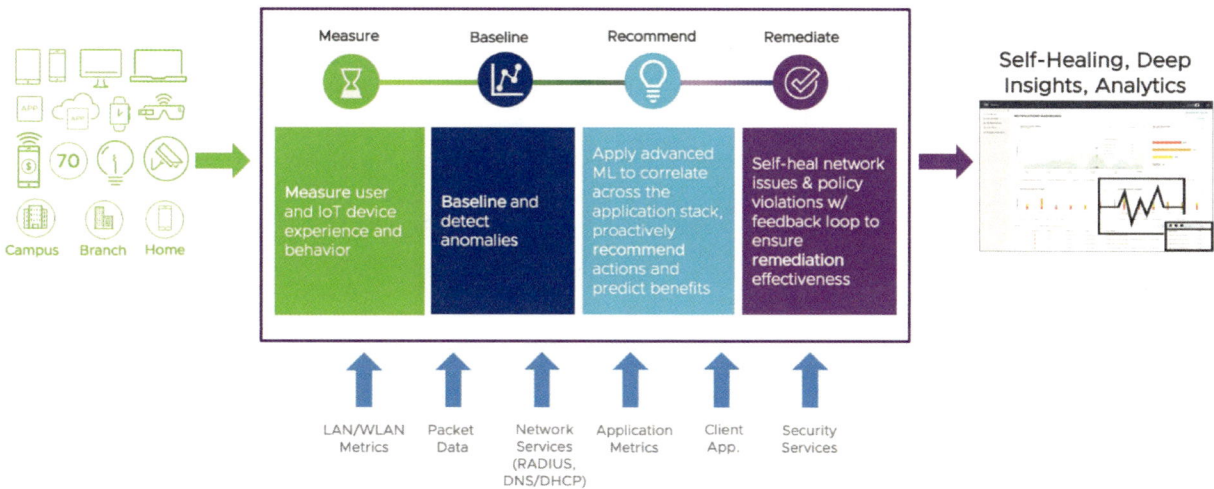

Figure 8.8: Comprehensive Cross Data Correlation and Analysis using VMware ENI

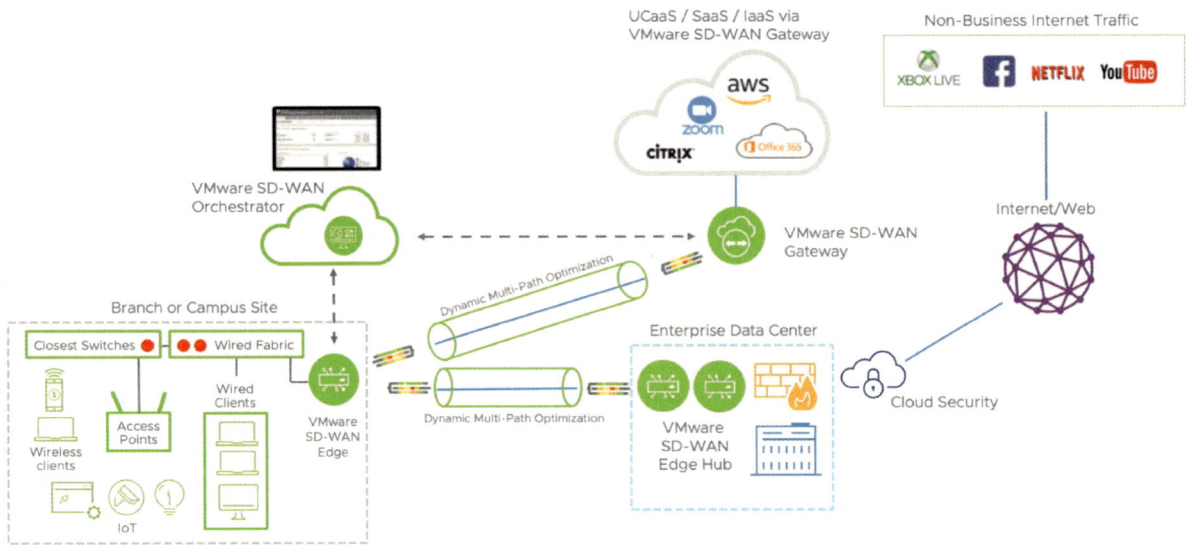

Figure 8.9: SD-WAN Viewpoint: Internals of the branch/campus is a black box (without AIOps/ML)

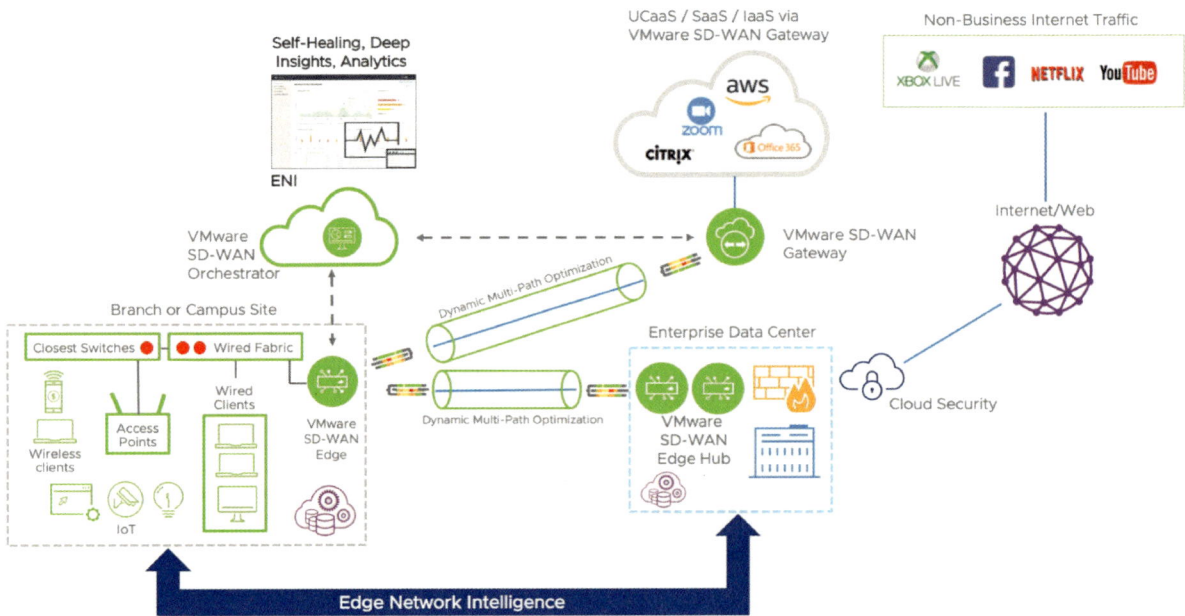

Figure 8.10: The new picture with an AIOps platform incorporating additional data sources describing end-client performance and behavior at the network edge. (With AIOps/ML)

Figures 8.9 and **8.10** show how VMware Edge Network Intelligence provides a panoramic network view.

As client devices access applications, they do so from an access network, a branch, or even a home office. These provide additional data sources that can be fed from SD-WAN into an AIOps platform. In many cases, this data arrives over a wireless system. This data includes information on the wireless access point, its location, signal quality, and whether there are any rogue access points interfering with the signal.

Wired devices, including IoT devices, provide another source of valuable information on SD-WAN network performance. This includes the wired devices connected to an access point, their physical locations, and the overall port health.

Get Insight into Network Services

Feeding all this data from wired and wireless devices into an AIOps platform such as VMware Edge Network Intelligence provides keen insight into network services. As an example, network administrators are able to verify whether client devices are able to authenticate to the network; when issues arise, determining the underlying problem becomes much simpler.

ENI can add insights from other network services (e.g., DNS, DHCP) either by getting data directly from the servers or from analyzing packet data within the enterprise premises. This lets IT look at individual network transactions to analyze the performance of every client device.

IT can also glean data directly from the client device itself as an additional data point. A VMware Edge Network Intelligence client application measures many of the data points previously mentioned but from the perspective of the client rather than a point in the SD-WAN infrastructure. The ultimate goal is to provide more insight into each leg of the journey as clients are connecting to applications.

Data from Applications

APIs offer application data that describes the user experience for every single client device. For example, Zoom provides data on voice, video screenshare quality, resolution, frame rate, and more. In healthcare, applications such as Citrix XenApp or VMware Horizon provide data that offers critical insight into the experience of client devices accessing the network. This allows network engineers to drill down into the root causes of any issues relating to the overall application experience.

Being able to analyze data from client devices accessing the network, as well as the applications those devices are using, offers visibility into the overall performance of the SD-WAN network. The ability to feed all this data into AIOps remains the key link in gleaning that actionable information from the masses of data supplied by the network, devices, and applications.

8.5.2 – How AIOps Helps Network Administrators Monitor SD-WAN

Using an AIOps platform such as VMware Edge Network Intelligence on this data goes beyond just the application insights on the WAN network. Its auto-discovery features can identify the actual devices accessing these applications from inside the branch, campus, or home. It also specifically recognizes IoT devices, such as a specific sensor, camera, or barcode scanner. The AIOps machine learning algorithms group discovered devices by their type as they learn how these device clusters are similar and different.

This approach adds efficiency to network troubleshooting processes. If multiple wireless devices in the same location are having problems, something may be causing wireless interference near that spot. Slow application access might be due to high latency on the DNS server used for that application. Network engineers become more effective at diagnosing and fixing issues as a result of these insights.

The ability to provide specific information on the root cause of a network problem improves based on the amount of data available to the AIOps platform. The internal algorithms leverage similar techniques employed for the WAN-only data. ENI automatically learns the performance baselines, detects deviations, and correlates those to a likely root cause. This additional data fed into AIOps expand insight, making it useful not only to WAN network engineers but also to other personnel across the IT organization, including LAN engineers and application teams.

8.5.3 – How AIOps Helps Address Work from Home

People who work from home mostly use commercial-grade networking hardware (e.g., Netgear, Apple, or basic ISP-provided Wi-Fi router). Because of this, many of the data sources mentioned above are not readily available to feed into the AIOps platform. Yet two critical data sources, when fed into an AIOPs platform, help shed light on work-from-home users:

- **Client Application Data:** Because it is measurements directly from the end-client device, client data is completely networking equipment/vendor agnostic.

- **Application Server Data:** Because data is coming directly from the application server, it describes the application performance of devices connecting from the office or the home

VMware Edge Network Intelligence uses machine learning on top of these data sources. It provides enterprise IT with a unified view of home users' experiences and the root causes of any critical application issues. For the previous Zoom example, it can determine that a Zoom performance problem was caused by poor Wi-Fi. Additionally, it can provide insight into the specific before-and-after ROI due to any change to help determine the user benefit of installing a VMware SD-WAN Edge. Finally, it can surface employees with problematic devices so that IT can proactively reach out to help improve their productivity.

8.5.4 – Applying AIOps to Network Security and User Authentication

VMware Edge Network Intelligence follows VMware's core security principle: rather than simply seeking to keep out bad software or people, the best practice is to establish a baseline of known good parameters and then detect deviations from that baseline. This comes into play with SASE data sources, such as a unified access gateway providing information about the security posture of a particular client device. Similarly, the next-generation secure web gateway and the next-generation firewall give important insights, both from a performance and a security perspective.

From the performance side, access control lists or deny lists configured on these devices have an important impact in terms of user experience. Perhaps specific endpoints cannot be accessed because of ACLs configured on these devices? From a security standpoint, it is vital to be able to baseline the normal resources accessed by a device and automatically figure out when it accesses something outside of those standards.

Ultimately, VMware Edge Network Intelligence ensures network branch sites receive superior performance in tandem with critical network security.

8.6 - Key Take-Away Checklist

✓ Automation and simplicity with a path to self-healing are essential to successfully transform IT into a proactive mode of operation.

✓ To deliver a rich end-user and IoT device experience at the edge of a distributed enterprise, IT Operations require an AIOps solution like Edge Network Intelligence.

✓ To manage the Post COVID transitions to a hybrid work environment and maintain high productivity, IT needs visibility into every end-user connected to the enterprise applications.

✓ With SASE, IT needs a solution like Edge Network Intelligence that can easily isolate faults across different domains, verify changes in the infrastructure and provide remedial insights for operational assurance.

Chapter 9

Rolling out SASE into the Enterprise

Chapter Objective

Few enterprises are just beginning their network modernization journey. Most have years or decades of legacy systems, architectures, and processes in place – WAN routers, on-premises security appliances, and firewalls, fiber loop contracts, change management systems. IT teams are always faced with the brownfield challenges of moving from where the company is to where the company needs to be; modernizing the enterprise strategy for Security and Networking is no different.

This chapter examines the individual steps of implementing an enterprise-wide SASE solution. It is designed to allow a company to identify where it is on the overall Networking and security journey, then move toward a more modern cloud-delivered solution. It will look not just at the technology and connections that move packets but also the policy and processes that ensure simplicity, quality of user experience, automation, network performance, and security.

9.1 – Migration Overview

Businesses interested in adopting a SASE solution are not required to immediately abandon existing practices and commit to significant change from the way they are conducting business. Migration to a SASE environment can progress at a pace that is both comfortable to the corporate culture and in line with available staffing and budget constraints.

IT teams can use the 5-phase reference framework shown in **Figure 9.1** as a template for their own migration planning. This 5-phases framework is referenced from ITIL (IT Infrastructure Library). This process consists of:

- Scoping
- Design Decisions
- Testing and Validation
- Implementation and Transition
- Continuous Improvement and Lifecycle Management

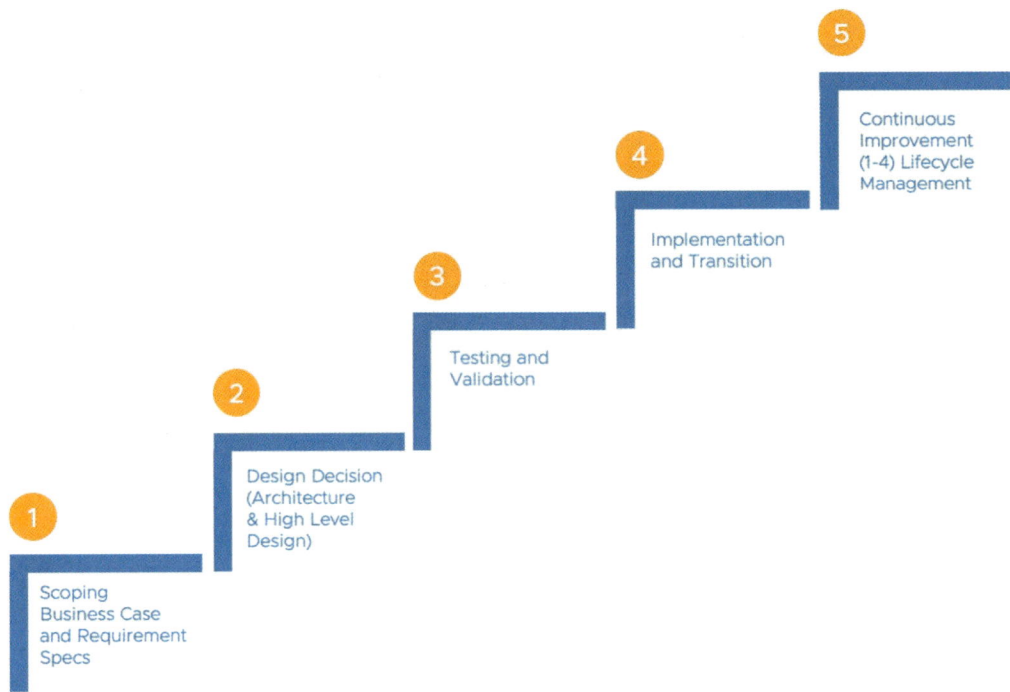

Figure 9.1: Five Phases Customer Journey for SASE

Begin with project scoping, identifying business goals, requirements, and constraints—document the technical requirements, deliverables, and acceptance criteria for each step. For the technical requirements, ensure the foundational Networking and Security is clearly defined.

Operationally, a business can begin to put in place the structures and processes necessary for a full SASE implementation while continuing existing operational practices without interruption. New users and applications can be immediately integrated into the new environment, while migration of existing resources can be performed when desired. Each step along the migration path builds on the previous, bringing the enterprise along from basic Networking and security enhancements through to fully unified policy and automated operations.

The best practice recommendation is to start small. Set up a proof-of-concept covering a limited number of branches and a single data center. Identify a set of users, devices, data, and applications for validation of end-to-end controls and traffic flow. Once that grouping has been successfully migrated, expand coverage to additional sets.

9.2 – Migration Phases

9.2.1 – Phase-1: Scoping

To properly scope a project, the business must understand both the issues they are working to solve and the resources they can bring to bear. Companies moving to SASE are working toward a number of business goals:

- Creating a flexible cloud architecture that can support dynamic changes to the environment.

- Achieving digital transformation without disruption by enabling a foundation that delivers any application, from any cloud to any device.

- Improving the end-user quality of experience and security efficacy.

- Ensuring high availability and scalability for the enterprise network.

- Reducing operational complexity, support tickets, and ongoing cost to maintain the infrastructure.

To help build mindshare, clearly define the problem statement for the enterprise. Identify specific capability gaps, security risks, operational challenges, compliance concerns, and business expenses. Finally, it is important to establish standards to judge the ongoing progress and ultimate success of the migration. These should be based both on industry standards and unique corporate criteria.

9.2.2 – Phase-2: Design Decisions

With an understanding of requirements and goals established, the next phase organizes the environmental framework and implementation details. The core of SASE architecture is well defined, but it can be customized to address the requirements of most any organization. Significant areas of design consideration that broadly apply are:

- Identification and inventory of resources and their locations – in the Cloud and across all corporate premises.

- Categorization of applications by type, physical requirements (e.g., performance, bandwidth, latency), business criticality, and sensitivity.

- Definition of user types, device postures, and authorization levels; establishment of ZTNA policies and authentication/authorization framework

- Network topology and Internet connectivity details between sites, including vendor selection, connection technologies (e.g., broadband, 5G, MPLS), bandwidth selection, and backup links.

- Security policy definition and connectivity to the broader corporate ecosystem

9.2.3 – Phase-3: Testing and Validation

The testing and validation bring together the planning efforts and afford early opportunities to show success. Establish a proof-of-concept project that is small in scope while providing the opportunity to demonstrate the benefits of the SASE model for Networking and Security. Identify a set of users and an application environment that can be migrated with minimal risk of disruption and no loss of data.

Prepare a validation checklist to demonstrate the success of the new environment for user experience and its alignment with the defined business goals.

Ensure there is broad representation from across the corporation when determining the exit criteria, both to foster mindshare around the project and encourage participation as the SASE environment expands.

9.2.4 – Phase-4: Implementation and Transition

Implementation is where the rubber meets the road. With success demonstrated in limited trials, expand the scope to include complete sites and application categories. New sites, applications, and users should be directly onboarded into the new environment while existing components are migrated over based on a well-structured plan. While this process should be able to be performed with negligible downtime for any given user or service, it is important to remain in close contact with all affected parties at all phases. Outside of general connectivity worries, be ready to address and validate concerns about compliance, security, performance, and process. All technology and user representatives—SoC, NoC, security architects, CISO, legal, HR, lines-of-business—should be on board with the process and active in communication. AIOps is in place to automate network optimization, link self-healing, and ongoing security oversight. Depending on business specifics and corporate culture, the pace of SASE transition may be rapid or restrained, but as highlighted in the final phase, it should be thought of as an ongoing effort toward modernization.

9.2.5 – Phase-5: Continuous Improvement and Lifecycle Management

Ongoing operation and growth of the SASE infrastructure can only be successful when it is incorporated into standard operational practices. New employees will join the company, and Applications will be adopted, upgraded, and phased out. Corporate acquisitions introduce new sites, cloud services providers, and geographies into the network. Ensure that processes are in place to manage the full corporate lifecycle within the SASE ecosystem.

As with all technology, Networking and Security are always evolving. Ongoing lifecycle management is essential for both optimizing performance and ensuring operations are running as expected. Connectivity into the greater management ecosystem will provide visibility to all interested parties (e.g., security, legal, HR, etc.) to aid in the risk-based assessment of future cloud service adoption.

After a successful migration and the SASE framework in place, it can be helpful and reassuring to validate end-to-end security. A best practice is to review the kill chain approach attacks would take and understand how SASE security and **risk assessment of the cyber security kill chain** protect the enterprise.

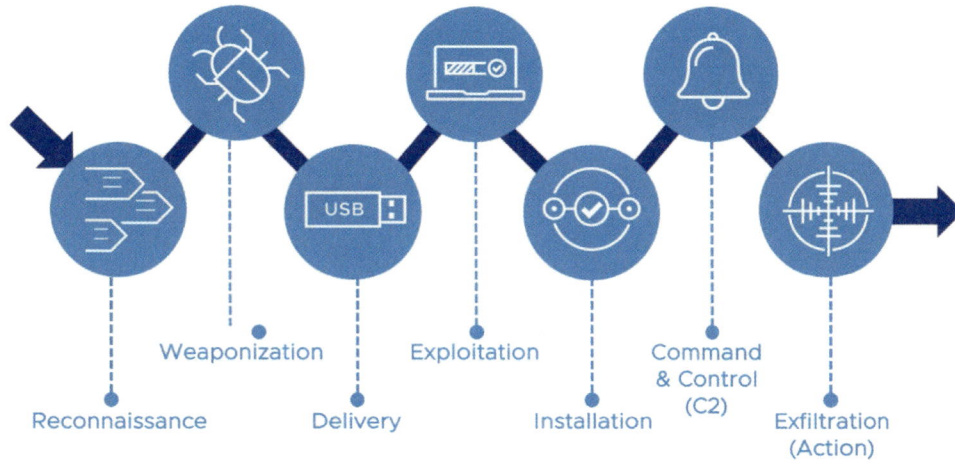

Figure 9.2: Cyber Security Kill Chain

Reference for ITIL:

For additional information on operational planning, service implementation, and continual improvement, refer to ITIL (IT Infrastructure Library) details and documentation.

ITIL is the most widely used approach to managing IT services. The guidance provided in ITIL® helps organizations to deliver their services in a customer-focused, quality-driven and economical way.

9.3 – Customer Case Study for SASE Migration

With the five phases of migration strategy established, this section examines uses cases and results from a VMware SASE customer case study. It breaks down the customer's motivations and challenging, examining decisions made during each phase of the project.

9.3.1 – Phase-1: Scoping

A medium-size (100-5000 employees) enterprise needed to transform its existing IT networking and security infrastructure to cloud services to support enterprise and remote users.

Figure 9.3: ITIL framework for Phase-1 Scoping

1. Problem Statement for enterprise is:

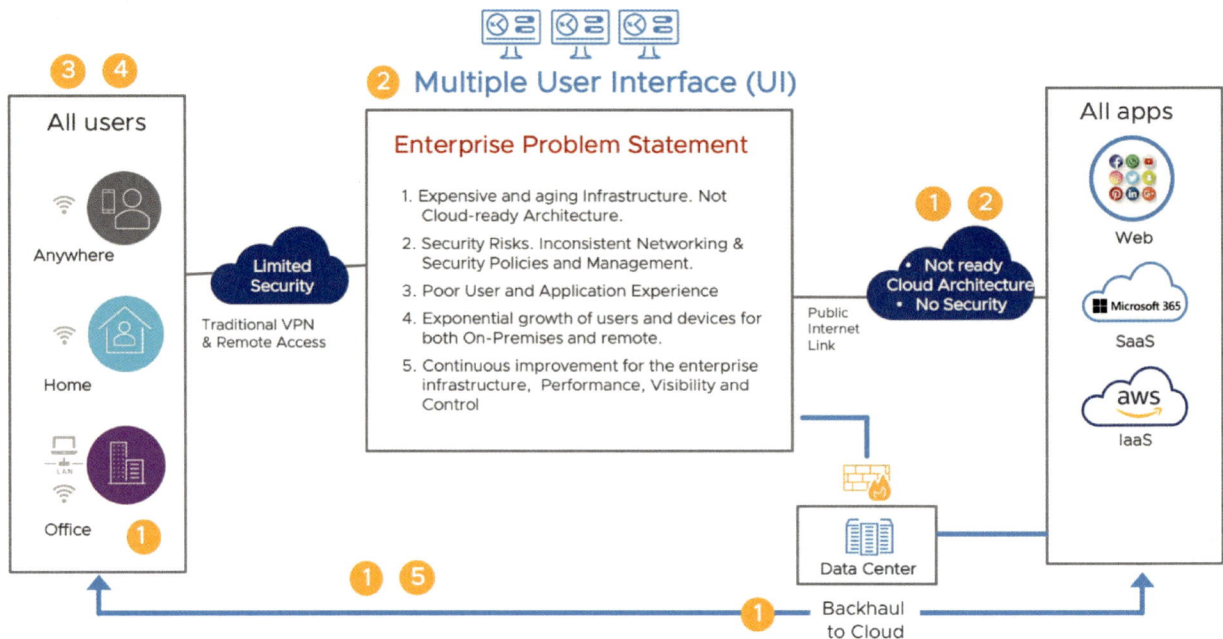

Figure 9.4: Enterprise Problem Statement

The enterprise identified high-level concerns, as shown in **Figure 9.4**, and their IT leadership reached out to VMware for assistance in investigating SASE solutions.

Enterprise Problem Statement:

1. **Expensive and Aging infrastructure.** Scaling infrastructure to meet today's business ongoing demand. Not Cloud-ready Architecture, application moving to the Cloud.

2. **Security Risks.** Inconsistent networking and security policies. Complex Networking and Security Management.

3. **Poor User and Application experience,** Slow customer adoption, costly and complex onboarding of new sites. Expensive and unreliable WAN Links for business-critical applications.

4. **Exponential growth of users and devices.** Managing the remote workforce and providing a consistent user experience.

5. Obtaining feedback from enterprise end users for **continuous improvement** for the enterprise infrastructure.

VMware professional services and enterprise IT architects met with developers, line-of-business stakeholders, and executives to understand existing frustrations, discuss expectations, and document requirements for a new remote user access service. The team collected and organized the results of those discussions into categories, including transformation motivations and user experience requirements.

2. Business Goals:

The **high-level business goals** driving these discussions including:

1. Boost Return of Investment (ROI)

2. Consolidation and consistency in networking performance and Security efficacy.

3. Improve User and Application Experience

4. Simplification of network and security management

5. Efficiency in day-2-day operations, end-to-end visibility, and control, and AIOps.

3. Requirement Details:

Working from the foundation of these general business issues, the project team focused on specific problems and their direct impact on user experience, enterprise networking and security, and operational complexity.

Business requirements are categorized as per IT Team needs:

1. Users/Devices/Data/Applications Requirements

IT was unable to effectively control access to corporate information when employees connected to SaaS applications from home. Users were unable to access all necessary corporate resources with personally owned devices, and associating a user profile with multiple devices was not always effective.

- All users should be able to work from a branch office, home, or remotely using a device of their choice.

- With proper authorization, a user should have complete, secure access to any application regardless of its location.

- IT-managed laptops and mobile devices are available on demand.

- Corporate applications are hosted in on-premises data centers, with SaaS providers, and in Cloud IaaS environments.

- The use of Internet/cloud services is expected to grow significantly over the next 36 months. Ongoing consolidation efforts are expected to move internal applications spread across multiple data centers to a single site.

- Corporate data must be secured per internal policy controls and should follow a robust GRC program or standards (e.g., PCI, HIPAA, SoC Type-1/Type-2)

2. Networking Requirements

Bandwidth was cited as a problem for multiple sites, but it was not possible to directly correlate this to user experience. Some branch sites had no backup connectivity, which led to network stability issues. Leased line costs prevented timely upgrades to site connectivity. WAN management was performed with different processes across multiple platforms.

- Align bandwidth connectivity capabilities with remote user profiles (e.g., light, normal, power)

- Branch sites have differing bandwidth requirements and a variety of connection technologies.

- WAN connectivity should support link aggregation and cost-effective commodity circuits.

- Support as wide a range of transport options as possible.

- Simple and quick deployment; provisioning of circuits and hardware should be able to be performed by a non-technical user.

- Provide high performance for SaaS/cloud applications through efficient routing

- Offer gateway connectivity close to user and application geolocations.

- The overall networking solution should be cloud-native and support an environment that focused on multi-cloud architectures.

- Single UI for management, configuration, Operations, monitoring, and troubleshooting

3. Security Requirements

The centralized security architecture had a significant performance impact on multiple cloud-based applications, leading users to find ways around corporate protections. The security organization had no real-time awareness of compromised user devices or ongoing server security problems. There were no automated controls to isolate a known-bad system.

- All traffic should be granularly inspected end-to-end – from endpoint source to application destination.

- Endpoint security is required for both managed and unmanaged devices.

- Guest user and 3rd party (e.g., business partner) traffic must be isolated/segmented from internal enterprise networks.

- Security should be delivered as a cloud-native service and unified with networking under a single management/architectural framework.

- A single set of policies should apply to both on-premises and cloud applications and be enforced through a common mechanism.

- Single UI for management, configuration, Operations, monitoring, and troubleshooting

4. Governance, Risk, and Compliance Requirement (GRC)

To minimize potential fallout in the event of a breach, the company wanted to begin encrypting all data at rest. While all sites and data repositories currently reside within a single region, they desired to report that could confirm compliance to regulations in other countries/regions where they expect future business.

- Corporate data must be secured per enterprise business model and should adhere to industry-standard compliance. (For example: PCI, HIPAA, SOC Type 1/Type 2)

- Address the Governance, Risk, and Compliance (GRC) for the new infrastructure.

5. Operations and Management Requirement

Understanding the health of any individual end-to-end connection required a significant amount of manual effort. Alignment of traffic shaping and security policy was managed on an individual, hop-by-hop basis. There was no self-healing or traffic optimization, where redundant links were available; functionality was limited to what was available from routing protocols.

- IT must have real-time end-to-end visibility of environmental health information and performance statistics.

- Visibility of and control over unsanctioned apps is essential.

- Infrastructure should be policy controlled and globally managed from a centralized orchestrator

- The environment must be self-optimizing and align with modern AIOps practices.

- The networking and security framework should programmatically ensure proper governance and compliance.

4. Project Timelines

Work with different team members, across business units, and external vendors on the timelines and milestones to come up with a project plan and deliverables for migration to SASE. Have clear ownership defined for each task specified in the project and success criteria.

5. Success Criteria

1. **User Experience:** Any user, any device, and from any location should be able to securely access the enterprise resources in accordance with their IAM role.

It provides end-to-end protection on/off the enterprise network to the closest Point of Presence.

2. **Application Performance:** Application Quality of experience to be measured using tools like Orchestrator QoE, vRNI, ENI with baselining, augmenting Private and Public WAN circuits for accessing application and leveraging VMware SD-WAN. The end goal is to have the quality of experience for the end-user during the brownouts and blackout conditions.

3. **Consolidation and Consistency in networking performance and security efficacy.** Networking and security as a service come from a single vendor reduces operational complexity.

With the migration to VMware SASE, VMware Orchestrator is used to configuring, manage, and troubleshoot networking and security policies.

4. **Return of Investment (ROI).** Reduction in on-premises security devices at the branch (lower CAPEX and OPEX cost) and moving towards VMware SASE framework (Cloud delivered networking and security services).

5. **Simplified Cloud-based centralized management.** VMware SASE has the Cloud delivered Orchestrator for visibility, control, and policy configuration

6. **Rapid deployment** with low IT touch for remote branch sites and remote users (WFH)

9.3.2 – Phase-2: Design Decisions

With an understanding of requirements and goals established, the next phase organizes the architecture design and infrastructure specifications.

Architecture and Design Specs

- With VMware cloud-native approach, Networking and Security services are offered by VMware SASE PoP. These PoP's are hosted and managed by VMware.

- VMware SD-WAN provides Networking as a service

- VMware Workspace ONE provides ZTNA, Secure Web Gateway, and Firewall as a Service provides security as a service.

- Use of any transport (Private, Public, LTE, 5G) can be leveraged using VMware SD-WAN. SD-WAN is a key building block for VMware SASE.

Infrastructure

- Categorize Sanctioned and unsanctioned applications in the public Cloud.

- Categorize application based on service class (real-time, transaction, bulk, etc.)

- Align business priority to the application traffic with High, medium, low priority.

- Define Bandwidth requirements for each site based on branch size (small, medium, and large) and DC. For e.g., small branch with 50 MB to 250 MB bandwidth, DC with 5GB to 10 GB, and beyond.

- Classify the user types, groups, and devices and what applications need to be accessed.

9.3.3 – Phase-3: Testing and Validation

IT followed a proof-of-concept (POC) test deployment plan developed by VMware professional services. They began by configuring business and security policies in the Orchestrator and redirecting three sites to use VMware SASE PoPs. These sites had consistent requirements for application access, and users had common membership in a small set of directory groups. Secure access was used for remote user and device postures to control access to both public cloud and enterprise data center resources. Over the course of two weeks, these test sites were monitored for performance problems and behavioral irregularities. The team identified where automated processes were able to address problems and where they manually had to intervene to make changes. After a successful trial case that met experience and behavioral evaluation criteria, SASE PoP migration was expedited for the remaining users and sites.

During the initial trial and throughout service expansion, specific attention was paid to the success of remote and branch users accessing different types of applications—on-premises, SaaS, IaaS, general Internet web—with distinct sets of policy permissions. For each category, where appropriates, the following aspects were continual areas of evaluation:

- **Identity & Context:** Proper identification of both user and device regardless of location; authorization of access based on enterprise directory group membership permissions; enforcement of restrictions on resource availability based on user location and device type.

- **Network connectivity:** ongoing stability of SD-WAN circuits; user/application impact during physical link problems/outages; ease of bandwidth tuning/resizing; PoP selection and proximity to user/site/application.

- **Security & Governance (GRC):** Real-time analysis of compliance posture; historical reporting on user authentication decisions; assurance of security policy implementation.

- **Operational:** unified policy definition and control; end-to-end visibility of network health; integration into enterprise ticketing and change management platforms; reporting against SLA metrics; flexibility of existing workflows to incorporate new tools and processes.

Overall VMware SASE Framework validation:

By this point, IT teams, application, networking and security architects, CISO, and SoC/NoC operations teams should be in sync with each other as well as their counterparts from different silos/technologies. Success with the SASE framework brings together not only the technical ecosystem but also organizational, operational practices. This highlights the responsibility across the corporation to ensure that proper policy is set for the user, device, and application access.

9.3.4 – Phase-4: Implementation and Transition

As noted in the testing and validation details, the success of the limited trial led to rapid migration of the rest of the infrastructure.

With the success of PoC, plan for actual migration of enterprise infrastructure to VMware SASE.

Start with bringing up network connectivity using SD-WAN, defining users Identity and device context, Business policy, Security policies and rules, Governance and compliance, and Validation and Visibility.

VMware SASE Implementation and Transition

Step ① Networking Connectivity

Step ② Identity and Context

Step ③ Global Policy (Networking and Security)

Step ④ Cloud Security Services

Step ⑤ Validation and Visibility

Figure 9.5: Phase-4: Implementation & Transition for VMware SASE

Step 1: Networking Connectivity

The **first step** of SASE migration is laying the foundation for cloud-native **networking connectivity.** It establishes day-0 operations practices, builds out initial SD-WAN infrastructure, begins application performance analysis, connects to cloud services, and develops a business policy framework.

Guidelines for SD-WAN Connectivity:

1) Branch and DC Site Deployment: Deploy SD-WAN edges and Configure DC site as Hub. Configure Hub-Spoke topology and Branch-to-Branch using Gateway or Hub device. The control and Managed plane for the SASE PoP are cloud-native maintained by VMware.

2) WAN Links: Provision a Public Internet WAN connection to be used for SD-WAN transport. This should at least be sufficient for an initial end-to-end connectivity testing.

3) Routing, LAN/WAN: Get the routing configured on LAN/WAN and start building up connectivity to Non-SD-WAN Sites or MPLS sites only. Additional links can be added to augment branch connectivity. These can be newly provisioned repurposed private circuits (MPLS), public Internet links, or a combination of these and other transport options.

4) Cloud Connectivity: Identify the enterprise application workloads located both within the corporate perimeter and in the Public Cloud, IaaS, SaaS, and build out secure tunnels and SD-WAN overlay tunnels to these destinations.

5) Traffic Rules: Develop and implement business policies (i.e., traffic rules) for individual applications based on service priority and security requirements.

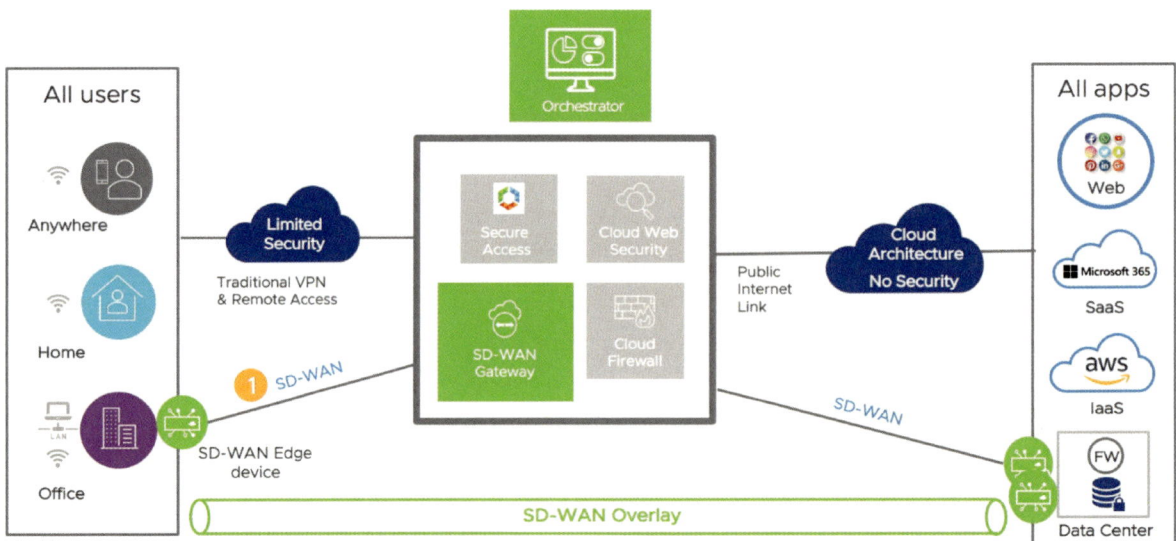

✓ Cloud Ready Architecture, Enhanced User and Application Experience

Figure 9.6: Step 1: Networking connectivity with SD-WAN

6) Security Policies: Configure security policies and rules for data center applications and for SaaS, IaaS connectivity. Furthermore, Segmentation was applied end to end for distinct routing domains with their own business policies, security policies, and topology.

Throughout this process, actively monitor and promote collaborative working relationships between Networking, Security, and application teams. VMware SASE unifies implementation and management of components spread across many traditional operational silos. It will necessitate an evolution of organizational mindset, and this should begin as early as possible.

Step 2: Identity and Context

With the Networking, SD-WAN infrastructure, and application policies in place, the effort can progress to user identification and authorization. VMware's intrinsic security capabilities allow IT to establish a ZTNA model that moves security from a network-based process to one built on identity and context.

- Develop application access policies based on user identity, group membership, and privilege. These should be managed through a central identity solution (e.g., Active Directory) that has visibility and control over the full scope of enterprise users.

- Similar to the users/groups process, establish device-centric policies. These take into account the coverage of any Mobile Device Management (MDM) systems as well as the use of unmanaged devices.

- Explicitly categorize all sanctioned applications. Any identified but unsanctioned applications should also be explicitly included/documented while allowing others to fall into this grouping.

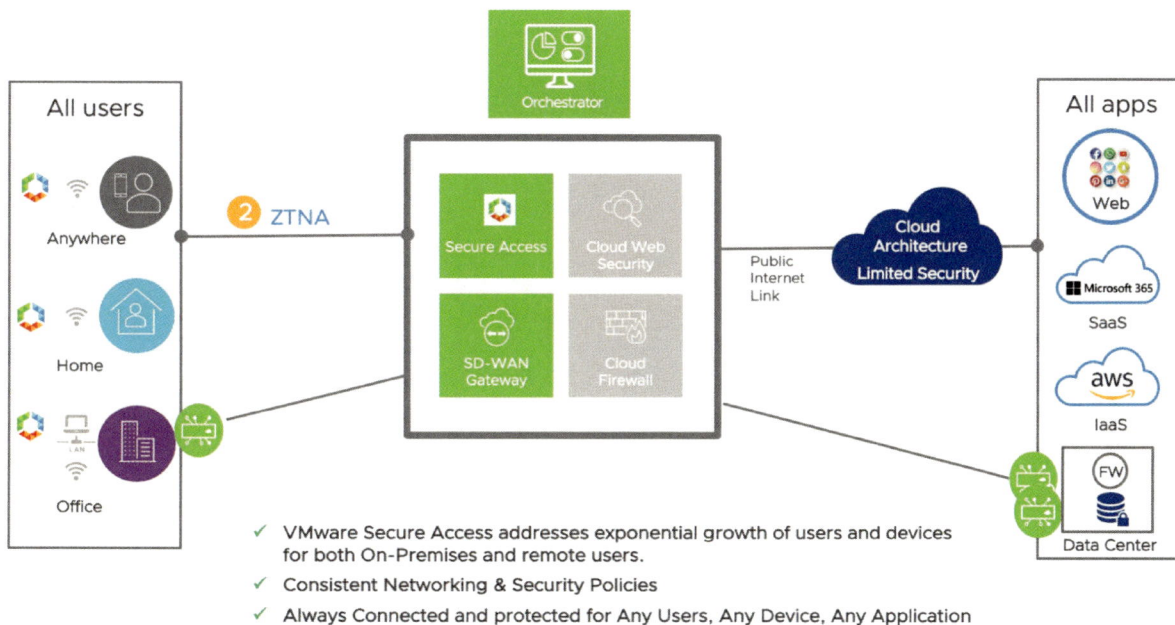

Figure 9.7: Step-2: ZTNA using Secure Access

Step 3: Global Policy – Networking, Security, & GRC

SD-WAN connectivity is half of the SASE promise; integrated security is the other piece. With physical connectivity and application access in place, the next step is the enforcement of a consistent end-to-end security policy. User, device, and application perspectives should all be taken into account – both for managed/sanctioned entities as well as those outsides of direct IT oversight.

The security policy may overlap with networking controls, such as allowing traffic on a specific port for application communication. It also includes higher-level decisions on approved protocols, acceptable applications, and device access restrictions. Concepts and actions include:

- A well-defined ZTNA process that connects individual components (e.g., FWaaS) into the overall SASE framework.

- Ongoing review of networking and security policies in relation to business mandates and compliance restrictions.

- Centralized configuration, visibility, and management of all policies through the VMware Orchestrator. This includes oversight of Cloud, branch, and data center environments.

- Ensure all parts of the environment are logging activity and submitting this information to the Orchestrator.

- Serving as the common consolidation point, the VMware Orchestrator distributes this data to other services to provide visibility, aid troubleshooting, and enable AI Ops activity (e.g., performance baselining).

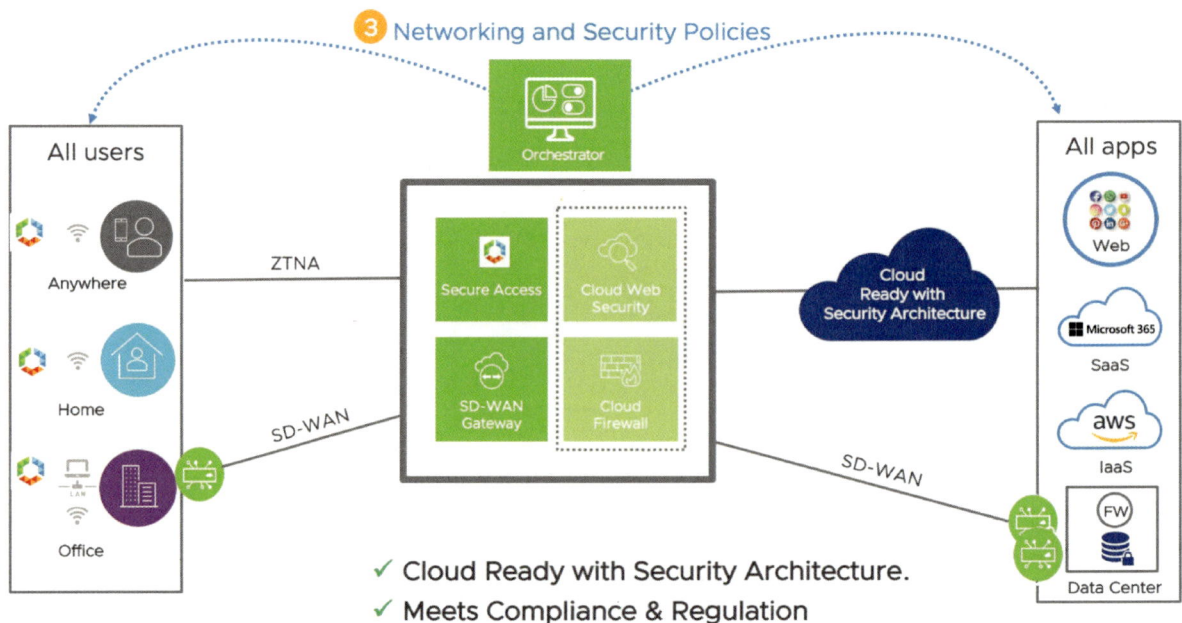

Figure 9.8: Step-3 Global Policy for Networking and Security

Step 4: Security as a service

Step 4 involves assigning users and groups for different business units access to different resources depending on their privilege levels and line of business through the use of granular cloud security services for Cloud Web Security and Cloud Firewall. This process further expands both the technical capabilities and organizational reach of SASE modernization. Control and visibility are extended beyond the corporate perimeter while organizations including HR, finance, and legal have increasingly direct roles in establishing enterprise-level security standards.

1. Incoming traffic flow will be inspected against the security policy. Incoming traffic flow will be inspected against the security policy. Traffic will be blocked or permitted to pass for further inspection. It may not be acceptable to intercept certain traffic per governmental regulation (e.g., banking data) while corporate policy dictates that other data (e.g., gambling) may be discarded entirely.

2. For granular security inspection, security rules are applied for Cloud web security and Cloud firewall components of SASE PoP. For instance, in Cloud Web Security (CWS), URL filtering, anti-malware, CASB, DLP, and sandboxing are the most common initial set of tools deployed. Verify these against a limited set of sites or a specific category to simplify validation and troubleshooting.

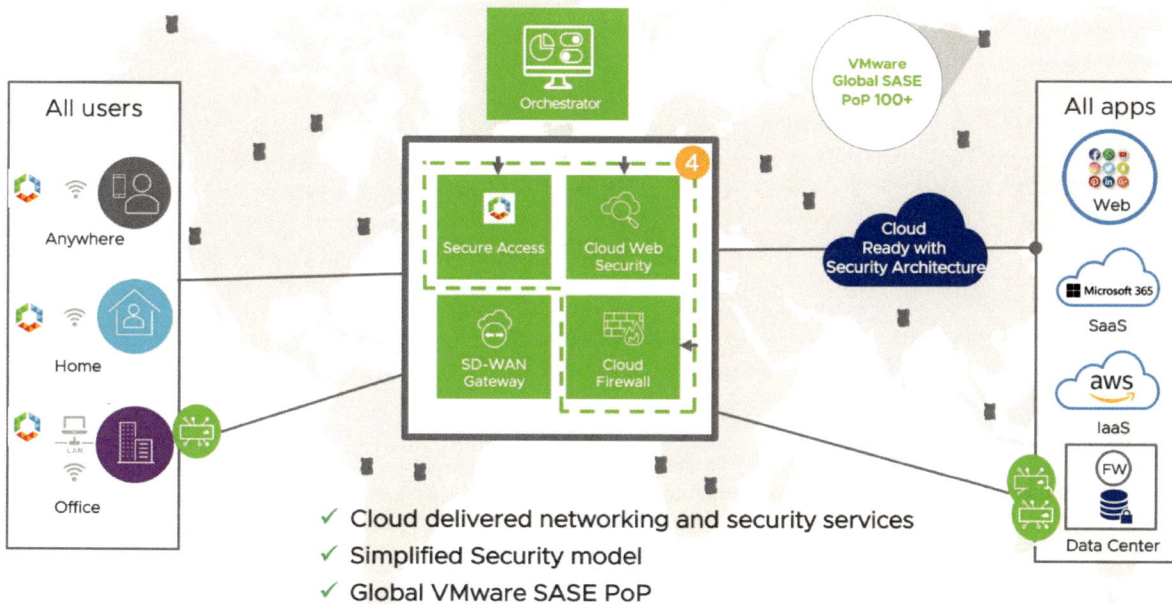

✓ **Cloud delivered networking and security services**
✓ **Simplified Security model**
✓ **Global VMware SASE PoP**

Figure 9.9: Step-4 Implementing Security as a Service: CWS & FWaaS

Problem Statement and solution Checklist for Enterprise deploying VMware SASE PoP

1. Expensive and Aging infrastructure. Scaling infrastructure to meet today's business on-going demand. Not Cloud-ready Architecture, application moving to the cloud.

   ✓ Cloud-Native VMware SASE Platform converges industry-leading cloud networking and cloud security to deliver flexibility, agility, security and scale for enterprise of all sizes. The VMware SASE Platform is offered as-a-service, helping offload IT staff from deploying and maintaining WAN/security saving enterprise operation costs.

2. Security Risks. Inconsistent Networking and security policies. Complex Networking and Security Management

   ✓ VMware SASE PoP components (Secure Access, Cloud Web Security, FWaaS), & Simplified Security Policy Configuration and Enforcement. Improved Security Posture.

3. Poor User and Application experience, Slow customer adoption, costly and complex on-boarding of new sites. Expensive and un-reliable WAN Links for business-critical application.

   ✓ VMware SD-WAN enhances user and application experience. Lower Capital and Operational cost.

4. Exponential growth of users and devices. Managing the remote work force and providing a consistent user experience.

   ✓ VMware Secure Access provides Secure and Consistent Access for Branch and Remote Users. Remote users will enjoy an improved performance as they no longer have to access the VPN concentrator hosted in a few data centers. In addition, users can benefit from the ability to leverage Global PoPs to eliminate hairpinning, and optimized traffic handling capabilities to help lower latency and drive better performance and resiliency in remote access

5. Obtaining feedback from enterprise end users for continuous improvement for the enterprise infrastructure.

   ✓ Advanced end to end path Visibility and Control using VMware ENI. VMware Edge Network Intelligence™ (ENI) is an artificial intelligence for IT Operations (AIOps) solution focused on the enterprise edge, ensuring end user and IoT client performance, security, and self-healing through LAN/WLAN, SD-WAN and secure access service edge (SASE)

Step 5: Validation and Visibility

- Validate that application traffic is addressed by SASE global policy and behaves as expected. Examples include user access regardless of location and application permission consistency across devices.

- AIOps and ML: Logging and performance data from different security components must be continuously analyzed and processed for actionable insights by VMware ENI. These actions may be automatically processed or raised for manual review but are central to the Alops and self-healing capabilities of the SASE framework. Poor user experience may be the result of a network problem or security constraint – correlation of this information can help determine the root cause and expedite resolution.

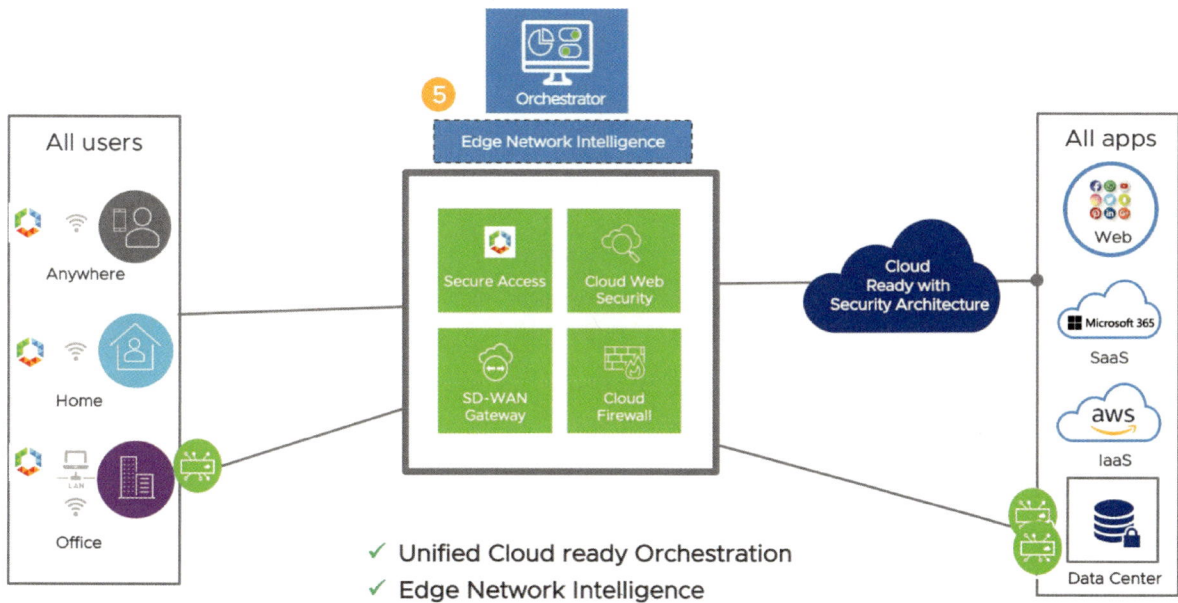

Figure 9.10: Step-5: Validation and Visibility

With VMware SASE unifying the implementation and management of traditionally siloed technologies, the company expects to align its IT team structure with this new model.

9.3.5 – Phase-5: Continuous Improvement and Lifecycle Management

Ongoing operation and growth of the SASE infrastructure can only be successful when it is incorporated into standard operational practices. For example, new users joining the company, Applications will be adopted, upgraded, and phased out, Corporate acquisitions will bring new sites, cloud services providers, and geographies into the network. Ensure that processes are in place to manage the full corporate lifecycle within the SASE ecosystem.

- Security policies should be regularly reviewed for applicability to both users and groups (e.g., line-of-business restrictions on read/write access to sensitive data).

- Ongoing alignment with compliance and government standards, including patch level review and configuration validation. Continuous monitoring of these parameters can alert IT well in advance of a security incident, allowing for proactive remediation of a problem rather than reactive response to an incident.

- Continuous monitoring also watches user experience and application performance, rapidly identifying drift from established baselines and acting to address problems before they grow and/or spread. As in other areas, this can take the form of automated remediation or active notification for manual review

Figure 9.11: Addressing the Kill Chain with VMware SASE Platform

The SD-WAN integrated firewall detects and protects against various attacks and combats exploits at all stages of execution. SD-WAN Orchestrator allows configuration and tuning of network and flood protections at both the profile and Edge levels. This can prevent against attack types, including general denial-of-service, TCP (e.g., flags, SYN fragmentation), ICMP (e.g., ping-of-death, fragmentation), and IP (e.g., unknown protocol, insecure options).

Firewall rule options can permit, drop, reject, or skip inbound and outbound traffic, matching on packet protocols, IP addresses or ports, VLAN IDs, system interface, MAC addresses, URL/domain information, object groups, application traffic type, and DSCP tags. The firewall offers protection against multiple layers of the kill chain, including reconnaissance (layer 1), command & control (layer 6), and action-on-objective (layer 7). Secure Access, Secure Web Gateway, and Cloud Firewall build out the rest of the picture, helping SASE PoP offer protections against all seven layers of the kill chain model.

9.4 – Key Takeaways Checklist

Adoption of a SASE framework, while not a trivial task, is one well within the capabilities of any business. Proper planning is required to understand both individual business requirements and technical solution capabilities.

✓ Take a phased approach; build out the SASE environment slowly in parallel with existing infrastructure.

✓ Act early to break organizational silos and foster collaboration.

✓ Continually review and evaluate policy, using the Orchestrator to manage and enforce consistency throughout the ecosystem.

✓ Data and visibility are central to automated remediation and actionable insights.

Chapter 10

Final Thoughts & Next Steps

10.1 – VMware Enterprise Edge Services Strategy

Perspective from Sanjay Uppal – SVP & GM VMware, VeloCloud Co-Founder

VMware SD-WAN started with the notion that the network must be where your business applications are - it must be in the Cloud. "The Cloud is the Network" has been our tagline since Day 1.

What does this mean for our future?

SD-WAN is evolving. It is no longer an "edge-to-edge technology." It is expanding to go deeper into the branch, to the individual clients—whether you work at home, on your mobile device, or in a large campus— through the Cloud, and all the way to the individual application container, wherever it sits—in the public or private Cloud. We call this client-to-cloud-to-container.

This strategy rests on six pillars – the "VMware Enterprise Edge Services Strategy."

1. Intrinsic Security – SASE

2. WFH/WFA (Work from Home/Work from Anywhere)

3. Multi-cloud Interconnect

4. Self-healing Networks

5. 5G Intelligence

6. Edge Compute

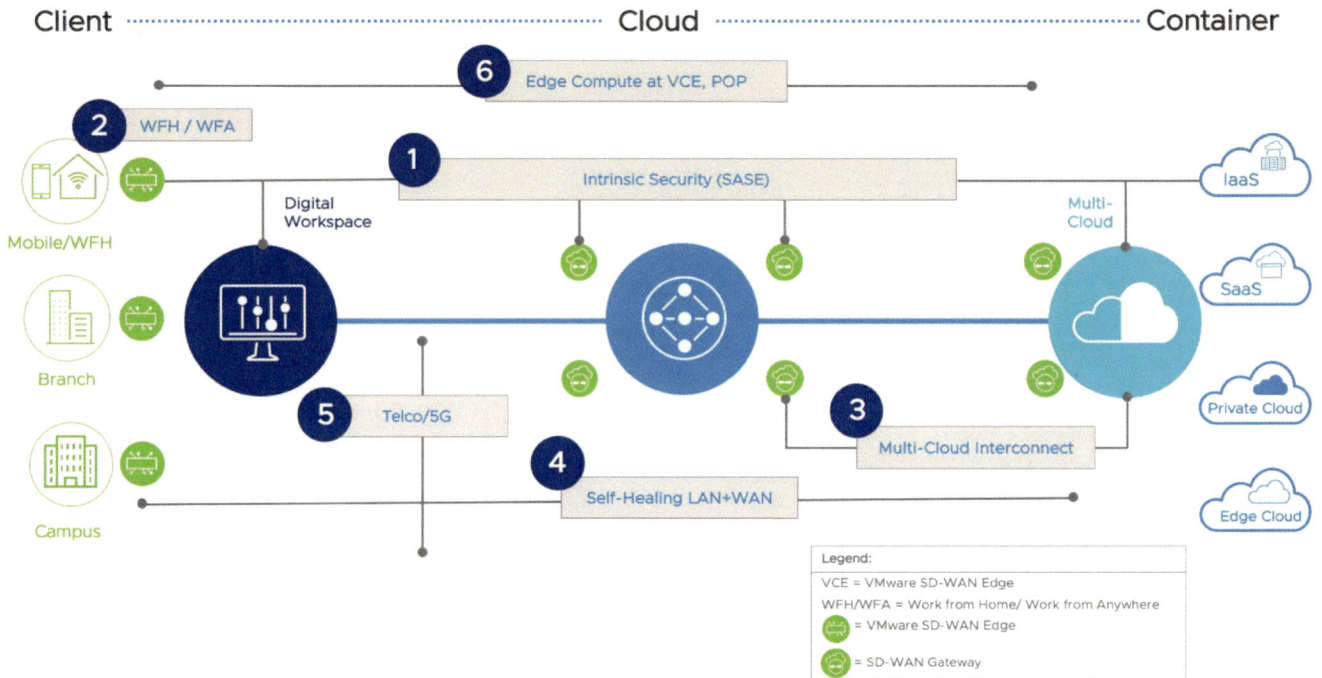

Figure 10.1: VMware SD-WAN Strategy

Intrinsic Security – SASE

VMware SASE Platform brings together cloud networking and cloud security. The power of our SASE architecture allows our customers to decide which traffic should go through specialized security services via policy-based rules. Additionally, our SASE platform provides users with secure remote access from anywhere.

VMware's unique architecture has provided, from the beginning, Cloud Gateways that serve as an on-ramp to SaaS and a network of other cloud services. This global footprint gives VMware a presence to continue to launch additional integrations and deliver incremental services.

With this set of capabilities, customers can:

- Continue to get a multi-tenant and elastic on-ramp
  for SaaS applications, with high quality, delivered using DMPO.

- Get a multi-tenant and elastic on-ramp for off-net devices using ZTNA from managed, unmanaged, and agentless devices using Workspace ONE + VMware SD-WAN.

- Get integrated services from VMware (e.g., NGFW, SWG/CASB) delivered as-a-service and automatically inserted as needed based on the customer's own business policies.
- Leverage high-quality on-ramp to security services provided by partners and sequenced via cloud handoff.

WFH/WFA

VMware WFH/WFA solutions bring optimal, secure, reliable, and automated application and cloud access experience to work-from-home users, regardless of the workloads' locations. VMware WFH/WFA solutions are powered by the VMware SASE Platform.

With this set of capabilities, customers can:

- Streamline provisioning and configuration through zero-touch deployment without the need for IT on-site.
- Optimize resource and application access to IaaS and SaaS through Cloud Gateways
- Enhance access experience and performance for VoIP, Unified Communications-as-a-Service (UCaaS), and collaboration services.
- Protect against network-based attacks through intrinsic security with an enhanced stateful firewall on Edge at home.
- Grow WFH/WFA deployments at their own pace through the unique architecture of Cloud Gateways and cloud-based multi-tenant SASE Orchestrator.

Multi-Cloud Interconnect

Simplified cloud on-ramp and multi-cloud interconnect provides automatic discovery of IaaS routing domains (e.g., VPCs and VNETs), automated and segmented full-mesh routing between domains, and connects ZTNA devices via Cloud Gateways to the same multi-cloud on-ramp provided today for SD-WAN branches.

With this capability, organizations can:

- Automate deployment of VMware Edges into IaaS.
- Auto-provision tunnels from Edges and Cloud Gateways to IaaS and Security providers
- Seamlessly extend network segmentation between data center, IaaS, branch, and ZTNA devices.
- Enable rapid cloud adoption and scale new operating models. They can rapidly interconnect multiple clouds through the global cloud-hosted gateway nodes.
- Support workloads in hybrid and multi-cloud natively and using VMC.
- Discover and audit new multi-cloud instances for consistent network security.

Self-Healing Networks

The VMware self-healing network is based on end-to-end visibility and algorithmic self-healing intelligence. It can detect anomalies, identify root-cause, and automatically remediate the issue or notify the network administrator. The Edge Network Intelligence (formally Nyansa) integration extends visibility to include LAN/Wi-Fi. This, combined with the AI/ML engine, will enable rapid diagnosis of issues from endpoints to applications.

VMware SD-WAN has been using the "Quality of Experience" of applications to identify and remediate problems with applications traversing the WAN. With Edge Network Intelligence on the LAN, Workspace ONE on the client, and NSX in the data center, VMware is uniquely positioned to extend this complete experience beyond the WAN: measuring application performance; using ML to do baselining and anomaly detection; using AI to identify potential causes, and remediating issues automatically.

With this functionality, customers can:

- Be notified of issues with application performance proactively.

- Have those issues automatically isolated to a specific area in the network (e.g., LAN, WAN, data center, SaaS).

- Identify potential root causes.

- Get a list of potential solutions that are either applied automatically or listed in order of confidence that they will resolve the issue.

- For customers whose solutions are applied automatically, machine learning detects whether the issue was actually resolved and if it increases or decreases the confidence score of the solution as a result.

- The system, over time, continues to learn what solutions best solve which problems to "heal faster" or provide better suggestions.

Telco/5G

Telcos and service providers represent a key route to market for VMware SD-WAN and SASE Platform. Today these providers bundle services as well as transport with the VMware offering, but VMware is partnering to enable them to add more value.

A case in point is 5G. 5G mobile technology will allow the mobile network to be a primary WAN link due to speed, low latency, and QoS options. Unlike MPLS or broadband, 5G can be dynamic underlay (i.e., "Network-on-Demand"). This allows the enterprise to change bandwidth and QoS dynamically, enabling enterprises to adapt their WAN quickly and easily when needed.

With this solution, customers can:

- Use 5G network slicing as an additional attribute to steer application traffic or to add more bandwidth.

- Enterprises can build the next generation of applications like IoT aggregation, loyalty, and IT on-premises break-fix, leveraging microservices-based applications that benefit from the low latency characteristics of 5G.

Edge Compute at VCE, POP

VMware SD-WAN will run compute primarily on the customers' premises at the Edge and secondarily at the SD-WAN Cloud Gateway. It is all orchestrated from the VMware SD-WAN Orchestrator, with its lifecycle managed by common VMware tools. Containers and VMs will run on a virtualized platform on-premises on VCE, and at VMware, SASE POPs are managed centrally by VMware Tanzu.

With this solution, customers can:

- Integrate with vSphere to enhance the security and scalability of deploying SD-WAN on commodity hardware.

- Integrate with VMware Tanzu to support seamless deployment, mobility, and lifecycle management of containerized applications.

- Integrate with VxRail and VMware Cloud Foundation to provide an automated and high-quality network on-ramp to compute stacks running in public and private Cloud.

- Take advantage of Cloud Exchange vendor partnerships (e.g., Equinix, Megaport, Pureport) and IaaS vendors (e.g., Amazon, Microsoft, Google, Alibaba) to facilitate one-click access to non-VMware compute.

- Use a single portal for provisioning, connectivity, and security for all computing environments as well as DMPO to ensure that the right compute venue is chosen and supportable based on real-world network conditions.

10.2 – Conclusion

VMware SASE is available today for enterprises ready to transform their access infrastructure.

This SASE architecture brings together VMware SD-WAN, Workspace ONE, Secure Access, and other components under a single management and orchestration framework. VMware's worldwide network of VMware SASE PoPs is the vehicle that delivers the solution.

VMware SASE simplifies application connectivity for any user—office, branch, home, mobile—on any device to any workload. It provides a common environment for end-to-end policy, ensuring both consistent security and optimized performance. Automation tools enable self-healing of ongoing network problems while data aggregation and event correlation streamline troubleshooting and root cause analysis. The centralized management model removes the need for highly skilled staff at branch sites and allows the enforcement of holistic business-centric policy across the network.

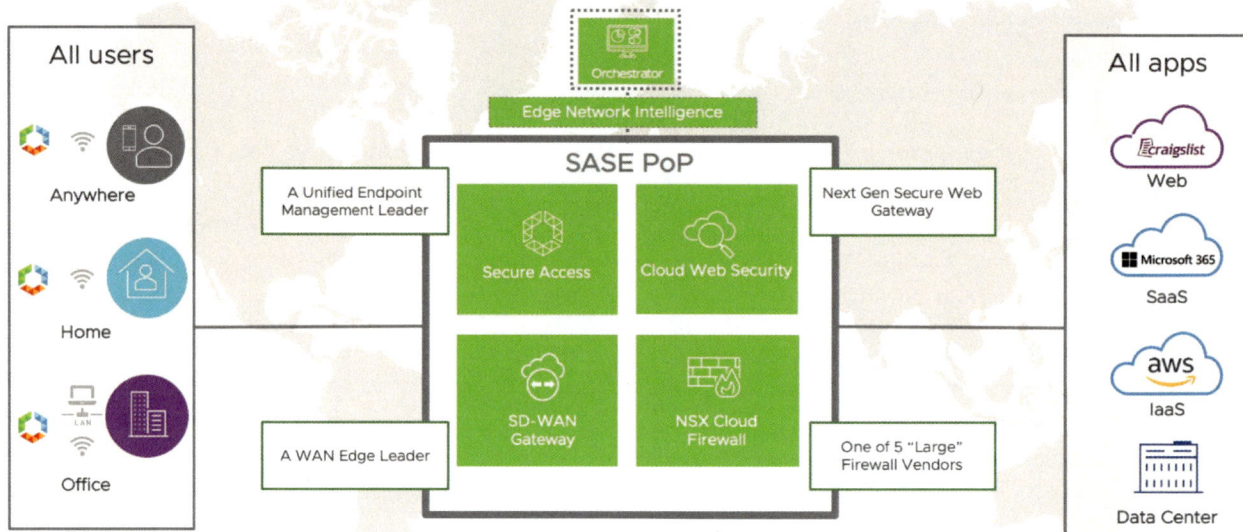

Figure 10.2: VMware SASE Platform

The VMware SASE Difference

VMware SASE services are delivered through a network of over 3000+ Cloud Gateways in hundreds of PoPs. This environment is supported globally by VMware and hundreds of service provider partners. Depending on business needs and preferences, it can be available as a managed service or a DIY offering. It is designed for easy adoption and consumption while taking advantage of the benefits of the Cloud for global reach, rapid scalability, and minimized operational complexity. This global reach allows IT to address the needs of all employees regardless of their location while simplifying the deployment, management, and maintenance of the infrastructure.

The solution provides customers with the intrinsic security required for operation in the connected digital world. The platform allows enterprise IT to:

- Operate a single multi-tenant platform that combines industry-leading SD-WAN, ZTNA, SWG, and firewall in a single PoP for secure access to public and private cloud applications.

- Access advanced analytics and intelligence on application performance.

- Manage business policies spanning multiple security and network services through a single-pane-of-glass management portal.

- Connect to third-party services (e.g., security, analytics, mid-mile) as well as integrated services to ensure flexibility and support for a large ecosystem.

The VMware SASE solution was specifically designed to address critical business pain points of operational complexity and financial impact:

- **Cloud:** SASE is designed with a cloud-first approach offering operational efficiency, instant agility, extreme scalability, and future readiness.

- **Security:** Intrinsic security provides built-in protection while the end-to-end solution brings together networking, endpoint, identity, and cloud security control points.

- **Quality Assurance:** Ensuring the quality of the application experience from office, branch, home, or away.

- **ROI:** Simplifying operations and reducing support complexity by unifying networking and security.

Cloud First

VMware SASE is based on the idea that the Cloud is the network. Through its global PoP network, it provides simplified, cost-effective connectivity to cloud- and SaaS-based applications while also ensuring end-to-end security with flexible deployment choices for work-at-home users. SASE leverages the power of cloud networking to support dynamic, flexible scaling. Organizations can start small, then grow their remote digital workforce through the unique architecture of Cloud Gateways and cloud-based management.

Intrinsic Security

Through a cloud security model that encompasses user identity, device posture, and network location, VMware SASE unifies network and application security policies for branch and remote workers. The solution's comprehensive suite of security features includes contextual access, network security, application protection, and network separation – allowing it to align with and realize the latest concepts in Zero Trust.

Application Quality Assurance

With the VMware SASE platform, organizations can ensure the availability and performance of mission-critical applications, even with degraded network conditions or congestion. By combining application recognition, traffic prioritization, and shaping with the ability to measure network path performance, the solution steers traffic on a packet-by-packet basis to achieve the highest quality of experience for end-users. The solution also employs artificial intelligence for comparative application performance benchmarking to identify sources of and solutions to network issues. The platform removes the requirement for VPN concentrators in the data center, eliminating a common bottleneck. This further reduces latency and improves network bandwidth utilization for users trying to reach the Cloud and SaaS destinations.

Operational Simplicity & ROI

The VMware SASE platform provides operational simplicity and lowers operational expenses. It allows the enterprise to procure, manage, and troubleshoot SD-WAN, ZTNA, SWG, and firewall functionality from a single vendor, avoiding the inefficiencies inherent in patching together multiple disparate solutions. The cloud-delivered network of VMware SASE PoPs spans the globe and is available as a service to minimize the internal operational burden.

VMware Edge Network Intelligence, a key analytics functionality of SD-WAN, constantly assesses the state of both LAN and WAN, producing actionable and insightful reports to aid troubleshooting and fault isolation.

10.3 – Next Steps and Take-Away Checklist

Now is the time to take action. Deploying and operating a global environment for user connectivity has never been easier or more secure.

✓ **Reach Out:** Engage with VMware and the service provider community to learn the most up-to-date information on SASE PoP solutions. Discover success stories from user groups to better understand the most compelling business benefits.

✓ **Start Small:** Identify small opportunities to demonstrate success – individual applications, small user groups, sites with problematic connectivity. Cloud agility allows each project to ramp up at its own pace then scale as necessary.

✓ **Build consensus:** Involve stakeholders throughout the enterprise to foster interest and drive adoption. Use the tools and visibility provided to break down traditional silos and highlight the full potential of VMware SASE.

✓ **Learn More about VMware SASE:** https://sdwan.vmware.com/secure-access-service-edge or SASE.vmware.com

List of Abbreviations

AAA – Authentication, Authorization, and Accounting

ACL – Access List

AI/ML – Artificial Intelligence/Machine Learning

AIOps – Artificial Intelligence for IT Operations

AMP – Advanced Malware Processing

ATD – Advanced Threat Detection

AP – Access Point

AV – Antivirus

BYOD – Bring Your Own Device

CA – Certificate Authority

CASB – Cloud Access Security Broker

CAPEX – Capital Expenditure

CISO – Chief Information Security Officer

CSIRT – Cyber Security Incident Response Team

DDoS – Distributed Denial of Service

DLP – Data Loss Prevention

DMPO – Dynamic Multi-Path Optimization

DMZ – Demilitarized Zone

DNS – Domain Name System

DNSSEC – Domain Name System Security Extension

DSLAM – Digital Subscriber Line Aggregation Multiplexer

DSS – Data Security Standard

EDR – Endpoint Detection and Remediation

ENI – VMware Edge Network Intelligence

EPP – Endpoint Protection Platform

FEC – Forward Error Correction

FWaaS – Firewall-as-a-Service

GDPR – General Data Protection Regulation

HIPAA – Health Information Portability and Accountability Act

HTTP – Hypertext Transfer Protocol

IaaS – Infrastructure-as-a-Service

IAM – Identity Access Management

IAM – Identity and Access Management

ICMP – Internet Control Message Protocol

IDS – Intrusion Detection System

IEP – Internet Exchange Point

IP – Internet Protocol

IPS – Intrusion Prevention System

IPsec – Internet Protocol Security

IT – Information Technology

LAN – Local Area Network

MDM – Mobile Device Management

NAC – Network Access Control

NAT – Network Address Translation

NDR – Network Detection and Remediation

NGAV – Next Generation Anti-Virus

NGFW – Next Generation Firewall

NIST – National Institute of Standards and Technology

OPEX – Operational Expenditure

OPSEC – Operations Security

OSI – Open Systems Interconnect

PaaS – Platform-as-a-Service

PCI – Payment Card Industry

PHI – Protected Health Information

PoP – Point of Presence

PPP – Point-to-Point Protocol

QoE – Quality of Experience

QoS – Quality of Service

RBI – Remote Browser Isolation

SaaS – Software-as-a-Service

SASE – Secure Access Service Edge

SDN – Software Defined Networking

SDP – Software Defined Perimeter

SD-WAN – Software-defined Wide Area Network

SIEM – Security Information and Event Management

SLA – Service Level Agreement

SOC – Security Operations Center

SSH – Secure Shell

SSL – Secure Sockets Layer

SSO – Single Sign-On

SWG – Secure Web Gateway

TCP – Transmission Control Protocol

TLS – Transport Layer Security

UCaaS – Unified Communications-as-a-Service

UCPE – Universal Customer Premises Equipment

UDP – User Datagram Protocol

UEBA – User & Entity Behavior Analytics

URL – Uniform Resource Locator

UTM – Unified Threat Management

VNF – Virtual Network Function

VoIP – Voice over IP

VPN – Virtual Private Network

VRRP – Virtual Router Redundancy Protocol

WAF – Web Application Firewall

WAN – Wide Area Network

WFH/WFA – Work from Home/Work from Anywhere

WPA – Wireless Protected Access

XDR – Extended Detection and Response

ZTNA – Zero Trust Network Access

Made in the USA
Monee, IL
27 April 2022